NEW DEVELOPMENTS IN COMPUTER-ASSISTED LANGUAGE LEARNING

NEW DEVELOPMENTS IN COMPUTER-ASSISTED LANGUAGE LEARNING

Edited by
DOUGLAS HAINLINE

CROOM HELM
London & Sydney

NICHOLS PUBLISHING COMPANY
New York

© 1987 Douglas Hainline
Croom Helm Ltd, Provident House, Burrell Row,
Beckenham, Kent, BR3 1AT

Croom Helm Australia, 44-50 Waterloo Road,
North Ryde, 2113, New South Wales

British Library Cataloguing in Publication Data

New developments in computer-assisted
    language learning.
    1. Language and languages — Computer-
    assisted instruction
    I. Hainline, Douglas
    407'.8   P53

    ISBN 0-7099-3780-6

First published in the United States of America 1987 by
Nichols Publishing Company, Post Office Box 96
New York, N.Y. 10024

Library of Congress Cataloging-in-Publication Data

New developments in computer-assisted language
    learning.

    Bibliography: p.
    1. Language and languages — Computer-assisted
    instruction. I. Hainline, Douglas.
    P53.28.N48   1987   418'.0028'5   86-12411

    ISBN 0-89397-253-3

Printed and bound in Great Britain by
Biddles Ltd, Guildford and King's Lynn

CONTENTS

Introduction

INTRODUCTION

One of the side effects of the relentless advance of the computer into every sphere of life has been an increase in the amount of contact and intellectual cross-fertilisation between the 'two cultures' of science/engineering/mathematics, on the one hand, and of the humanities, on the other. Computer Assisted Language Learning (henceforth abbreviated CALL) is a field in which this sort of collaboration has been going on for a long time, and the last few years have seen a substantial increase in it. One result of this has been the appearance of many interesting new developments in CALL applications and techniques. The documentation of these has tended to be rather widely dispersed.

This book is aimed at those who already have an appreciation of the value of enlisting the computer as a language-tutoring assistant. Its primary purpose is to bring together a number of detailed and concrete reports of work in progress, with a certain degree of bias towards novel applications.

Many readers will probably already have some background in CALL, but the field continues to attract the interest of both language specialists with little experience of computing, and of computing specialists with little experience of the problems of teaching foreign languages. For those for whom this may be their first extended exposure to the subject, we have begun the book with three chapters designed to provide a basepoint from which the balance of the contributions might be assessed.

The first chapter, by the editor, presents a view of CALL's place within the Computer-Assisted Instruction tradition in general, and offers some predictions as to how its evolution is likely to be affected by current developments in computer networking.

The next two chapters are symmetrical: in Chapter Two Alan and Pamela Maddison of Thames Polytechnic (UK) provide newcomers to microcomputing with a survey of its most important terms and concepts, and in Chapter Three the same authors present those readers who come from a purely technical background with a summary of what we know about the teaching of second languages which may be relevant to its partial incorporation into computer systems. The latter chapter will, it is hoped, be particularly useful for the growing number of computer scientists who have been attracted to this particular form of language-centred computing in the last few years, only to discover that this subject supports a whole body of research work whose terms of reference, theories, conclusions and controversies should be understood if serious work is to be undertaken it it.

Next, the reader will find examples of applications of the computer to new CALL fields: in Chapter Four, Gary Palmer of the University of Nevada (USA) reports on the economical production, 'in the field', of high-quality language-teaching materials using the latest generation of microcomputer which allows the integration of text and images. This particular work was done in aid of language preservation for a small American Indian tribe: a host of related applications should suggest themselves to other social scientists. Chapter Five, by Olivia Saracho of the University of Maryland (USA), surveys work being done with microcomputers in the United States to teach second-language literacy to the children of immigrants, an application which should be of great relevance in the United Kingdom and the rest of Europe as well.

The programs described in Chapters Six and Seven, by Peter Saunders of the Inner London Education Authority (UK), and Betje Klier of the University of Texas (USA), respectively, address what is surely a major problem in language teaching: student motivation. (More precisely: lack of student motivation.) Both report results obtained in using two very different computer games to teach French. Saunders describes a French-language adventure game, and provides useful guidelines for anyone contemplating writing similar programs. In particular, the 'context-sensitive' on-line dictionary he describes should become a standard feature of all similar future programs. Klier's report highlights the value of systems designed to promote group work, and also makes some possibly controversial observations relevant to the psychology of pedagogy.

The latest generation of microcomputers allows us to break out of the Latin alphabet/ASCII standard, although not without some effort. The next section describes three CALL systems in which the representation of the alphabet is a central concern. In Chapter Eight, Martin West of Salford University (UK) presents solutions to the problem of presenting the ornate Hebrew script, which requires a 16 x 16 matrix for its representation, on the BBC microcomputer. In Chapter Nine, Taj Bhatia of Syracuse University (USA) demonstrates a method, implemented on the PLATO system, for representing the Devanagari alphabet, as part of the system to teach Hindi. This alphabet, with its ninety-plus characters, non-linear script, and syllabic orientation is a major challenge to the CALL programmer. And in Chapter Ten, Ian Press of Queen Mary College (UK) describes how to design a Cyrillic character set for Russian language instruction on the BBC microcomputer.

Chapter Eleven, by Theodore Braun and George Mulford of the University of Delaware (USA), should be of interest to anyone contemplating the serious, full-scale adoption of computing technology to language teaching, using a large mainframe computer or a system of equivalent scope. The story of the 'computerisation' of an American university's French department, and the results achieved so far, based on the records of over 6200 hours of student use, will be relevant in the coming period to hundreds of similar institutions. Of particular interest is their experience with random-access audio devices.

In Chapter Twelve John Collett of the University of Waikato (New Zealand) gives a comprehensive description of the techniques used to design an authoring language particularly suited for (but not limited to) CALL systems.

A major problem for CALL programs, as for CAI in general, is to be able to respond informatively to 'near miss' answers from students, in the way a human instructor would do. The last two chapters describe in some detail sophisticated methods for such 'intelligent word processing' in the CALL context. In Chapter Thirteen Robert Phillips of Miami University (USA) presents the technique of 'masking'. This method allows his Spanish verb drill programs to recognise student inputs which, although wrong in the immediate context, represent 'the right answer to another question'. The approach detailed in

Chapter Fourteen by Harald Trost and Georg Dorffner of the University of Vienna (Austria) is an algorithm which can recognise or generate all grammatical inflections of German words. This algorithm can be incorporated in a wide variety of CALL applications, including that of text generation. Both approaches can be applied to other languages.

The contributors hope that current or intending CALL workers will find these chapters a rich source of ideas for their work.

Chapter One

COMPUTERS IN LANGUAGE INSTRUCTION: TRENDS AND POSSIBILITIES

Douglas Hainline, School of Computing and Information Technology, Thames Polytechnic, London

The computer as a language-teaching assistant promises much. In its first twenty years it has not fulfilled its promise. But the next twenty should see advances that will more than compensate for the somewhat slow start.

CALL's first two decades

Some light on the probable evolution of CALL can be shed by considering the progress - or lack thereof - of Computer Assisted Instruction (CAI) in general. Early development work in CAI, beginning in the mid 1960s, necessarily involved the use of terminals tied to a mainframe in time-sharing mode, and was not cheap. Thus a major preoccupation of research into CAI in this period was to test its cost effectiveness, as well as its educational effectiveness.

By either measure, research results were not overwhelmingly convincing for the value of the computer. Suffice it to say that almost everyone directly involved in developing CAI programs became convinced of their utility - and that almost no-one else did. A survey carried out in the winter of 1978-79 of 1,810 foreign language departments in American higher educational establishments revealed that, of the 602 who responded, only sixty-two made use of CALL systems. (Solveig Olsen, 'Foreign Language Departments and Computer-Assisted Instruction: a Survey', Modern Language Journal 64:1980). Cost was most frequently cited as the reason for non-use. Nor were foreign language departments out of step with other academic disciplines in the application of computers to their teaching. With the partial exception of its use in privately-financed specialised short-term training courses for highly-

1

motivated adults, CAI remained marginal to the educational process throughout the 1970s.

Looking back at this period, one suspects that there was a certain naive, if unstated, expectation during the early days of CAI that the demonstrated great utility of computers in other fields would be evident in education also, and in the same way: through the partial replacement of expensive labour. But education is a profoundly <u>social</u> process, sometimes possessing subtleties beyond our present ability to perceive, much less to measure. What we can say is that the role of the teacher is only secondarily that of a 'delivery system' for facts and techniques, and that the process of learning is as yet dimly understood. So the educational system could not be automated the way payroll systems were. If computers were to be more widely used, they would <u>not</u> be a way of saving money.

Furthermore, the 'political' problems involved in attempting to integrate mainframe-oriented computing into the educational environment were not trivial, whatever the educational benefits. In analysing the survey cited above, Olsen concluded that another reason for the slow expansion of CALL systems was 'the attitudes of many in our profession who are suspicious of computers and modern technology in general'. Such advances as CAI systems might have brought to education were simply outweighed by the barriers, financial and otherwise, to setting them up and maintaining them. Now all that has changed (as Olsen predicted it would).

The Impact of the Micro

The appearance and development of the microprocessor and supporting technology have rendered the financial consideration involved in CAI almost moot. In addition, the ease of use of micros has been developing in rough proportion to their spread into daily life. The computer is no longer exotic technology. Soon it will be safe to assume that both teachers and students will have had exposure to the use of a microcomputer in one role or another. The micro is not yet, but is becoming, simply another information tool, like the telephone, or television. This means that the CALL pioneer in a language faculty has a much easier time of it when he or she proposes to add CALL packages to the repertoire of mechanical aids available to language learners. A repeat of Olsen's survey seven years on would surely show dramatic growth in the use of computers in teaching languages.

Thus we are seeing a great expansion in the 'market' for CALL packages. CALL research has become more academically respectable, and even has a certain overlap with currently 'hot' disciplines like Artifical Intelligence and Human-Computer Interface studies. CALL is also a potential customer for such emerging technologies as digitalised speech processing and interactive video.

Technological Evolution and CALL

The changes in the status of CALL which have occurred in the last few years have been caused entirely by bringing formerly expensive but rather ordinary computer technology into the mass market. By and large we are now using the technology available fifteen years ago, subject to an orders-of-magnitude shrinkage in size and price. Almost everything currently being done in CALL was technically possible from the mid-1960s, which is why many papers on the subject written in this period still make useful reading. In fact, many contemporary CALL packages are implemented on limited-memory micros and therefore offer <u>fewer</u> facilities, such as the ability to record student progress, than were available on the systems which originated fifteen years ago.

This observation must, however, be qualified on two counts. In the first place, the storage deficiencies of microcomputers are rapidly being overcome by progress in providing them with inexpensive, powerful disc drives and communications facilities. In the second place, even the least expensive of the current generation of micros are superior to their mainframe ancestors with respect to the hardware available for their user interface. In nearly every computer system of the previous generation user and computer communicated via a scrolling line-at-a-time monochrome 'glass teletype' (or even an actual teletype). Now almost all current microcomputers have sophisticated colour monitors and the possibility of input via alternatives to the keyboard, such as light pens or 'mice'. Both monitors and dot-matrix printers typically afford the possibility of user-defined character sets, solving the vexing problem of the diacritical marks necessary for most European languages and even permitting the use of non-Latin alphabets.

Very cheap home micros will no doubt always be available. But a machine powerful enough to sustain good CALL facilities will probably fall into the small business machine, rather than the games machine, category. In order for such machines and their peripheral devices to be affordable in sufficient quantities, they will almost surely have to be systems which are sold on the mass market to business and professional users. For such 'off the shelf' systems, we may expect soon to see 256K bytes to be the absolute minimum available RAM, with about ten times as much storage on exchangeable discs, ten times as much again on hard discs, and yet again ten times as much on optical read-only discs. Powerful data communications facilities will be standard. These developments are being driven by the demands of the business and professional user markets. The naive extrapolation which predicted £50 super-micros is almost surely wrong. What we are likely to see is a 'bottoming out' of the price curve in the £500-£1500 region, with further improvements reflected in increased power rather than substantial price cuts. This will still keep micros within the budget possibilities of most educational establishments.

Many other lines of hardware development can be forecast, such as interactive video, random-access audio discs coupled to speech output capacity, very high resolution monitors driven by fast graphics processors, to name but some. Indeed, all of these are available in some form now. What is not clear is whether or not these will be in such demand for general use that they will be produced in mass quantities at relatively low cost. If not, their application to CALL will remain in the category of interesting experiments which cannot be widely replicated.

Assuming a rather conservative development in technology, what new developments can we expect to see CALL utilise? The remainder of this chapter discusses some of the potential CALL applications of the rapidly advancing phenomenon of computer networks. The development of national and international data communications facilities which are open to use by anyone with a microcomputer and a modem may be the most significant social impact of the new technology.

Networks as facilitators of language study

We have recently seen the appearance of a cheap packet-switched international data network, paralleled by technology permitting the proliferation of open-access 'bulletin boards' which can be set up and run by anyone. These promise to be a new tool which may provide language learners with a new motive to pursue their studies and the opportunity for practice in a linguistically-authentic environment. Perhaps the future will see such developments as: bi-national 'twinning' of pairs of language classes studying each other's language, with daily communication via a dedicated bulletin board system; regular participation by language students in trans-national bulletin board sessions conducted in the country whose language they are studying; or their participation in the specialist hobbyist 'conferences' which are another off-shoot of computer bulletin board technology. Some language departments already make use of international television broadcasts distributed via satellite, and this practice will certainly spread as the price of receiving equipment falls. An analogous development in which computers will play a central role is waiting to occur.

Networks and the Incompatibility Problem

One very serious shortcoming of CALL software - shared by all computer software - may be described with one word: incompatibility. Ten of the fourteen chapters of this book report on existing CALL programs: only three of the authors could readily exchange their software with each other. Barring the total conquest of the world by IBM, we can expect to see this situation continue into the indefinite future. We may express this as a law: at any given instant, only a minority of potential users of CALL will be able to run a given piece of CALL software. This is clearly a wasteful and undesirable situation. Is there anything that can be done to alleviate it?

CALL programs are mainly manipulators of strings of words: printing text on the screen, receiving the user's input and testing it against other text held in memory. It is only a slight over-simplification to say that a text file which is held as a simple string of ASCII character codes can be read by any program, running on any computer. This is the situation currently obtaining in the large databanks of publication abstracts, which can be accessed by any one of several different information retrieval systems.

CALL programs will necessarily be written in a language specific to a particular machine and using its peculiar features; there will possibly be externally-stored data used by these programs which are also tied closely to the specific hardware on which the CALL program is implemented. However, many

5

CALL systems can be designed such that much of their externally-accessed data consists entirely of simple bodies of text, which can be held as physically separate files. These files can be relatively easily turned into straightforward collections of ASCII character codes. If, for each of these files there is an associated description of its structure, they would then be usable by anyone developing CALL programs. Some candidates for such treatment would be: lexicons (of varying degrees of sophistication); files of 'drill-and-practice' material; and adventure game texts.

Since nationally- and internationally-access- ible networks are developing rapidly, it would then be feasible for these files to be available as a resource to researchers all over the world developing CALL programs, saving much re-inventing of the wheel.

Therefore a goal of the CALL community - indeed, of everyone who sees the promise of CAI - should be to facilitate the development of an on-line system whereby text files are freely or cheaply available to anyone who can connect to the network. The technical side of implementing such a proposal presents few difficulties. Rather, the problems lie in the political/economic/administrative sphere. The con- crete possibilities for the construction of such a resource will be constrained by the way in which national and international networks develop in the next decade. What is needed is an expansion of the concept of the 'public library' to match the progress being made in the technology of information storage and transmission.

Increasing Access to CALL Systems

Many, if not most micro-based CALL systems in educational establishments are implemented on microcomputers which are confined to 'language labs' or 'computer rooms', perhaps linked in a Local Area Network (LAN). The power and practical usability of these systems may, in some cases, be enhanced by connection to the local mainframe if one is available. One can occasionally detect a tendency in certain quarters to equate 'computer' with 'microcomputer'. This predilection is particularly strong among those in the Further and Higher Education sector for whom the micro represents liberation from an unsympathetic and distant Computer Centre. Thus we presently see many campuses where one or more isolated clusters of microcomputers co-exist alongside a mainframe-and-terminals system.

But the current trend in networking technology is making it increasingly easy to attach micros to the central computer, where they can either simply serve as sophisticated terminals to the central mainframe, or use the latter's high-volume disc storage capacity in support of their autonomous functioning. CALL researchers and implementers working in an institution with a mainframe, but whose work is currently confined to stand-alone or only-locally-connected microcomputers would be well advised to remain alert to the possibility of taking part in the development of such a relationship. An accessible mainframe system can yield at least three advantages for CALL work: (1) The practical availability of CALL systems can be greatly enhanced if microcomputers can be put in many parts of the institution, each with access to a central store of programs held on large-capacity hard discs. The most practical way to provide this facility will probably be in co-operation with the already-existing mainframe-and-terminals network. (2) The disc storage capacity of the typical mainframe system is always likely to be much greater than that available on isolated microcomputer-only systems, and may allow student access to a much larger store of programs and data than presently possible on the latter. (3) A growing number of students will have access to microcomputers-plus-modems at their places of residence and will be able to take advantage of CALL packages which are accessible via the telephone system. For the next few years, centralised mainframe computers will represent the most practical way of providing distance access to CALL software via dial-up facilities. The CALL systems which get the most use are likely to be those which are available via mainframe-mediated gateways, whether or not they themselves are implemented on mainframes.

As is the case with utilisation of national and international networks, the technical problems involved in implementing the above suggestion will usually be overshadowed by the administrative and 'political' problems. But the rewards of success are potentially great and make the effort to tie a local CALL system into the wider computer network well worthwhile.

Conclusions

The next few years will see dramatic improvements in the quality of CALL systems, made possible by the greater memory available on sixteen-bit systems

backed up with hard discs. Widespread utilisation of
the many possible developments in new peripherals,
such as interactive video and speech output, remains
dependent on whether or not these technologies become
mass market items. One development which is occuring
right now is the provision of cheap and uncomplicated
access to national and international data networks.
This provides an opportunity to extend CALL in
several new directions: the possibility of
communication across national frontiers giving
direct access to other language communities; placing
into the public domain dictionaries and other files
of text which can be used by many different CALL
programs; and increasing access to CALL systems.
Utilisation of these opportunities will increase the
effectiveness of the computer as language-teaching
assistant.

Chapter Two

THE CURRENT POSITION IN MICROCOMPUTER HARDWARE AND SOFTWARE

Alan and Pamela Maddison, Thames Polytechnic

The important parts of a computer, to the user, are a keyboard similar to a typewriter, and a screen, which resembles a television. Also important are a memory device, to store information when the computer is switched off, and something to make a permanent record (hard copy) on paper. Linking these together, and doing the actual work, is the central processor unit (CPU). This machinery is called hardware; we also need sets of instructions, called software, that make the computer do what we want. All the user should need to know is which buttons to press, but those involved in the preparation or selection of educational software and hardware need more; in this chapter we aim to cover the basic material relevant to Computer Aided Language Learning (CALL). A fuller treatment is given in "Microcomputers in the Classroom" (Alan Maddison, published by Hodder and Stoughton, or by Love in the U.S.A.).

The Central Processor Unit (CPU)
This can be divided into two parts, a memory and machinery to carry out computations. In essence all computers are similar; a large machine can tackle larger tasks, or be split among a number of users to give each access to a common store of information but size does not alter the basic mode of working. The essential feature of microcomputers is that they can be used in ways that would not previously have been cost-effective.

The memory holds both the program (instructions) to be obeyed, and the data (information) that this program acts on. A program for giving vocabulary drill would have, as data, a list of the words to be tested - which can be altered each time the program is used - the user's latest answer, a record of the

9

number got right and so on. Some people confine the term data to information supplied to the program, and exclude items, such as the score, generated by the program during its execution. (The (British) Data Protection Act defines data to include information generated by the computer.) This central memory comes in two types: read only memory (ROM), which cannot be altered, and whose use is discussed later, and random access memory (RAM), which can be altered. The computer's power comes from the ability of RAM to hold an infinity of different programs and sets of data.

Computers store and manipulate information in binary form, i.e. in terms of sets of 'switches' which may take one of two values (0 or 1). The details need not bother the average user. Memory is generally measured in terms of bytes, units of 8 such binary digits, which may be used in various ways. It is common to record memory in kilobytes (K) – 1 Kbyte = 1024 bytes. Most relevant to our purpose is the use of a single byte to hold a character, which is generally done using the ASCII code. This includes both upper and lower case forms of the basic Roman alphabet and English punctuation marks, and there is a draft international standard (ISO 6937) extending it to cover other alphabets. Equipment used for CALL should allow the user to handle any characters required.

The Central Processor gets instructions from the memory and carries out the operations required. On microcomputers this is done by a single silicon chip called a microprocessor; the same type of microprocessor may be used in different micro-computers. Other chips will act as memory and perform tasks such as communicating with the outside. It is very expensive to develop a new type of chip, but, when this is done, it costs little to manufacture in quantity.

The microcomputers originally used for CALL were 8 bit machines, i.e. they operate on one byte at a time. This limits the amount of memory they can conveniently use to 64K. This has to include the ROM containing the operating software, a record of what is on the screen and a rough working area for the processor, as well as the user's program and data. The more facilities provided in ROM and the better graphics facilities, the less space left for the user. Some machines provide extra memory by switching between different memory areas, but this slows them down. Newer machines use 16 bit microprocessors, which can use much larger memories, and are also faster.

Auxiliary Memory

The main memory of a computer is both limited and
volatile, i.e. the information is lost if we switch
the machine off. The cheapest long term storage
device is an audio style cassette recorder; a good
quality tape is necessary and many users prefer tapes
made for computer use. Special tape recorders are
made for use with computers, and are essential with
some machines - an extra cost not always mentioned -
but ordinary domestic recorders are often used;
paradoxically a high quality machine may be useless,
as noise suppression circuits can filter out the
computer signal.

We can only reach the information we want by
starting at the beginning and going through the tape
to the desired position. Discs, flat surfaces coated
in a recording medium, allow us to go direct to the
information needed. Floppy discs are fairly cheap,
but have a limited capacity and are comparatively
slow. Rigid discs are faster, and have greater
capacities, and are falling in price; the term
Winchester disc is often used.

A compromise is to use the high speed tape loops
originally developed for dictating machines. The
best known example is the Sinclair microdrive, used
with the Spectrum (Timex 2000) and QL computers.
This gives a reasonable performance at low price.

Other alternatives include the use of magnetic
bubble memories, which are very robust and so
suitable for rough conditions, and, soon, optical
discs. It is possible to link computers and video
recorders.

Input Devices

Information is usually entered into a computer via a
keyboard, with the characters typed appearing on the
screen. It is generally possible to correct what has
been typed before the computer has to act on it, so
learners can check they have made no apparent
mistakes in their answers. In English speaking
countries the keyboard would have the QWERTY layout;
it is simple to program the computer to give the
effect of, say, an AZERTY layout for use with French;
an overlay can be put on the keyboard to show the new
meaning of the keys.

An alternative class of input devices is
exemplified by the Concept Keyboard. This is a flat

surface, about A4 size, which can be covered by an overlay. It is divided into 128 regions, and the computer can detect which of these has been pressed. The overlays can show a keyboard, a set of objects, a picture etc; possible uses are only limited by the teachers ingenuity.

There are various methods of selecting a position on the screen. Touchscreen devices, which respond when the user touches the screen, and which can be mounted on existing equipment, are now becoming sufficiently cheap for CAL use. A cursor (marker) can be moved round the screen from the keyboard - some machines have special keys for this purpose - though it is more convenient to use a joystick or a lightpen for this purpose. Pictures can be entered by a variety of devices which move a marker over a flat surface; the name tablet is often used for devices where the user holds a stylus like pen and digitiser for other systems, but this is not invariable. These devices can also be used to control a cursor.

Speech recognition systems exist, but these are unlikely to be good enough for language CAL in the foreseeable future. One study found that, even in an application where speech recognition equipment was adequate, users still preferred to type commands in.

Output Devices
Output is normally shown on a screen similar to a domestic television, and, indeed, one is often used. The name monitor is used for high quality displays, which give better pictures; normally they cannot be used as ordinary televisions, but dual purpose systems are becoming available. A black and white display will give a sharper picture than a colour one of comparable quality for technical reasons.

A printed record (hard copy) may be required from the computer. This will usually be produced by either an inpact or a matrix printer. Impact printers work like typewriters, often with replaceable heads (e.g. daisywheel printers) in matrix systems characters are formed from of an array of dots. Impact printers give a sharper edge, though many matrix printers can now provide almost equally good results. On the other an impact printer has a limited range of characters at any one time; matrix printers are less restricted, and may offer the ability to define your own characters. 'Pin addressable' matrix printers can be used to make a copy of what appears on the screen as can some impact machines.

It is also possible to produce pictures by using a graph plotter, where a pen is moved over the paper. Voice output is possible at a fairly low price, but is unlikely to be good enough, in the near future, for foreign language learning - except, perhaps, for special groups such as air traffic controllers, who have to be able to follow English spoken by non-native English speakers, and heard under poor conditions. Current equipment is designed for a particular language; systems designed for English would not be suitable for French. It is possible to control an audio cassette recorder by a computer; Atari have used a stereo cassette system this way, with one track being used to inform the computer of the position of the tape, and similar systems are offered for other microcomputers.

User Defined Characters and Graphics
In CAI systems, the picture on the screen is made up of small dots called pixels. In systems for the British market, technical factors generally limit them to 256 rows of pixels, though some systems may have 612 pixels per row.

Each character occupies a number of pixel positions, typically 8 rows of 8, and is formed from a pattern of dots. Most microcomputers now allow users to define their own characters by specifying their own patterns (user defined graphics); this can provide an extended alphabet or help produce pictures. The number of characters that can be defined varies from computer to computer; on the Sinclair Spectrum, (Timex 2000), 21 such characters may be immediately be defined but it is possible to completely redefine the whole character set, and to switch between character sets. This could be useful when teaching languages, such as Russian, with a non Roman alphabet. It would even be possible to provide a Chinese vocabulary of several thousand words, though it would be necessary to form each ideogram from several computer characters. A lot of work would be required to define the characters, and also to program the computer to display them. Languages, such as Arabic, which run from right to left would also require a small amount of special programming.

Pictures (high resolution graphics) are formed by specifying each pixel individually. Though normally be used for pictures, they can be used to add diacritics, but the use of user defined graphics is more convenient. The computer would normally provide basic drawing operations, and one might have

13

programs or libraries of routines to help produce
complex pictures. Many computers provide graphics
commands which can be used to build up pictures.
Alternatively one can define one's own characters; a
character may form a complete picture element - e.g.
a man - or several could be combined to form a single
element.

Colour is produced by a combination of red, blue
and green; specifying which of these is present in a
particular pixel provides 8 colours, including black
and white, but requires three times as much memory as
just black and white. By specifying the strength of
each, we can obtain more colours, but need more
memory. Similarly we can highlight a picture element
by making it flash, or by altering its brightness.
However, the extra memory needed for the picture
reduces the space available for users' programs and
data, and some computers provide a range of modes,
providing a trade off between number of colours,
degree of resolution and space needed.

Networks and Viewdata

Computers and associated equipment may be linked in a
network; a Local Area Network (LAN) links equipment
within a site, while a Wide Area Network (WAN)
operates over greater distances. For CAL a number of
microcomputers, probably in a single room, could
share common disc units and printers. This reduces
costs, and allows each user access to common files.
Each computer on the network is known as a station,
and the disc (printer) will be accessed through a
special station known as the file (printer) server.
The computers on the network may require some slight
modification, and extra software; this presents few
problems, but some commercial programms need
modification to be used on a network.

The Viewdata idea was developed by British
Telecom to provide easy access to a large volume of
information, in what is now known as the Prestel
service. Information is organised into screen
displays, and the user can select which page to see
next. Systems have been developed for microcomputers, which can be used to form databases, and
one publisher provides a package with the text in
French.

System Software

This covers programs that do not directly perform any
useful task, but make it easy (!) to write and use

14

programs that do. It includes operating systems, language translation programs and utilities. The essential parts are often included in ROM, and are effectively part of the computer.

The operating system provides communication between user and computer. It receives the users instructions, loads programs and other files, handles communication with peripheral equipment, and controls access to files. Operating systems are either proprietary, specific to one make, or machine independent; in theory programs developed for one of the latter will run on any computer that uses it.

The most common system on 8 bit micros is CP/M, though many machines used for CAL have proprietary systems. 16 bit micros almost all use machine independent systems; in Britain MSDOS may become the standard for educational work.

The actual instructions obeyed by the computer are in binary form, (eg 00110111), but we can write programs in more comprehensible forms, and have them translated by a special program. At the simplest we can use machine code - the actual instructions obeyed by the computer, but written using octal (base 8), decimal (base 10) or hexadecimal (base 16) numbers rather than binary. Above this we may use assembly code, which has broadly the same structure, but uses terms like 'ADD' instead of numbers. This will be specific to one type of computer, or rather microprocessor. Assembly code programs, also known as low level programs, are translated into binary by a program known as an assembler.

High level languages, also known as machine independent languages or problem orientated languages, are designed to be easier to use, and a program may be used on any computer for which an appropriate translation program is available. Unfortunately there can be large differences between different dialects of a language. Translation may be either by an interpreter, which translates each instruction as it is required, or by a compiler, which translates the complete program into binary before it is run. Any language may be interpreted or compiled.

A number of general purpose languages have been used to prepare CAL material. Procedural languages consist of a series of instructions to the computer. Probably the best known, particularly for microcomputers, is Basic, which is comparatively simple to learn, but far from ideal for writing long programs. Pascal is better for this, as is Fortran, which has been widely used on large computers, and

has been extensively revised as ideas about what
should be in languages has developed. The language C
has been attracting interest lately, and is worth
considering if a program will have to run fast.
Snobol was designed to handle and manipulate text.
Two 'exotic' computer languages, which can handle
gramatical transformations and inflexions conveniently, are Lisp (List Processing) and Prolog
(Programming in Logic). The latter is provided with
statements of facts from which it draws conclusions,
including what responses are appropriate.

Other facilities that might be available
include editors used to alter and correct the
contents of files; and libraries of routines (part
programs) to perform particular tasks, these can be
included in programs. For example these may be used
to handle the learner's input, manipulate text and
produce pictures, providing the user of a general
purpose language with many of the features of the
author languages discussed below.

Applications Programs
These are programs that do something directly useful,
e.g. teach languages. Many books give lists of things
to look for when selecting programs; too often a good
educational idea is spoilt by poor implementation.

Producing good computer programs is an
expensive and lengthy process - in 1984 it was
estimated to cost about £4.50 per instruction. It is
necessary to decide what a program should do, and to
test the final product with learners; writing the
instructions should be a small part of the total
task. This is particularly true with commercial
products, which will be used by people unfamiliar
with the program. Piracy, obtaining commercial
program products without paying for them, is theft,
and its prevalence among school teachers has made
firms reluctant to produce and market educational
programs.

The types of teaching program most relevant to
language learning are:
(a) Drill and Practice
(b) Computer Aided Instruction (CAI). The
presentation of new material, and testing a learner's
grasp of it,
(c) Adventure Games, giving practice in the use and
comprehension of language,
(d) Word Processing, allowing learners to write and
modify text in the language being learnt.

It is also possible to use the computer

(Computer Managed Learning - CML) to monitor a learner's progress, and to decide what should be done next; this can be combined with teaching activities. Teachers using programs that record learners' progress should be aware of any legislation concerning personal data; in Britain the Data Protection Act would apply.

If you write your own programs, there are some basic rules. Think before you start writing, and design your program to be flexible, so it can be changed in the light of experience. Separate the logic, what the computer does, from the lesson material, e.g. if words for vocabulary drill are put in files or data statements they can be replaced by new sets for other classes. All messages must be in terms that the learner can understand, not of what is happening inside the computer. The program must not 'crash' if the user makes a mistake, but must make a helpful response. Making a program user friendly often involves much more work than programming the teaching activity.

In language CALL it may be desired to store large numbers of words. There are various encoding techniques, described in other books, which reduce the space needed by up to 75%. Sometimes the space needed can be reduced by making the computer generate inflected forms from the root; see Chapter Thirteen for an example of this. Pictures can also be stored in condensed form, using runlength encoding or quadtree techniques - see specialist texts for details - and it usually requires much less space to store the drawing instructions than the finished picture.

Languages exist for writing instructional material. These generally provide a teaching process in which some information is shown to the learner, who has to make a response; this response determines what is shown next. This approach can be used for drill and practice, and for CAI. Usually the learner has to select from a number of alternatives or to provide a particular word; understanding human language can demand too much of the computer. These languages allow the writer to specify what is shown, and the responses appropriate to different answers. It is generally possible to provide pictures, and to make the response depend on past performance. Such systems reduce the computing knowledge needed, but still require a lot of work; one university which makes extensive use of such tools has found it generally takes a year to learn to use them to full advantage, and not all teachers manage it. These systems allow one to alter teaching material in the light of experience, or to meet different needs; in effect writing becomes a continuous process, under the teacher's control. Chapter Twelve describes one such system, and how it evolved to meet requirements.

Akin to such languages are adventure game generators. The user specifies setting, possible actions and items and what happens next. Teachers could use them to produce material using different scenarios; getting up, in French, can be as much an adventure as finding gold, in English. In a system such as 'The Quill', from Gilsoft, it would be simple to change the language used so that the same basic 'adventure' could be used for different languages. Teachers could produce games to exercise particular language areas, or to provide an insight into different cultures and settings. Systems are also available for producing pictures on the commonly used microcomputers, and could be useful for producing teaching material.

Animation
Computers, unlike books, allow the use of animation, whose potential is discussed in the next chapter. Apart from the use of videotape and videodisc, whose potential is, as yet, more obvious than realised, there are several possibilities.

The pictures may be produced by the computer. Film quality animation is very expensive, but reasonable effects can be produced comparatively easily. It may be necessary to use assembler or machine code to get the required speed.

We can make objects move against a static background by redrawing them in a series of positions (and restoring the background). This can conveniently be done using user defined graphics; a car could be represented by, say, 6 characters (two rows of three). Sprite facilities, available on many computers, make it easy to do this. It is generally possible to scroll all or part of a picture, move it across or up and down the screen, or even diagonally.

Alternatively we may store several of pictures, either swopping memory (this needs a lot of memory) or manipulating the colour value table (this reduces the number of colours usable). Both methods only allow a limited number of pictures, but can be particularly useful for before and after type illustrations. What is possible will depend on your particular computer. If pictures are stored in condensed form it is unlikely that they could be reconstituted fast enough for animation.

Word Processing

Computers are often used as word processors, 'intelligent' typewriters, allowing users to enter and modify text. This could enable learners to produce and correct material in the language being learnt; as corrections will not show in the finished product, they may be more willing to make them. It separates the tasks of composition and of producing the required letters and also reduces the unnecessary work involved in exercises such as rewriting a passage in a different tense. Word processing is also convenient for producing teaching material, particularly where a basic text will need alterations or updating.

Word processing packages are available for most popular computers, but if they are to be used for language teaching it is necessary to ensure that they, and any printers used, will handle the character sets used.

Chapter Three

THE ADVANTAGES OF USING MICROCOMPUTERS IN LANGUAGE TEACHING

Pamela and Alan Maddison, Thames Polytechnic

We confine ourselves to specifically language issues; for a general discussion of CAL and its problems see Maddison (1982).

We do not propose to discuss the basic principles of language teaching, but it is worth examining some fundamental points. One major problem is that there is not much solidly based data on the language learning process; Palmer and Rodgers (1983), in a "State of the Art" article examining the use of games in language teaching, could find only three studies, one of which gave no data. Anecdotal evidence, though illuminating, is often dangerously misleading. We can hope, however, that now that more work is done with observing children and less with rats and flatworms, useful ideas will emerge.

In discussing both problems and ways in which computers may be able to help solve them in the teaching of second (and subsequent) languages we shall also consider the teaching of a first spoken language to deaf students, as there is a great deal of common ground; this is stressed by Goldberg (1982), who has had wide experience with both.

The introduction of computers into teaching may be as revolutionary an innovation as the introduction of writing, far more so than printing. Printing merely mechanised one stage of the dissemination process; mass production of books preceded it, and probably brought about its spread. Literacy, on the other hand, brought about a major revolution in the storage, transmission and retrieval of data. Computers represent a further step, partly through their potential for interaction, and the consequent availability of immediate feedback for the student. A book is not a teacher; outside the tedious mazes of programmed texts, which can cover very few eventualities, it can tell students that they are wrong, but not why; and it can neither make positive suggestions nor give encouragement. With the 16 bit computers now available, it should also be possible to explain errors of grammar or vocabulary use as easily as errors of arithmetic or spelling can be handled on 8 bit machines. It must be remembered, however, that though computers can be better than books, they are not, on their own, as good as teachers.

It is essential to decide on one's objectives; these can be categorised as strategic, or what one is trying to do, and tactical, or how one is trying to do it.

Whether or not computers are used, and certainly before they are introduced, it is a salutary exercise to ask oneself what, eventually, the students are expected to achieve. When computers are to be used, these objectives must be explicitly decided in advance. It appears from such sources as Hayes (1980), in his Presidential Address to the British, Association for Language Teaching, that this is not being done at any level in Britain, and a similar picture emerges for the United States. In some courses, the aim is simple and explicit: for example, a reading knowledge for scientists, or language courses for holidaymakers. Others are more nebulous; there is an assumption in many degree courses that the student should be able to handle the literature of the chosen language, and survive in a country where it is spoken. The latter should be a major objective of any course not concentrating purely on a reading knowledge, and obviously benefits from teaching something about the country itself - if only how to recognise the police. What is less obvious to some people is that an ability to read the language is essential, particularly where the link between the written and spoken word is as tenuous as in French. The question of what is meant by "survival" may need to be considered; it is likely to involve what is acceptable to native speakers, which can vary from language to language - any attempt to speak Swedish is likely to be received more sympathetically than anything but near perfect French, as is emphasised by Ensz (cited in Omaggio, 1983). There is no magic CALL approach that can be applied regardless of aim.

Once the objective has been decided, we reach the stage of tactical planning: what particular topics are to be taught? and what is the best way to teach them? Here again the dearth of evidence is disappointing; Partington (1981) has carried out a survey to see what methods teachers of secondary age children use, but has not yet been able to publish anything on which methods are most effective.

It has been fashionable to suppose that, as young children acquire a fluent knowledge of their own language without specific teaching of vocabulary and grammar, the same can be accomplished at any age. This idea is not new; it has been around for at least a millenium and a half, and the fact that it does not appear to work was one factor that led to the formulation of the theory of critical periods in language acquisition. Although this theory is no longer generally accepted, the fact remains that a need for it was felt, to account for the difficulties found by adults in learning languages; arguments for the direct method also miss the point that it normally takes about seven years of constant exposure and considerable feedback for the child to produce consistently fully acceptable language. Merry (1980) stresses the fact that "the 11-year-old beginning a second language already has a large store of concepts and strategies inextricably tied in with his native language, and it is pointless to expect this language not to intrude, especially if teachers are dealing, as they are advised to, with ideas and situations that are already familiar", and Krashem et al. (1979) found distinct differences between adults and children both in approach and speed of learning and in eventual fluency.

In both cases, it appears that the learners' task is easier if structures are pointed out to them; in spoken French, it is extremely difficult for the learner to isolate elements within the sentence. The specific teaching of grammatical points is even more important with non-Indo-European languages; if the quasi-verb nature of Japanese adjectives is not understood, their modification to past and negative forms can only cause utter confusion. Omaggio (1983) quotes Higgins and Clifford on the necessity of teaching grammar explicitly and requiring language with correct grammar, it not being the case that "the same communication skills that allow one to obtain food in a restaurant would also serve to negotiate a business contract or an international treaty". We might note Papert's findings that children attempting to produce computer-generated poetry discovered the necessity of grammatical categories.

Another factor to be considered is the manner of learning: whether the learner is one of a class or learning without support. Most work has dealt with the former situation, but the market for home tuition of languages is large and healthy, and computers can provide help of a kind that would not otherwise be available. Obviously, when a teacher is available, less actual teaching may be necessary, and the teacher can determine what stage and what topic the learner should tackle next. The fact that a learner at home would be in a one-to-one relationship with the computer is not the advantage it may look; in other areas of CAL, it has long been realised that neither self-pacing nor individual use are the best way of learning; over many years, Hartley's work has shown that pairs or even larger groups are best, and that few individuals work at their optimum pace spontaneously - this may be one reason why programmed learning texts failed.

Transformational grammar offers a useful approach, avoiding the problems that have arisen from using methods to analyse English utterances that were developed for use in Greek and adapted for Latin; besides producing more valid results, they are highly suitable for computer based methods. Whether or not such grammars can generate all valid sentences in a given language, if the idea has any validity it can be used to teach the student how to generate a large number of acceptable utterances, and how to understand them. If the rules are adequate, the computer can be used to generate kernel sentences and carry out transformations; and to match sentences generated by the student. Such an approach could be combined with something analogous to the John Lea scheme, a programme used with children with developmental language disorders; by colour coding parts of speech, it teaches the child to generate sentences to progressively more complex patterns. This approach can be particularly useful when word order differs markedly from the first language, by drawing attention to the problem. On the screen, words can be placed on coloured lines, or even coloured backgrounds, though contrast can be a problem; using different colour characters for different types of word could cause difficulties with words that have colour connotations, and one would not be able to provide "templates" for the pupil to fill with the appropriate class of word and care must be taken not to make the material so colour dependent as to cause problems for students with problems in colour vision; as such problems are estimated to affect about 10% of all males, this is obviously important.

Learning vocabulary is also a major problem. Although few things are more tedious than the learning of long lists, there appears to be no real alternative. Goldberg tried dispensing with it, and found the results so unsatisfactory that he was forced, against his own inclinations, to return to the practice. The commonest words can usually be learnt easily by reading and talking; but whenever any specialised vocabulary is involved, such as that for car repairs, either the words have to be learnt or the student has to carry round dictionaries and phrase books.

The mapping from one language to another is rarely very close. Distinctions are made, and concepts are grouped in one language that do not occur in another; so for many years learning from context and from pictures have been favoured methods of avoiding the word/word link. These, however, both have problems: in the first place, learning from context may not be accurate; if there are only a few instances, the word may be completely misunderstood, as when one of us assumed "chantier" to mean "footbridge" and not "work in progress"; fortunately without fatal results. Pictures have even more problems: Hammerly (1974) found that 70% of children immediately thought of a native language label for the picture shown; in some cases only 40% of the children interpreted a picture correctly, with a maximum of 75% correct, and we found two major problems with our youngest daughter's alphabet book: D for Dinosaur elicited first "monster" and then "Stegosaurus" (which it was), and the picture of a nurse with a brown face led her to assume that the word "nurse" meant "black person", not "someone who looks after sick people".

Other evidence reinforces Hammerly's suggestions; indeed, Sperling (1963) suggests that all visually presented material is aurally mediated. Fontana and Evans (1980) emphasise the point that "at all stages of junior schooling material presented aurally is likely to evoke superior short-term memory performance in children than material presented visually", and Hicks (1980), considering what is actually involved in a visual sequential memory test, points out that "... visual memory is characterised by quick decay and limited capacity". In the context of reading, she suggests that "it might be more profitable to provide general strategies for transferring information into a verbal memory store"; the same may well be true for language learning. It is indeed possible that these problems associated with processing visual, and particularly pictorial information, may account for some of the problems deaf children find with non-verbal tasks.

If labelling will occur, regardless of the teacher's desires, the obvious solution is to make sure the labelling is accurate. Merry found great advantages in using the Keyword system, whereby an idea is used to link the word in the language being learnt with one in the learner's own language. Turner (1983) found similar results, but noted that care has to be taken as some children were spending all their time and energy on the learning strategy, with none left over for the task itself. The advantage of the computer in this approach is that the learner is not restricted to what someone else finds a useful mnemonic: each can supply their own, as the computer can enable each learner to build up a file with their own mnemonic.

Some of the problems with pictures can be minimised by following the example of the John Lea scheme and using a large number of different instances; very good high resolution graphics are desirable, and in the future the use of video discs may be particularly valuable. Winston (1975) has done important work on concept formation by computers which is highly relevant: the computer was taught to recognise an item by means not of descriptions but of examples and counter-examples; an important feature of this work is the idea of the "near-miss", the counter-example that only fails to meet the criterion by, ideally, one feature; another important factor that emerges is the large number of examples needed. There is no reason why a similar approach should not work with human learners; the advantage of using a computer is that examples, counter-examples and near misses could be presented until it is clear that the learner has indeed grasped the intended meaning. Computers have a great advantage over other media in that the use of animation can make the demonstration of verbs, and anything else that can benefit from a dynamic presentation, far clearer. Work has been done on programs where the typing in of a valid descriptive sentence leads to a picture being built up on the screen.

Where rote learning cannot be avoided, computers can be used both to make it more interesting and to check on the type of mistake made; the type of reinforcement used should vary according to the learner. The biggest advantage in using computers in this type of task, however, is that feedback can be immediate: if a mistake is made, indicating that the learner has failed to understand something, it can be indicated and rectified at once instead of a habit being set up that would later take a considerable time to dislodge. Answers in the back of the book do not provide this immediate feedback, and are much less effective. The importance of the interactive aspect of the use of computers is stressed in a recent paper by Ward et al. (1985) who found considerable improvement in the language produced by deaf children after using a program where the computer carried out instructions, asked and answered questions and prompted the child when a grammatical mistake was made. Fox (1982), who considers the most relevant uses of computers to be in drill and practice, reading comprehension and games and simulations, lays great emphasis on the importance of immediate feedback in all of these fields as the great advantage that computers have over other media.

Ideally the learner should be exposed only to the language being learnt for long periods, with access to native speakers for conversation. This is rarely possible, and one must do the best one can. If computers can help teach grammatical points, sentence construction and transformations, and assist in the learning of the vocabulary needed for even the simplest conversation, the teacher can concentrate on the use of language. However, computers can also help here: an area that has only recently started to attract attention is that of adventure games. These need not be purely of the "dungeons and dragons" type, though they may well motivate some otherwise reluctant learners; they can also emulate real-life situations such as catching trains and ordering meals in restaurants. They can be used to give some idea of specific towns, particularly useful when the language is being learnt for holiday purposes; equally, they can place the student in business situations. In school use, more adventurous episodes can be set in a realistic background, enabling the learner to practice the language while learning something about the country and the way people live. In the case of the humble Sinclair Spectrum, an excellent adventure game generator is available (The Quill) that can allow messages to be presented in any language or level of difficulty, with or without graphics, allowing the teacher to concentrate on producing the adventure.

Similar approaches can be used for deaf students, though here obviously the setting will be their own country. Practice in social interaction is equally valuable, and enables the learner to carry out the task without the additional problem of oral communication at this stage.

Another approach, which appears to have great potential, is based on the classic ELIZA program, where certain words from the user were picked up and used to generate dialogue that at a glance seems remarkably naturalistic. Underwood (1982) used a variation on this, called FAMILIA, to simulate conversation in Spanish. A user who carries out such a conversation would end up with a sound knowledge of all the language used; grammatical mistakes are pointed out so that they can be corrected and statements from the student such as "No se" or "no entiendo" will get a help message.

Although little is apparently known of what methods are most effective in the teaching of languages, Partington (1981) has carried out a detailed and valuable survey into what methods are actually in use in the teaching of foreign languages to 14/15 year olds. He found seven to be in common use in the classroom: oral question and answer; learning vocabulary lists; translation into English; guided composition; reading comprehension with questions in the foreign language; blank filling exercises and sentence building. A further twenty were used to some extent, in some cases very occasionally by a few teachers only. Some of these methods are easily adaptable to computer use; others would need some software or hardware not currently widely available, but which could become so within the near future. The use of computers may influence which methods are most suitable and practical.

One such development would be either improved speech synthesis or an ability to integrate either with audio cassettes or, even better, with video discs. Some systems are available for controlling audio equipment, but these are expensive. The other main development would be the provision of a "smart word processor" for the language in question; this could check for accents, agreement and other endings, and conceivably for word order. The computer would not correct the input; it would check with the learner whether the word used was that intended, pointing out the possible error, immediately the word was typed in.

Of the methods listed by Partington, some of those most often used are highly suitable for using with computers: the learning of vocabulary lists, blank filling and sentence building are obviously well suited. Of the less often used methods, translation to the foreign language (both sentences and continuous prose) is suitable given that the range of acceptable answers at this level is likely to be very small. Role playing can be done with adventure games; multiple response questions (in either English or the foreign language) for reading comprehension are particularly easy to arrange, and written questions and answers are also suitable, with the same constraints as translation.

The availability of satisfactory speech output, either by speech synthesis or recordings, would make it possible to carry out exercises in listening comprehension; Partington listed separately four forms the questions could take: questions in English or the foreign language; multiple choice in English or the foreign language. Dictation would also be possible for the individual learner.

The "smart word processor" could be used for reading comprehension with questions in the foreign language and guided composition; also for free composition and résumés in the foreign language.

Some methods present problems, but the computer still might be useful: for translation into English, summaries in English, comprehension with questions in English and some language games. The only ones where we cannot see any way of using computers in the foreseeable future are oral questions and answers; playlets; reading aloud; songs and oral pattern practice. These would require a very sophisticated level of speech recognition.

It is a little disturbing to note that he did not find anyone to be using explicitly transformational approaches; unless this was covered by "sentence building". As suggested above, the computer is well suited to help with this, probably the most important conceptual development in the understanding of language learning. Roberts (1981) has used it in this way, as a "language calculator" that generates sentences according to rules.

No-one should use a computer in language teaching simply because it is there. There should always be a positive reason, even if it is only to deliberately make use of its novelty value. Its use does not of itself commit the teacher to any particular philosophy of instruction; where rote learning is thought to be desirable, it can mitigate the disadvantages of this method, and it can produce graded and structured practice in freer situations. The computer's value in drill and practice should not be ignored, as Fox points out; a number of people dislike drill and practice on philosophical grounds but its pragmatic value is undoubtable. The objection is sometimes also made that its use in this area is a waste of its capabilities; but it is surely more important to do well a job that needs doing rather than show off the more flamboyant tricks of CAL in a manner that may be more distracting than helpful. At present its use is really limited to the written word, at any rate until speech synthesis makes a major jump. In the fields of syntax and vocabulary, it can supplement the teacher's work; with adventure games and the like, it can do what no teacher or book can do. Roberts stresses the usefulness of the computer in motivating teenage boys unenthusiastic about the idea of learning languages; even rote learning became attractive, and it seems that language learning developed pleasant associations in consequence.

The ethical aspects must be considered, whatever method is used. This is more important when the introduction of computers is considered, but should be thought of whenever a change of method takes place; should a method not known to be better be introduced? The question of what provision should be made for helping students who suffer from a new method is rarely considered; for a fuller discussion of this problem, see Maddison (1985).

Apart from the educational rationale for the use of computers, which should be paramount, the most important consideration is cost. The initial cost of the hardware, including storage devices, has to be considered, and also that of software; it must be remembered that while more and more powerful machines are becoming available at lower cost, the price of software is a significant item, particularly if it is fully to exploit the capabilities of the machine. However, the price of books is also rising, and one copy of a good program is likely to be cheaper than a set of books for the whole class. It should not be thought that it is essential to have one computer per student: Hartley's work, confirmed by the experience of others, has shown that pairs or even small groups can work more efficiently than individuals. When software is designed for home use, this consideration is unlikely to apply; where it is to be used by a class, consideration must be given as to whether more than one student will be dealing with a particular topic at the same time.

Where languages use different scripts, there may be extra hardware and software costs. Indeed, where character forms are affected by their position relative to other characters, computers have so great an advantage that they are the chosen method of typing in languages such as Arabic and Hindi; word processing packages have been developed for use in

29

Japanese, where the appropriate syllabary may have to be selected, and the computer can inform the user when a kanji character should be used, and what alternatives the selection should be made from.

There are considerable advantages to the learner in not having to learn the formation of written characters before being able to produce work in the script. These are analogous to the advantages found for young children in using word processing equipment; Perera (1983) found that where writing is slow and effortful, written work lacks resemblance to the writer's spoken language as ideas run on ahead and small grammatical words are left out. A learner using a new script, particularly when it differs markedly in basic approach, is in a very similar situation, both in reading and in writing, and the writing of connected prose would be greatly facilitated in the early stages. It might be worth bearing in mind Chandler's description (1984) of a three-year-old child who learnt to type words, sentences and stories using a word processor without being able to handle a pencil well enough to write with it.

References
Boden, M. (1977) <u>Artifical Intelligence and Natural Man</u>, Harvester Press
Chandler, D. (1984) <u>Young Learners and the Microcomputer</u>, Oxford University Press
Ensz, K.Y. (1982) <u>French Attitudes towards Speech Errors</u> (cited in Omaggio, 1983)
Fontana, D. and Evans, H. (1980) <u>Mode of Stimulus Presentation and Short-Term Memory Efficiency in Primary School Children</u>, British Journal of Educational Psychology 50, 229-235
Fox, J. (1982) Computer Assisted Learning and Language Teachers, <u>British Journal of Language Teaching</u> 20, 89-92
Goldberg, J.P. (1982) Teaching Verb Usage: Another Past Tense Pattern and some Reflections upon Previous Comments, <u>Teaching English to Deaf and Second Language Students</u> 1, 4-15
Hammerly, H. (1974) Primary and Secondary Associations with Visual Aids as Semantic Conveyers, <u>I.R.A.L.</u> 12, 118-125
Hartley, J. (1966) Personal Communication
Hayes, H. (1980) Presidential Address to the British Association for Language Teaching, <u>British Journal of Language Teaching</u> 18, 5-10
Hicks, C. (1980) The ITPA Visual Sequential Memory

Task; an Alternative Interpretation and the Implications for Good and Poor Readers, British Journal of Educational Psychology 50, 16-25

Higgs, T. and Clifford, R. (1982) The Push Towards Communication (cited in Omaggio, 1983)

Krashem, S.D. et al. (1979) Age, Rate and Eventual Attainment in Second Language Acquisition, TESOL Quarterly 13, 573-582

Maddison, A. (1982) Microcomputers in the Classroom, Hodder & Stoughton.

Maddison, P. (1985) Ethical Aspects of CAL (in: Smith, D. Information Technology and Education; Signposts and Directions for Research, ESRC)

Merry, R. (1980) The Keyword Method and Children's Vocabulary Learning in the Classroom, British Journal of Educational Psychology 50, 123-136

Omaggio, A.C. (1983) Methodology in Transition: the New Focus on Proficiency, Modern Language Journal 67, 330-341

Palmer, A. and Rodgers, T.S. (1983) State of the Art: Games in Language Teaching, Language Teaching Abstracts

Papert, S. (1980) Mindstorms, Harvester Press

Partington, J. (1981) Teachers' Strategies in the Foreign Language Classroom, British Educational Research Journal 7, 71-79

Perera, K. (1985) 'Do your Corrections' - How can children improve their writing, Child. Lang. Teach. Ther. 1, 5-16

Roberts, G. W. (1981) The Use of Microcomputers for the Teaching of Modern Languages, British Journal of Language Teaching 19, 125-129

Sperling (1963) A Model for Visual Memory Tasks (in Fontana & Evans, 1980)

Turner, G. (1983) Teaching French Vocabulary: a Training Study, Educational Review 35, 81-89

Underwood, J. (1982) Simulated Conversation as a CAI Strategy Foreign Language Annals 15, 209-212

Ward, R., (1985) The Evaluation of 'The Language and Thought' Software, Journal of Computer Assisted Learning 1, 66-72

Winston, P.H. (1975) Psychology of Computer Vision (cited in Boden, 1977)

Chapter Four

THE MICROCOMPUTER AND THE CULTURE LANGUAGE APPROACH TO AMERICAN INDIAN LANGUAGE MAINTENANCE

Gary B. Palmer, Associate Professor, Department of Anthropolgy and Ethnic Studies, Associate Director Center for Computer Applications in the Humanities University of Nevada, Las Vegas

Introduction

For technophile language educators, the lure of microcomputers lies in CAI (Computer Assisted Instruction). In most cases, this means that the computer displays linguistic subjects to the screen of a cathode ray tube monitor. With CAI, presentation routines can interactively await student responses and adjust the subsequent presentation sequences accordingly. For those who can afford the hardware and software, the potential benefits are enormous, because languages are best learned interactively, but the majority of communities in the world can not yet afford computers in the classroom. For them, the benefits lie out of reach for at least a decade. Amidst all the hoopla over CAI, the potential for microcomputers to enhance traditional classroom instruction goes almost unnoticed. Just as important, the new technology can support an approach to language teaching which emphasizes the 'culture language', that is, the culture-loaded items of vocabulary (Eastman 1981). The implementation of this approach can be enhanced with hard copy materials produced with the assistance of microcomputers.

This article is about the use of a microcomputer system costing under $2,500 for the production of textbooks in the language of the Coeur d'Alene Indians of Idaho, USA. The system discussed is the first popular computer in the United States to make use of bit mapping technology which permits the relatively facile mixing of alphanumeric text with graphics figures which can be viewed on the screen and printed on paper. The cost is one which could be borne by most American Indian language programs, and by many other communities which need native language materials. It is especially appropriate in situations where the target population of native speakers is relatively small, making it difficult to justify more traditional and expensive methods of typesetting.

In this paper I discuss the significance of bitmapping technology for the production of instructional material and I describe the use of the microcomputer in the Language Preservation Project of the Coeur d'Alene Indian Tribe of Idaho. I argue that the computer offers hope for greater intertribal co-operation in the production of language lessons. I include a few remarks on the design of lessons. I discuss costs. Finally, I explain why modern computer technology can enhance the production of lessons based on the culture language approach.

Bit-mapping

The human species has been developing graphics technologies at least since the Upper Paleolithic when the peoples of Altimira, Spain drew images of bison on the walls of their caves. With the emergence of hieroglyphic writing in Egypt and ideographic writing in China a mere four millenia ago, graphics and writing technologies merged into unified modes, but in the Mediterrean cultures phonetic alphabets ultimately replaced hicroglyphics, while in China ideographs evolved into complex characters whose function as images is today marginal. For publication, Western culture has relied upon the Mediterrean tradition of phonetic alphabets up to the present day, with iconic and representational images being a relatively clumsy adjunct achieved of late primarily by means of expensive photo offset devices. However, a new imaging technology has again tipped the balance toward more direct visual representation of ideas, with a more facile mix of text and image.

The advent of microcomputers in which text and images are bit-mapped makes it possible to overlay the two modes, to print them as they appear on the screen, and to store the mixed images in computer files, from whence they can be later recalled, edited, and printed again, as many times as necessary. Prior to the advent of bit-mapping, computers stored text character images in permanent read only memory. It was possible to create graphics images, by painstaking specification of each bit. Programs which painted images were available prior to 1984, but the images could not be used in the same document with text, nor could the keyboard be used to overlay text on graphics. In brief, text and graphics were poorly integrated at best, but most often they existed in separate computing domains. Micro-computers with faster central processing chips and larger internal random access memories have changed all that by removing text fonts from read only memory and placing them squarely in the graphics image. The marriage is not yet perfect, but it is definitely utilitarian. As the technology becomes cheaper and more widespread, its influence will be as strongly felt as that of other historical revolutions in publishing, such as the use of paper, the printing press, and the typewriter.

Currently the greatest interest in the new technology focuses on computer assisted instruction, the use of the machine to present instructional routines directly to the student. I share this interest, but I also believe that in the near future more important practical consequences will flow from the ability to use bit-mapped computer systems to produce high quality hard copy (paper) instructional materials. The bit-mapping technology makes the production of illustrated instructional workbooks a relatively inexpensive endeavour compared to the situation which existed as recently as 1983. Furthermore, the skills necessary to produce final copy are well within the reach of the average intelligent layman who is willing to practice and read reasonably simple manuals.

The new technology would appear to be particularly beneficial to small communities with minimal budgets. For an investment of less than ten thousand dollars, they can purchase the equipment necessary to produce fully illustrated workbooks for classroom use. This level of expenditure is within the reach of education programmes of many American Indian tribes in the United States and many small communities elsewhere in the world. Hitherto the tribes have been handicapped because their populations were too small to justify expensive publications costs for native language instructional materials. The new microcomputer graphics technology offers a means for them to self-publish native language materials which would hitherto remain in the memories of tribal elders or on the dusty linguistic shelves of university libraries. Because the tribal need for instructional materials is great, the potential influence of bit-mapped microcomputer self-publishing on American Indian native language programs is immense.

The Current State of American Indian Languages

The linguistic legacy of American Indians is rich and diverse. It is likely that over 300 indigenous languages were spoken in North America prior to the settlement of Europeans on this continent. The major groupings of related languages include (1) Uto-Aztecan of the Southwest, a group including the Nahuatl speakers of the Aztec kingdom in the valley of Mexico, (2) Salish of the Northwest Coast and the Interior Plateaus, (3) Algonquian of the Northeast Woodlands, (4) Hokan-Sioux, a group widely distributed across the continent, (5) Penutian of the Northwest and the central valley of California, (6) Athabascan of Canada, Alaska and the American Southwest, and (7) Eskimo. Many small isolates, such as the Zuni of the Southwest and the Kutenai of Idaho and British Columbia, cannot be confidently related to one of the major groups. Some would divide the major seven into as many as 62 distinctive groups (Campbell and Mithun 1979). Within each of the major groupings are many languages which are mutually unintelligible, and within those exist many dialects. While representatives of all the major groupings still survive, many languages within them have become extinct. Such was the fate of Beothuk, Nicola, Chumash, Vanyume, Salinan, Natchez, Esselen, Yana, Alliklik, Tubatulabalic, Timucua, and Halchidoma.

With the arrival of Spanish missionaries in the 16th Century, American Indian languages came under attack. In the Southwest, Spanish became an Indian lingua franca at an early date (Bright 1976). The early Catholic missionaries, and the hundreds of Episcopalians and Protestants who followed up to the 20th Century, almost invariably attempted to teach modern European languages while suppressing native tongues. Extirpation of native languages was essential to their program of winning the Indians away from shamanism and the nature spirits which the missionaries believed to be the puppets of the devil (See, for example, Gill (1983) and Point (1967)). While Indians have borrowed heavily from the phonological and grammatical forms of neighbouring Indian languages, their contact with Europeans and Americans of European background, not to mention Africans, Chinese, and Polynesians, resulted in little structural borrowing. Bright (1976) has speculated that obsolescence and extinction have overtaken most Indian languages before structural borrowing could occur. Furthermore, deep level borrowing may require congruence of world views or a recognition of the necessity of adopting a world view imposed by imperialist and colonial powers, but many anthropologists who have worked with American Indians have been impressed by the tenacity of basic values in the face of overwhelming cultural imperialism (1).

Perhaps there has simply not been time for Indian languages to reflect non-Indian language structures, because in spite of inundation and appropriation of Indian homelands by EuroAmericans during the past four centuries, at least 200 distinct languages survive today in various states of integrity (Leap 1981). Navajo, for example, can listen to radio broadcasts in their native tongue as they drive through the reservation. The Oglala Sioux boast a substantial linguistic community on the Pine Ridge Reservation. Some of the more populous Salish and Athapascan groups of Canada and Alaska have hundreds of speakers. Reliable data on numbers of native speakers and the state of language preservation are unavailable for most and perhaps all tribes (Leap 1981). It is probably true that among most Amerindian tribes, fewer than 500 native speakers maintain their linguistic heritage, and among those who do, the native language of the younger generation has degenerated greatly from that of their parents and grandparents. Nevertheless, native speakers and non-speakers alike place a high value on learning and speaking native languages, regarding the language as a premier sign of ethnic identity.

Difficulties in Learning Native Languages

In spite of the high value placed on language maintenance, few, if any, programs of native language instruction are successful in producing fluent speakers. This is not to imply that all such programs are failures. Many can claim success in introducing students to native language concepts and constructs, and in exposing them to the sounds of native languages. These are useful goals in themselves, but if the goal is to produce speakers, there are enormous obstacles, including the following which I have observed among one or the other of the several tribes with whom I have worked:
*   Few classroom teachers boast native language skills and few native speakers possess skills in classroom instruction. Classroom teachers are typically non-Indians with minimal interest in learning difficult phonologies of complex languages

possessing limited utility beyond the reservation. To gain their participation, instructional materials must have intrinsic interest beyond their value in teaching language basics.
*   Few youth have the opportunity to participate in native language conversations. Native speakers may make little use of their language, even in the home, often in reaction to old instances of ridicule in school or in neighbouring non-Indian communities.
*   Elderly native speakers may use the language, but criticize the faltering first attempts of youth and teachers, thereby discouraging further practice. Even middle-aged native speakers receive severe criticism from older, more traditional speakers. The embarrassment of public criticism is sometimes sufficient to discourage native speakers from participating in instructional programs.
*   Good native language workbooks and readers are scarce and even good materials may be difficult to use.

Good workbooks are scarce because linguists and highly literate native speakers are in limited supply and they are expensive personnel. Few tribal education programs can afford a full-time linguist. More often, workbooks are produced by non-linguists. Often, a linguist is obtained for a few weeks on a grant from the state office of the National Endowment for the Humanities. He or she is funded for a time which is sufficient to produce a short introduction to the phonology and a few simple question-answer frames, vocabulary lists or verb paradigms. Alternatively, a graduate student produces a comprehensive grammar, essentially the doctoral or master's thesis rendered in a practical orthography. The resulting workbook is far too advanced for beginning students. Seldom, if ever, do American Indian language programs produce a comprehensive series of workbooks spanning the gamut from beginning to advanced materials.

Materials written by linguists often make the mistake of plunging native speakers into interactive question and answer lessons before the students have become familiar with phonology and the orthography. They may use orthographies which native speakers find alien, as when the numeral '7' is used to represent a glottal stop, or the character 'i' is used to represent the high front vowel which Indians with an English education more naturally try to represent with 'ee'. The orthographic conventions of linguists can be strongly justified in terms of consistency and reduction of ambiguity, but they require more preparation of the students and the language community than do more natural conventions. I have seen very high community resistence to potentially useful, but novel, orthographies. Still worse, unusual orthographies can become the focus of factional differences arising from other sources. It is important that new conventions be field-tested and introduced carefully.

Where reasonably consistent orthographies exist and have found employment prior to a program of language instruction, it is best to use them. When I began work on the Coeur d'Alene Language preservation project, I encountered the problem of conflicting orthographies at first hand. The existing Coeur d'Alene practical orthography was very consistent, but I had difficulty accustoming myself to using right and left parentheses to represent conditioned variants of a pharyngeal phoneme, such as the word Hn(us(uskwe' 'Lost Waters'. My attempts to substitute capital R were met with polite but firm resistence until I eventually capitulated. A similar fate met my attempts to use the more common stress mark in place of an underlined vowel. Now reconciled, I am glad I surrendered , because the result supports and provides continuity with previous indigenous work.

* School administrators may give native language instruction low priority, particularly where the language is thought to be moribund or where uncertainty and rivalry exist concerning the relative jurisdiction of school administrators and administrators of native language instruction programs.

* Failure to develop speaking skills may be taken as a sign of program failure, even though reading skill and cultural appreciation may be developing. This is an important point which is insufficiently recognized in language maintenance programs. Eastman (1981:302-303) has suggested the useful concept of a 'culture language' which can be stressed in curricula of language programs 'where American Indian languages are no longer used by people to communicate with each other but where they are important symbols of the group's identity'. The approach requires a shift in emphasis from teaching language for its own sake to teaching local Indian history and culture using the native vocabulary and concepts. This leads away from a culture-free approach and towards the teaching of vocabulary which is culture-specific. I believe Eastman's formulation will gain widespread acceptance and will be found to be most appropriate for the majority of Indian language maintenance programs.

Although I had not seen Eastman's work when I produced the Coeur d'Alene workbooks, the basic approach was my primary working principle. Because of many technical constraints of introductory phonetics, it was difficult to follow, but I was able to introduce such interesting vocabulary as qhasi'qs, the word for moose, which means 'good nose', and 'L'Lkhwi'lus, meaning little hole in the head;' referring to a spring on a hillside and to the Indian and Jesuit mission town of DeSmet, which is built on that hill. Though difficult to integrate into introductory phonetics lessons, the culture language approach is well suited to such topics as geography and personal names which provide the focus of the current Coeur d'Alene language preservation project. Eastman refers to the idea as 'language resurrection'. The culture language 'consists of a stock of vocabulary reflecting Indian cultural concepts (e.g. unique cosmology, counting systems, mythology, fishing and hunting techniques, oral tradition)' (Ibid:302). While Eastman emphasizes vocabulary, it is not hard to envision lessons in which morphology and syntax also reveal Indian thinking and culture, but this is not the proper forum in which to develop culture language theory, which is in essence an applied branch of Whorfian linguistics. It is important to realize that fluent native speech is not necessarily the goal of a culture language program. Understanding and appreciation of Indian culture have priority. I will return to the relation between the culture language approach and the computerized production of language lessons in the summary.

Difficulties in Producing Educational Materials

A host of influences make the production of native language instructional materials a difficult task.

Unusual characters and unusual sequences of letters are difficult to type, an especially serious problem where tribal secretarial services are minimal. In Coeur d'Alene, a typist using the practical orthography faces such constructions as 'L'Lkhwi'lus and hnχp'χp"mi'n'n. To cope with a text of more than a few words, a typist must be bilingual or make a serious commitment to the program. Typists who can reliably reproduce the orthography are difficult to find.

Tribes with minimal financial resources may be

unable to afford graphics production and typesetting. Each tribe must produce or contract for its own materials because there is little sharing of materials among tribes. This is due partly to the diversity of languages and partly to the inability or failure of tribal education departments and linguists to coordinate programs and share materials as they develop. As scholars, linguists have an ingrained dislike to plagiarism, but this scholarly attitude may be inappropriate where the interests of education would be better served by the mass production of materials in many languages. Coordination of tribal education programs could promote greater sharing.

Some of the blame for the lack of sharing can be laid to technical barriers. Good educational materials, especially at the primary school level, often require a mix of text with expensive camera-ready graphics. Where text and graphics are mixed, the originals must be modified or partially reproduced. The economic efficiency of such re-use of existing materials may be less than 50 per cent. It may require a full order of magnitude improvement in production efficiency to justify the added costs of coordination and sharing. The difficulty of modifying original manuscripts makes it difficult to share materials among greatly diverse linguistic groups. Dissolving the thrombosis in technical production would stimulate tribal education programs to coordinate with one another and release the energies of applied linguists to produce more lessons.

The Macintosh as a Solution (2)

Computers provide the obvious solution to the problem of preserving and modifying original manuscripts in which text and graphics are mixed. I have been using the Macintosh microcomputer with 128K of internal memory, at first with a single internal drive for storage on cartridge diskettes and later with an external drive. Through June of 1985 the Macintosh, made by Apple Computer, was the only popular computer offering a well integrated text and graphics system of bit-mapped graphics and the easy-to-use windowing environment in which the user issues commands by manipulating icons on the screen and choosing 'pull down' menu items with a mechanical 'mouse' pointer which rolls and clicks. Atari and Commodore corporations have both announced their intention to produce similar machines at lower prices, and by 1986 it is expected that all new microcomputers will offer similar features.

The design of software is critical to the usefulness of the Macintosh and its imitators in language programs. Every item of software must integrate text and graphics and it must allow the transfer of both text and graphics information between programs. The paint program enables the convenient mixture of text with graphics. Duplicates of graphics files can be sent through the mails on diskettes or over the telephone to any office with a Macintosh computer. On arrival, they can be printed as is or modified to suit the recipient. A linguist could sit down at the computer with a native instructor and a diskette copy of language lessons from another tribe. Together, they could go through the lessons, call up the files, and substitute text in the target language for that in the previously used language.

Of course, it is not all so simple, because it may be difficult to adapt lessons to a new environment. One problem arises when different illustrations are required to support similar demonstrations of grammar in two languages. For example, it may be feasible to illustrate transitivity with verbs for gathering roots and accompanying illustrations in one language, but another language may have no single word for root gathering, or the word may be so complex that it should not be used because it would exceed the current level of the students' knowledge. Thus, the graphic illustration of gathering roots would be useless at this point in lesson development, however, it might be useful for illustrating quite a different point in Indian grammar, possibly one involving a noun for 'root' or 'root digger' or an intransitive verb for work. Thus, it would have to be moved to another position in the lessons. Each group of lessons has its own syntax. The lesson developer would then face a trade-off between producing new illustrations and sifting through old files to match illustrations to instructional problems. There is a need to experiment to determine just how much file sharing between languages is useful. A joint project involving three languages, two of which are closely related, would provide some answers to these questions.

If some file browsing is inevitable, then a cataloging system is needed. The Macintosh permits at least two different approaches to storing and sorting graphics files: desktop and filing. The most elementary approach, and the only one available at the time of this project, is to use the 'desktop' of the Macintosh operating system to organize files hierarchically by placing related files in 'folders' which appear on the 'desktop' screen as icons. Unfortunately, these folders are inaccessible from within programs. Returning to the desktop can be a time consuming process, so one inevitably resorts to naming files carefully, with prefixing or suffixing to represent common themes. This system also raises the question of what to name the folders. Should files be sorted by topic or by features of grammar? Sorting by grammar may be most efficient for the developer, but topical sorting may be required to render them useful to developers for other languages. The solution of maintaining two filing systems with duplicate files is both time consuming and expensive. This brings us to the filing approach.

With a filing or database program it is possible to sort by either subject or linguistic criteria, or both. In fact, one can sort by many criteria. Until the advent of the Macintosh, it has not been feasible to archive graphics files with personal computers. Now, it is possibe to store graphics files in a database and sort them by key words. When a desired file is located, it is sent to a buffer called the 'clipboard', from which it can be retrieved by the paint program for revision. At the present time, this is accomplished most effectively with a 512K-byte Macintosh and a program called 'Switcher' which acts as a shell to alternatively activate either of two or more programs residing in internal memory. Switcher enables rapid switching between database, word processor and paint programs, with the clipboard buffer acting as the conduit between them. The program FileVision also permits the stored files to be represented as icons on the screen, so that, for example, a dozen files representing cut-outs in a large map could be represented as icons on the map itself. From here, it is only a short step to interactive instruction if tribal budgets support microcomputer purchases for classroom use.

A filing program which accepts graphics images requires adequate storage devices. Graphics files vary from 6 to 30 K-bytes per screen. With five megabyte cartridges or a fixed disk all the images used in the Coeur d'Alene workbooks could be indexed and stored in a single database, making future recovery more convenient. And one is not limited to drawings. With devices costing as little as $200, including software, one can digitize photographs, figures and maps. Devices which capture video images are available at about $500. The image files can be edited with the paint program, then indexed and stored in the file program.

Using this extremely versatile technology, it would be a relatively easy matter to produce a native language geography workbook complete with maps and digitized photographs or a book of biographical sketches with photographs. These two projects are currently in progress in the Coeur d'Alene language preservation program. The technology completely circumvents expensive photo offsetting. The quality is not as high, but for many purposes it will suffice. For illustrating language workbooks, the iconic quality of edited digitized images will often prove superior to detailed photos just as the casual traveller prefers a road map to an aerial photograph of the same terrrain.

If possible, the language program using a bit-mapped microcomputer should also purchase a fixed disk, an item which costs from $1,400 to $2,000. The fixed disk is much like the standard external disk drive except that it holds from 6 to 15 times as many images. The standard 400 K-byte cartridge holds only one or two dozen screens of graphics images. But even more important than storage capacity is the speed of operation. Much of the time involved in producing the Coeur d'Alene workbooks was actually spent listening to the sing-song whir of the disk drive as the paint program shuffled data and subprograms back and forth from the cartridge diskette. A fixed disk could speed up these operations by at least a factor of three, yielding a reduction in development time of up to 50 per cent. Inexpensive RAM disk or emulated disk drive software is not preferred because it does not work with the switcher program.

The Macintosh computer also solves the problem of special characters in a convenient manner. A program called the font editor enables one to modify the appearance of the entire ASCII character set in point sizes from 9 to 72. A new user-defined font is easily installed in the system files of any diskette with a program called the font mover. The screen display and the printer drivers of the graphics paint program, the two available word processing programs, and at least one filing program, MicroSoft File c, make use of the system fonts handled by the font mover. The filing program DBase Master c will display special fonts but it cannot print them. It is also limited to records of 3000 characters or less. Thus, it does not adequately support a culture language approach where each field might be required to store a text of over 3,000 characters. Microsoft File supports fields up to 64,000 characters, or about 20 single spaced typed pages, in length. If one has the external storage capacity to support it, each of hundreds of fields in hundreds of records can be of this length. Several other commercial database programs are available.

Text and graphics can also be mixed within the word processor files, but they coexist less conveniently in this program. The mix is accomplished by copying graphics files to the clipboard or to a file called the scrapbook, from whence they are 'pasted' into the main buffer of the word processor, where they appear to act as a separate paragraph. In my experience, it is more convenient to print all pages which mix text and graphics from the paint program. Of course, the graphics program lacks automatic page numbering and other formatting functions of the word processor. The graphics capability of the word processing programs is most useful where a stock graphics character is used repeatedly amidst a substantial quantity of text.

The Coeur d'Alene Language Preservation Project

The 1000 plus enrolled members of the Coeur d'Alene Tribe of Idaho (CDI) live on the reservation near the southern boundaries of their aboriginal territories. After suffering severe epidemics in the late pre-contact period, the Coeur d'Alene accepted the Sacred Heart Mission of the Jesuit order in their territory in 1846. Conversion was swift and thorough. Under the tutelage of Fathers Joset and Diomedi, several Indians became prosperous commercial farmers by the late 19th Century. In 1890 the population of over 500 Coeur d'Alene was augmented by about 100 Spokan, another language of the Salish family. Boarding schools for both boys and girls were built at the mission town of DeSmet. In the late 19th and early 20th centuries, children who learned Coeur d'Alene and Spokan in the home, were required to speak English at school and study other European languages as well. Indian languages were discouraged.

Today, the survivors of that cohort from the boarding schools make up the native speaking population of the Coeur d'Alene tribe, an elite group of no more than twenty elders, not all of whom are mobile enough to visit and converse on a regular basis. Two of these work part time as teachers in the native language instruction program in the tribal

school. One of the instructors, Lawrence Nicodemus,
worked with linguists in the 1920s and 1930s and
later himself produced an excellent two volume
practical dictionary of Coeur d'Alene and a book of
language lessons printed in the same practical
orthography. The latter is useful, but most Coeur
d'Alene find it difficult.

The Nicodemus orthography uses standard
typewriter characters, with apostrophes for
glottalizations and parentheses for pharyngeal-
izations. The one exception to the standard character
set is the slashed-l, which appears as 'γ' or '$\mathcal{L}$'.
This frequently used character causes infinite grief
to tribal typists who are unused to reproducing the
Coeur d'Alene language. Nor do they appreciate the
trigraphs used for glottalized consonants: ch', k'w,
ts'. Until 1980, there was only one Coeur d'Alene
text available in the Nicodemus practical
orthography.

The Coeur d'Alene Language Preservation project
was undertaken in January 1984 at the initiative of
the department of Education, CTI, Armando Da Silva,
Director, with a grant from the Association for the
Humanities in Idaho. It provided for the
collaboration of two native speaking tribal elders
with the author to produce a set of native language
lessons suitable for the primary grades of the tribal
school at DeSmet, Idaho. Linguistic elicitation for
the project took place during two weeks in January,
after which I returned to Las Vegas and began
producing lessons on an Apple II Plus computer and
Epson printer which uses a standard installed
character set. The most convenient way to render the
'γ' character was to draw in the slash by hand. The
product was unattractive and no funds were available
for typesetting and graphics production.

In late February I purchased the Macintosh
computer, and began learning the graphics
procedures. My first efforts produced only one page
per day, but the situation improved as I learned the
procedures and built up a library of figures which
could be pasted onto the screen and rotated or
otherwise modified. A tribal artist produced a
muskrat figure which I copied on the computer and
then shrunk, expanded, rotated and dressed to make a
whole series of muskrat characters. Though I boast no
particular artistic gifts or experience, the
computer graphics pleased both myself and the tribal
Department of Education. When reproduced on a modern
photocopy device at 2.5¢ per page, the effect is
almost as good as typesetting and far superior to

45

materials produced on ditto machines.

Of course, graphics are not the only problem to consider in producing a native language workbook. It would be easy to produce graphics which distract from the lessons. Graphics must complement and augment the text. One must introduce the orthography and phonetics in understandable fashion. Then one must systematically, and interactively, provide a series of increasingly complex forays into the culture language, if that is one's approach, or into morphology, syntax, semantics and pragmatic speech acts, if one's approach is more traditional.

All of this represents an investment which should be utilized beyond the boundaries of the original language. When one considers the many Indian children who need good instructional materials, the idea of confining a set of lessons to a single tribe seems unpardonable. Therefore, it is my hope that other tribes will try to adapt the lessons to their own languages and that the Coeur d'Alene muskrat characters will become multilingual, perhaps learning to speak Kalispel, Thompson and Shuswap among closely related languages, and Nez Percé, Shoshone, and Kutenai among the unrelated but neighbouring languages. For this to take place, those tribes would have to acquire computers which can read the Macintosh diskette format. Tribes which cooperate in this way will acquire the ability to produce a series of workbooks for what it formerly cost to typeset only one. The new technology offers the opportunity to develop a community of tribes which share lessons as they are produced, thereby reducing the cost of production and greatly expanding the horizons of the next generation of students.

Design of the Workbooks

In any discussion of computer graphics there is a tendency to turn the piece into a tutorial. Microcomputer trade magazines abound with hints for coaxing the paint program to produce amusing expansions of figures and subtle shading effects, so I will purposely avoid that in favor of more significant issues in the use of graphics for language instruction.

Selection of the content of figures is a most difficult task. Too many bury the text, while irrelevant images distract attention from the lessons. Even great artistic inspiration and talent will not produce a useful workbook if relied upon exclusively. The content should reflect the language, call attention to important points and assist the memory. The moose below illustrates not only the term for the animal, but also the suffix meaning 'nose', one of over 30 anatomical suffixes which play an important linguistic role in Coeur d'Alene. The panel also introduces Coeur d'Alene vowel harmony for the alert student (Figure 4.1).

Figure 4.1: Qhasi̱'qs

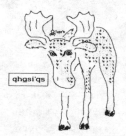

qhes means "good."
-i'qs means nose.
Write a word that means "good nose" or "moose."

The "e" in **qhes** changes to an "a" in **qhasi'qs**.
That's because of the "q" in **-i'qs**.

An illustration of muskrat children making the sound of wind howling on Halloween night was intended to remind students of the phonetic features of the trigraph 'khw' (Figure 4.2).

Figure 4.2: wind on Halloween night

KHW is the sound of wind
on Halloween night.

How many letters in the sound **khw**?

Circle the right answer.

ne̱k'we'   e̱sel   chi̱'ɬes

An Indian theme might have been better, but none was ready at hand to illustrate the sound. Muskrats of varying sizes illustrate the formation of diminutives (Figure 4.3).

Figure 4.3: Chch'likhw

CHE-lekhw ⟶ ch-ch-'LIKHW

WHAT HAPPENED?

CHE ⟶ ch-ch

lekhw ⟶ LIKHW

LIKHW ⟶ 'LIKHW

What did the **che** in **chelekhw** change to?_____
What did the **e** in **lekhw** change to?_____
What did the **l** in **chelekhw** change to? _____

A path which must be traversed by spelling the names of resident figures provides an instructional game. Parts of figures and small scale figures drawn for previous lessons provide graphic reinforcement. With the graphics software, one can retrieve partial figures and scale them down if necessary (Figure 4.4).

Figure 4.4: Spelling Pathway

Name the Picture

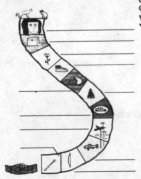

Smiyiw and Chch'likhw are having a race to the basket of sqigwts at the end of the path. Choose whether you want to be Smiyiw or Chch'likhw. If you can give a Coeur d'Alene word for the picture, you can move to the next square. If you miss, you have to sit tight while the other player gets a chance to move ahead.

If you can't think of a word, look it up in Nicodemus' dictionary and get it next time. GAME IDEA BY JAY POWELL, ET AL., IN <u>THE SOUNDS OF KWAK'WALA, BOOK 5</u>.

A map of modern Lake Chatcolet is used to illustrate
the typical construction of lexemes of geography
which begin with a prefix of contiguity (Chat-, 'on a
flat object'). This page also reveals that the modern
name for the lake derives from a Coeur d'Alene word
with the meaning 'the lake where it is flat like a
meadow' (Figure 4.5).

Figure 4.5: Chatq'ele'

Q'ele' means "lake"
Chat- means on a flat, like a meadow
-ip means "bottom"
Chch'likhw lives at Q'ele'ip
Who lives at Q'ele'ip?_____
What is a word that means "bottom of the lake?"

_____

What is a word that means "flat lake?"

_____

Illustrations in the Coeur d'Alene workbooks
reflect a broader purpose than mere instruction in
the forms of language: they were intended as a
vehicle for teaching Coeur d'Alene culture as well.
Figures illustrating traditional basketry and food
plants reflect the more comprehensive scheme of the
culture language approach. The illustration of
pattern in basketry, fabric, or native construction
materials is remarkably well served by the paint
program. It is a simple matter to create a shape,
fill it with a pattern and multiply it. Shapes can be
inverted horizontally or vertically; they can be
rotated, or reversed in shading to yield dramatic
representations of authentic native patterns. The
workbooks contain traditional patterns never before
seen by most Coeur d'Alene children. While it is
useful to present authentic native patterns for their
own sake, the combination of culture and language
should generate more interest and a richer, more
integrated, learning experience (Figure 4.6).
The relatively low cost of computer graphics
compared to traditional typesetting exerts an
important beneficial influence on content. Because
illustrated books of good quality can be economically
produced for very small groups, they can reflect the
personality of the local community. Learning becomes

more personal when characters and places in workbooks
have local names.

Figure 4.6: Qaqepe'

The Coeur d'Alene Indians
once made beautiful corn husk bags.
Write the word which means "corn husk bag."

Fix the word which means "corn husk bag."

_____a_____epe'

Frequent use of localisms doesn't prevent the
introduction of more universal themes. The Coeur
d'Alene wrapped their discussion of American
government and politics in native humour, as revealed
in the proclamation of Skunk when he returned from
the capital bragging "Ch'n uχ te'l khwe 'Wash'n," 'I
have come from Washington'. Skunk spoke always in
diminuatives, signified here by the two apostrophe's
(glottal stops) in 'Wash'n. If the workbooks undergo
another revision, Skunk will certainly appear, but
having gone to considerable trouble to develop a set
of muskrats, I was not able to do justice to another
major character. This illustrates the potential
advantage of assembling a production team of
specialists consisting of illustrator, linguistic
anthropologist and native speaker. The Coeur d'Alene
Language Preservation Project included the latter
two, but lacked the first.

Practical Considerations
Costs. The bulk of the first draft of the workbook
was accomplished on a machine which cost the author
$2,500, including software, in February, 1984. Work
speeded up rapidly after the acquisition of an
external disk drive for $425. Today both items could
be obtained for about $1,600. High speed production
would require a hard (Winchester) disk or its

equivalent at about $1,500. A tribal or educational office should be able to acquire the equipment for even less.

Time. Producing one page of text with graphics can absorb anything from a few minutes to a few hours. When I started the workbooks I was a complete novice on the Macintosh operating system with its 'desktop' metaphor. While I did not keep a log, I would guess that I averaged one hour per page for the 200 page pair of workbooks. The operating system, which uses a mouse to move a cursor to icons on the screen in order to manage files and control programs, has been justifiably touted as a lure to the computer novice, because anyone can learn to use it without recourse to a manual, but it is also true that efficient and effective use requires a great deal of practice. An experienced user would require much less time to complete the same set of lessons and would probably produce a better set.

Summary
A bit-mapped microcomputer system has proven highly useful in the production of hard copy lessons for the teaching of the Coeur d'Alene Indian language. The system permits text and graphics to be mixed freely. The ease of filing items of vocabulary with relative cultural information and with graphics files of figures, photographs and maps means that the system provides suitable support for the production of lessons using the culture language approach proposed by Eastman (1981). In the culture language approach the object is to teach culture and history through the presentation culture-loaded items of native vocabulary. The object is to resurrect or highlight the semantic structure of the language culture. For some tribes the approach and the computer systems will come too late. Those tribes which recognize the utility of bit-mapped microcomputers and can afford them should realize substantial benefits in culture and language maintenance.

Notes
1. For a discussion of Oglala cultural persistence see Powers 1977.
2. The author has had no communication with the Apple Computer Company concerning this article. The company has in no way subsidized this work,

except that a program for designing fonts was supplied by a local dealer. The author has no obligations to Apple.

References
Bright, W. (1976) 'North American Indian Language Contact' in Thomas A. Sebeok (ed.), Native Languages of the Americas: Vol. 9, Plenum Press, New York. pp. 59-72.

Campbell, L. and M. Mithun (1979) The Languages of Native America: Historical and Comparative Assessment. University of Texas Press, Austin.

Eastman, C. (1981) 'The American Indian's Language and Culture in USA Education'. World Yearbook of Education, Kogan Page Ltd., pp. 293-305.

Gill, S. (1983) Native American Traditions: Sources and Interpretations. Wadsworth Publishing Company, Belmont, CA.

Leap, W. (1981) 'American Indian Language Maintenance', Annual Review of Anthropology, 10, 209-36.

Point, N. (1967) Wilderness Kingdom: Indian Life in the Rocky Mountains: 1840-1847. The Journal and Paintings of Nicholas Point, S.J. Joseph P. Donnelly, S.J., Trans., Holt Rinehart, Winston, New York.

Powers, W. (1977) Oglala Religion, University of Nebraska Press, Lincoln.

Chapter Five

TEACHING SECOND-LANGUAGE LITERACY WITH COMPUTERS

Olivia N. Saracho, University of Maryland Department of Curriculum and Instruction Reading Center, College Park, Maryland 20742

Matching Language and Culture in Second-Language Teaching

Many children face academic problems, but even the simplest academic problem can be converted into a series of complex problems when the students' home language and culture differ from that of the school. Students discover that the standard language of instruction of the school excludes them and their native language and culture. This disrupts the continuity of their everyday living.

Students respond differently to the mismatch of language in an instructional situation based on the degree to which they are able to function in their own language and culture and the school's language and culture. Four levels can be identified:

Level 1 (lowest level): Students become confused when they experience a drastic difference between the two languages and cultures.

Example: A series of charts is used to teach the unit on the family. The father usually is blond, has blue eyes, wears a suit and holds a black attache case. Dalia, who does not speak or understand English, sees the charts and discovers that the family on the chart does not resemble her family. Her father has black hair and wears greasy overalls, because he is a mechanic. This experience confuses her.

Level 2: Students deny their language and culture, pretending that their language and culture is the same as the school's.

53

<u>Example</u>: Miguel Jimenez, a Spanish-speaking student, changes his name to Michael and may even go a step further and change the pronunciation of his last name from Himanez to Geemes.

Level 3: Students adapt to those new or different customs in the culture in which they perceive to have more advanced patterns. Therefore, children will assess each language and culture to adapt only the best patterns or customs to make them their own.

<u>Example</u>: Juan Jose enjoys eating the food from his culture. He makes it a point to celebrate birthdays and holidays with his family and friends, because he usually gets to eat and has a good time. However, when he is with his English-speaking friends, he refuses to speak his native language and only listens to English-speaking stations on the radio.

Level 4 (highest level): Students are able to make the transition back and forth from one language and culture to another language and culture with ease.

<u>Example</u>: Juanita is a fluent bilingual student. She speaks her native language and the school's language. She carries a conversation in the language that is used in the group. Her behavior is appropriate in the different situations or settings such as at home, school or gatherings.

Sociocultural factors influence all human development factors including child rearing practices, family styles, sociolinguistic patterns, political and economic systems, and socialization and behavior patterns. These factors have an impact on the individual's development in their cultural differences, because their ancestors contributed in developing their culture and history. For approximately sixty years, the appropriate education of the children whose native language and culture differed from those of the school has been an educational, sociological, psychological and in many respects a political issue. Two major issues have been raised and debated in this context: (1) Children learn to read in their native language easier and better than in their second language. Should they first be taught to read in their native language with instructional materials which reflect their culture?

and (2) Children achieve more general knowledge in subject matter areas in their second language if they are taught these subjects in their native language. Should they be taught using instructional materials which reflect their language and relate to their culture? These issues have not been resolved. The different atmospheres can identify the effects of the social status of the two languages or the linguistic relationship of the languages on reading and academic learning. Research evidence provides conflicting results, possibly due to the vast number of factors involved, in the world-wide nature of the problem, and its magnified social, political and economic importance. In promoting students' learning, it becomes essential that educators, especially classroom teachers, recognize, understand, respect and accept the students' language and cultural differences by taking into consideration what these students bring to school (Saracho & Hancock, 1983) and including them in the instructional curriculum.

The curriculum for these students include four educational areas: communication, language expression and acquisition (in both the students' native language and culture and the school's standard language and culture). Teachers develop a healthy atmosphere for continued learning in the students' dominant language and their second language. Second-language learning must be relevant to both the students' school and the community lives. The students' language has an impact on their thought patterns and patterns of expression; thus, they need more than just language instruction. The curriculum must integrate the students' cultures to help them acquire flexibility in their thinking and functioning in both culutres (Saracho & Spodek, 1983), allowing them to achieve the highest level (level 4) of functioning in two languages and cultures.

The curriculum educational goals established need to consider the students' developmental levels, strengths and needs. This process requires teachers to work with the local community and with parents to formulate expectations for the students' learning. They also select and translate pertinent research outcomes to relate them to their knowledge about classroom students and their community as well as to place into perspective all efforts to carry out the specified educational goals.

The curriculum integrates both the students' and school's cultural and linguistic similarities and differences such as in language patterns, social structures, family organizations, patterns of authority, knowledge forms and art forms. Teachers also must be cognizant of the effects of socioeconomic factors and cultural factors on the students' learning. They must consider these factors in establishing educational goals.

Goals are specified into objectives and learning alternatives are designed in obtaining such objectives. The teachers' awareness of these curriculum models, approaches, materials and resources which are available in their school can help them select the ones which are appropriate for second-language teaching. They must know a wide range of alternative teaching techniques, which integrate the relevant aspects of the students' culture including language, music and art in the curriculum. They also need to identify resources available in the community to support educational learning alternatives, which are relevant to such aspects of the students' language and culture (Saracho & Spodek, 1983).

In teaching a second language, teachers must be aware of the greater needs created by the students' linguistic and cultural differences. Many of these students need individualized instruction, extensive opportunities to practice, and materials that are stimulating.

Using the Computer to Teach Second-Language

Computer Assisted Instruction (CAI) has become one of the most instructional strategies used in individualizing instruction. Teachers use the computer to keep the students' records up-to-date and to analyze continuously student responses, test scores and progression of school work. The computer's display allows students to view their responses in a visual, aesthetically pleasing way. Students also practice their tactile skills as they type commands and responses into the computer. Students learn the language and the demands of computer technology without pressure while they simultaneously enjoy learning academic subjects through the computer.

The computer has three special operations which make it a promising educational tool: (1) it prestores programs, assesses students' responses, gives immediate feedback on students' responses, and records the students' progress to keep it up-to-date; (2) it provides each student with the opportunity to respond continuously during the session to as many questions as possible; (3) it individualizes the students' instructional levels and paces their instruction at their own achievement level, specific interests and capacities in areas such as reading, language arts and mathematics. The computer keeps a profile of students' progress individually and as a whole class to modify their instruction based on the individual students' performance with the materials.

Students learn through CAI as they interact with the computer. According to Saracho (1982b) there are three approaches to instruction using computers: (1) drill and practice, (2) tutorial and (3) dialogue. These are described below:

Drill and Practice

Drill and practice is the simplest type of computer instruction. It usually supplements the teacher's regular classroom activities (Suppes; cited in Callahan and Glennon, 1975). It is one of the most widely used and its applications range from drill in arithmetic, spelling and language arts at the elementary school level to drill in key medical concepts for nursing students. A problem or part of an exercise is displayed in the computer's screen, much like in a workbook. Then students type their answers on the computer keyboard. CAI drill and practice gives the students instant feedback in order that they can quickly find out if their responses are right or wrong. This process is not possible with the workbook or other forms of drill and practice used in school.

Tutorial

The tutorial instructional system presents a concept and develops skill in using that concept. This system provides instruction which is more meaningful to the student than does the drill and practice system. The instant feedback tells students whether their responses are right or wrong, and also gives students tutorial assistance to help them understand the source of their errors and guides them to correct their mistakes through specific additional exercises. The tutorial system instructs students on a one-to-one basis, teaching concepts and skills through continuous interaction between the student and the computer.

Dialogue

The dialogue system offers a complex and continuous

interaction between the student and the computer where both student and computer join to explore the curriculum. For example, if students request instruction, the computer surveys the students' records to determine their reading levels and then presents appropriate exercises on the screen. The students type their responses on the computer's keyboard. The computer evaluates the students' responses, lets them know if their responses are correct or incorrect, and continues the dialogues. If correct responses are offered, the computer raises the level of difficulty of exercises. However, if incorrect responses are given, the computer will lower the level of difficulty of the exercises. The students learn the language required to command the computer for specific types of instruction and for appropriate feedback. Instructional areas where dialogic CAI can be used include mathematics, language and reading with specific basic skills, descriptive instructions, testing procedures and reinforcement methods. The CAI curriculum with skill building exercises consists of (1) descriptive instructions and examples; (2) testing questions and simulations; and (3) reinforcement involving immediate feedback on correct and wrong responses.

Reviewing Research Studies in Teaching a Second-Language

Research on CAI indicates its effectiveness in teaching subject areas such as reading, language arts and mathematics with low achievers in Freeport, New York (Holbrock, 1976); Fort Worth, Texas; Seattle, Washington (Macken & Suppes, 1976); Southern California: Shawnee Mission, Kansas (Poulsen & Macken, 1978)); Los Nietos, California (Crandall, 1976); and Drew, Mississippi (Petty, 1978). The students in these studies had a positive attitude toward this kind of instruction (Crandall, 1976; Macken & Suppes, 1976), suggesting that CAI can be used to increase the students' achievement levels and gains on standardized achievement tests in a favorable way.

In a recent study, Saracho (1982b) examined the importance of CAI in reducing the educational deficiency of Spanish-speaking migrant students. The computer based instruction in this study consisted of instruction in reading, language arts and mathematics. CAI supplemented the regular teachers' instruction in reading, language arts and mathematics. Students worked independently on the computer at their own pace. All students started at the same grade level (third, fourth, fifth or sixth grade) and if they succeeded with the material, they rose to higher levels; while students who had difficulty with the material in their grade level were given easier items from a lower grade level. Individual lessons consisted of a mixture of exercises from various skill areas to provide students with a variety of exercises from different types of items instead of a series of similar items.

The results in Saracho's study showed that those students who used CAI performed better on language, reading and mathematics than did those students who did not use the CAI program. In addition, the students did better in language than they did in reading and mathematics. Thus, the outcomes in Saracho's study support that assertion on the CAI program may have an impact on the Spanish-speaking migrant students' achievement gains, with more learning in the second-language, which in this case was English. It is important to note that the students in this study were Spanish-speaking migrant students who entered school with little or no knowledge of the English language. These students were members of families who worked in the fields and followed the crops from one part of the United States to another. Their migratory route leads to a lack of continuity in the students' schooling and the economic and social factors in the migrant workers' lives, which tend to have a devasting effect on the students' education. The students in the study participated in the CAI program between October 30 and March 31 of the following year. The use of computers for instructional purposes for these students seems particularly appropriate. In this study, instruction on the computer supplemented the teacher's instruction in the classroom and increased practice opportunities. The computer's system provided a record of student's performance on a print-out. Information on the students' strengths and needs can assist the teachers to improve the planning for instruction.

In relation to the students' attitudes scores, the results showed that the students who did not use CAI had more favorable attitudes toward the computer than did those who used CAI. This was an unexpected outcome; however, Garraway (1974), Crandall (1976), and Macken and Suppes (1976) found that attitudes of students who used CAI were highly positive. Saracho (1982b) attributes this conflicting result to those students with various learning styles. Students in a classroom differ in their ways of thinking which influences their reactions to different kinds of instruction. Differences in the individuals' thinking process is referred to as "cognitive style." Some of these differences relate to ethnicity (Ramfrez & Castaneda, 1974; Saracho, 1983). For instance, some students may prefer independent, impersonal and direct instruction; while others may prefer the opposite kind of instruction (Saracho, 1980; Saracho & Dayton, 1980; Saracho & Spodek, 1981, in press; Saracho, 1983). The students who used the CAI program were probably in favour of a more dependent, personal and indirect form of instruction. Differences in the students' cognitive styles may account for the differences in the attitudes in this study.

The studies reviewed indicate that CAI programs are effective in increasing student achievement levels and are an effective form of supplementary instruction. While studies suggest that CAI programs should be encouraged in schools that educate students who have a native language different from the one used for instruction in the schools, further studies on the use of computers to teach a second language need to be conducted before making any generalizations. These studies need to provide further support on the effectiveness of CAI programs and provide information on meaningful computer instruction for students who need to learn a second language.

Planning Instruction In Teaching a Second Language with Computers

Planning is one of the essential elements of effective teaching. An instructional plan provides a guide for teaching that clarifies the presentation of material. It should have some degree of flexibility to help teachers organize content into a sequence of experiences and to provide information for evaluating learning and for diagnosing areas for future learning. Planning must be based on the students' learning styles, levels, needs and interests. Since student responses are of foremost importance in teaching and learning, any lesson should be modified on the basis of student-teacher interaction in each learning setting.

When using CAI, teachers need to consider individual differences to plan for those students who will be using the computer. Teachers must employ appropriate experiences for students in relation to the computer. The students' learning style should be integrated in their instruction. For instance, teachers can encourage those students who prefer to work in groups and in discovery experiences to meet before and after using the computer and can provide these students with opportunities for them to share their work with their peers (Saracho, 1981).

Although computers can interact with students and can be adapted to a range of circumstances, they may not fulfill each student's needs, particularly in the affective domain. The students' learning styles influence their learning according to instructional strategies. Students who have a similar learning capacity can differ in their ability to process several kinds of information. An instructional program can be created and organized to develop relationships or frameworks which are adjusted to a number of different types of varied input (Saracho, 1981).

Planning must also consider the students' perceptions of CAI instruction. Students need to perceive CAI as a valuable and enjoyable learning experience instead of remedial instruction, which often stigmatizes slow learners. Students who experience negative labelling may develop negative attitudes toward the computer (Saracho, 1981). The computer room should also be available to students before class, after class and during lunch time. Teachers can take turns taking duty in the computer room to help students who wish to work with the computer. Having the computer available to the children at all times can alleviate the children's fear of being scheduled more time into the computer room, because they need remedial instruction. This way it is their choice instead of the teachers'. The computer should also be made available to all students rather than just to speakers of other languages. This process can also reduce any negative attitudes toward the computer.

Students' attitudes toward the CAI program are an important aspect in their learning. It is essential that teachers help students develop a positive attitude toward the computer system. The CAI materials become a major determiner of students' attitudes. These materials need to integrate the students' native language and culture as well as maintain their interest.

Employing Instructional Techniques in Teaching a Second Language with Computers

An instructional technique is a specific indirect and ingenious way, stratagem or contrivance used to achieve the educational goals and objectives. Techniques depend on the teachers' background, philosophy and values as well as the composition of the class. Particular problems can be overcome equally successfully by the use of different techniques. For instance, in teaching the difference between the pronunciation of English /l/ and /r/ to some non-English-speaking students, teachers may use imitation as a technique. Other teachers or the same teachers at another time may depend on drawing or a chart of the human vocal apparatus.

Laboratory tape-recorders, phonographs, computers and machines which are used in teaching situations are considered instructional techniques. Machines have enjoyed great favor recently. A number of claims have been made for their effectiveness in language teaching. In fact, many consider them to have great educational value. Computers, however complex, are considered to be more valuable and are most widely used as instructional techniques. Their operative element depends on the kind of approach and equipment that are used in teaching situations to motivate the students' learning.

In a series of studies, Malone (1980) examined which computer games and which characteristics in these games captivated students in different grade levels (kindergarten to eighth grade). In Malone's first study, the students selected computer games which made learning interesting. Students preferred to play in the computer the following games (listed in the order of preferance):

1. Petball - simulated pinball with sound.
2. Snake2 - two players control motion and shooting of snakes
3. Breakout - player controls paddle to hit ball that breaks through a wall piece by piece.
4. Dungeon - player explores a cave like "Dungeons and Dragons"
5. Chase S. - two players chase each other across an obstacle course with sound effects
6. Star Trek - navigate through space and shoot Klingon ships
7. Don't Fall - guess words like Hangman but instead of a person being hung, a person or robot advances to a cliff
8. Panther - guess who committed a murder by

questioning witnesses who may lie
9.   Mission - bomb submarines without getting your ship sunk
10. Chaser - capture a moving square with perpendicular lines
11. Chase - like Chase S, but without sound
12. Horses - bet on horses that race along track
13. Sink Ship - bomb a ship from an airplane
14. Snake - like Snake2 but snakes can't shoot
15. Lemonade - Run a lemonade stand: buy supplies, advertise etc.
16. Escape - escape from moving robots
17. Star Wars - shoot Darth Vader's ship on screen
18. Maze Craze - escape from randomly generated maze
19. Hangman - guess letters of a word before man is hung
20. Adventure - explore cave with dragons, etc.
21. Draw - make any design on the screen
22. Stars - guess a number (clues given by number of stars)
23. Snoopy - shoot Red Baron by subtracting Snoopy's position on number line from Red Baron's position
24. Eliza - converse with simulated psychiatrist
25. Gold -fill in blanks in story about Goldilocks

Students preferred games which set goals, keep score, provide audio effects, and involve randomness in the game.
     In the second and third studies, Malone (1980) examined several versions of certain games. He found that the versions were isomorphic to each other except specific key characteristics consisting of fantasy, feedback or scorekeeping. He attributed the differences for each version to their specific characteristics. The first game he analyzed was "Breakout", a computer game requiring sensorimotor skill. The game was analyzed in relation to its characteristics in the visual display, in the motion of the stimulated ball, and in the scoring. Students consider the most important characteristics of the computer game to be the graphic display which simultaneously presents a score and goals at multiple levels. Those versions without obvious goals were not as appealing as the other versions.
     In his fourth study, Malone (1980) analyzed "Darts", a computer game, and found significant sex differences in appeal between sexes. Boys preferred the fantasy of having arrows pop balloons but disliked its verbal constructive feedback; while girls disliked the fantasy having arrows pop balloons but preferred the music played in the game. Both

63

fantasy and music were found to be more appealing than simple feedback. Computer games with such characteristics as responsive fantasy, captivating sensory effects, and individual adaptability have an unprecedented potential in producing learning atmospheres.

One of the advantages of using a computer assisted instructional system is the ease with which second-language can be assessed and intervention materials be used with a common graphics base. Speech digitization can be employed with a speaker of any language. A native speaker of the language used expresses or communicates some thoughts and feelings. In speech digitization a native speaker can be used to produced phrases. This differs from phonetically generated synthesis which depends on a phoneme system of a specific language. This attractive characteristic helps meet the needs of students whose language and culture differ from those of the school. Often recent immigrants, older siblings and parents are the only persons in the communiy to speak the bilingual students' language and share their culture. These people can be used to help with speech digitization.

Until recently CAI required students to have some degree of literacy. New developments in inexpensive and intelligible speech synthesis units have provided computers with appropriate non-reading materials which integrate the students' native language and culture.

Picture generation has been achieved with the use of the Apple Graphics Table, a device which enables the user to draw pictures using six high resolution colours. It is unique because it is equipped with a variety of selected programmed subroutines to provide the user with an easy approach to develop and store pictures. Pictures of familiar objects can be used to teach vocabulary. These vocabulary items developmentally preceed comprehension. Teachers can demonstrate to the children manually how to type their responses. Pictures can be employed to provide situations which take place outside the classroom and is of interest to the students. These events are appropriate to be used in second-language teaching. Graphics loading and display, employing only the software which accompanies the Graphics Tablet, is too slow for courseware use with children. Wilson and Fox (1982) suggest using a machine language routine to code the graphics. This compression and subsequent elaborate routine permits one to load multiple pictures into active memory to display on the front screen; thus, decreasing both load and display time. The combination of the audible component with the computer graphics has provided the opportunity to create dynamic materials for second-language teaching.

The Mountain Computer's "SuperTalker" originates synthesized speech. It is a device which accepts human voice input and stores it the way it is said. If it is activated, the digitized speech develops under software control. One of its limits is that the highest digitization level in the "SuperTalker," restricts the number of phrases on the computer disc. However, Wilson and Fox (1982) found that they were able to get enough phrases on a disc for at least twenty minutes worth of instruction, although they used young children who typically work in short modules.

Evaluating Teaching Second-Language with Computers

Evaluation is an important aspect to improve an educational program. It is employed to identify and understand the different components which contribute to the effectiveness of the program and the ways these components create their effects. Sufficient information about an education program must be obtained through the evaluation process to be able to modify instruction. Evaluation is an essential approach in modifying a program. Its careful planning becomes an asset to an educational program (Saracho, 1982a) and program components.

An evaluation can become a source of information to develop an appropriate approach to use the instructional materials in teaching a specific content. Educational products are often constructed based on a theory without an awareness of practical problems. To utilize blindly an educational product hoping that it will serve some educational purpose is a waste of both the teachers' time and effort (Saracho, in press).

To discourage these practices in teaching a second language with computers, a careful assessment of the strengths and weaknesses of computers must be conducted. In addition, the effectiveness of each item by means of item analysis must be evaluated. Simple procedures can be used to determine the difficulty and discriminating power of an item and the effectiveness of each item. This evaluation must suggest and guide ways that instruction on the computer can serve the teacher's purposes.

The evaluation of a computer system must integrate a variety of evaluation techniques to assess the computer program effectively. Educators need to reduce any educational errors by using the computer program skillfully, although it provides the teacher with little or nothing about how the students are able to perform in an actual situation where knowledge is applied or where knowledge influences the students personally or academically.

Computers in teaching a second-language must be assessed in relation to their effectiveness. The major consideration in this evaluation should be the degree to which the product fits the particular uses for which it is considered (Saracho, in press).

To achieve the full potential of computers in education requires that educators, programmers and computer manufacturers will need to evaluate the computer-based materials for the schools. Second-language teching presents the challenge for creating and locating courseware which encourages students to think creatively about language. Software programs can be used as a vehicle to teach a second-language. Computer experiences can stimulate discussions (in any language) among the students or between students and teacher that would not occur under different circumstances and can motivate students to think about both languages.

Chomsky (1984) suggests that the following questions be asked in evaluating software in language:

- Is the program interesting to you?
- Does the thinking the program requires seem worthwhile?
- Is the emphasis on thinking rather than on repetitive practice?
- Does the program involve two or more students at a time?
- Does the program introduce activity or thought that is different from that provided by books or pencil and paper?
- Does the program allow users to customize material?
- Can the program be used many times by a student and remain interesting and worthwhile?
- Does the program allow time for reflection?
- Does satisfaction in using the program come from the content itself? (pp.61-62)

Second language teaching programs which provide students with an enhanced sense of the intrinsic power fascination and diversity to both languages are the type of software that will earn computers a place in a curriculum which includes the students' native language and culture.

References

Callahan, L.G., and Glennon, V.J. (1975). Elementary School Mathematics: A Guide to Current Research. Association for Supervision and Curriculum Development, Washington, D.C.

Chomsky, C. (January 1984). 'Finding the Best Language Arts Software', Classroom Computer Learning. 61-65.

Crandall, N.D. (1976). 'Its role in the education of ethnic minorities', The Journal of Technological Horizons in Education, 9, 24-26.

Garraway, T. (1974). Computer Assisted Instruction in the N.W.T. Northwest Territories. Alberta University, Edmonton Division of Education Research Associates (ERIC Document Service No. ED 152 285).

Holbrook, J.I. (1976). An Analysis of Achievement in Mathematics and Reading in the Freeport Public Schools During the Period 1970-1975. Unpublished Manuscript.

Macken, E., and Suppes, P. (1976). 'Evaluation Studies of CCC Elementary School Curriculums 1971-1975', CCC Education Studies, 1 (1), 1-37.

Malone, T.W. (1980). What Makes Things Fun to Learn? A Study of Intrinsically Motivating Computer Games. XEROX Palo Alto Research Center, Palo Alto.

Petty, G.G. (1978). Personal communication, October 19, 1977. In G. Poulsen and E. Macken. 'Evaluation Studies of CCC Elementary School Curriculums 1975-1977', CCC Educational Studies, 1 (2), 1-68.

Poulsen, G., & Macken, E. (1978), 'Evaluation Studies of CCC School Curriculums 1975-1977,' CCC Educational Studies, 1 (2), 1-68.

Ramfrez III, M., & Castaneda, A. (1974). Cultural Democracy, Bicognitive Development, and Education. Academic Press, New York.

Saracho, O.N. (in press). 'Evaluating Instructional Materials Using the Educational Products Information Exchange Product', Education.

Saracho, O.N. (1981). 'Planning Computer Assisted Instruction for Spanish-Speaking Students', Journal of Educational Technology Systems, 11 (3), 257-260.

Saracho, O.N. (1982a). 'New Dimensions in Evaluating the Worth of a Program', Education, 103 (1), 74-78.

Saracho, (1982b). 'The Effects of a Computer Assisted Instruction Program in Basic Skills Achievement and

Attitudes Towards Instruction of Spanish-speaking Migrant Children', American Educational Research Journal, 19 (2), 201-219.

Saracho, O.N. (1980). 'The Relationship Between the Teachers' Cognitive Style and Their Perceptions of Their Students' Academic Achievements', Educational Research Quarterly, 5 (3), 40-49.

Saracho, O.N. (1983). 'The Relationship of Teachers' Cognitive Styles and Ethnicity to Predictions of Academic Success and Achievement of Mexican-American and Anglo-American Students', in E. Garcia and M. Sam-Vargas (eds.), The Mexican American Child: Language, Cognitive and Social Development, Notre Dame Press, Southbend, Indiana, pp. 107-122.

Saracho, O.N., & Dayton, C.M. (1980). 'Relationship of Teachers' Cognitive Styles to Pupils' Academic Achievement Gains', Journal of Educational Psychology, 72 (2), 544-549.

Saracho, O.N., & Hancock, F.M. (1983). 'The Culture of the Mexican Americans', in O.N. Saracho and B. Spodek (eds.), Understanding the Multicultural Experience in Early Childhood Education, National Association for the Education of Young Children, Washington, D.C., pp. 3-15.

Saracho, O.N., & Spodek, B. (in press). 'Cognitive Style and Children's Learning: Individual Variations in Cognitive Processes', in L.G. Katz (ed.), Current Topics in Early Childhood Education, Vol XI. Ablex Publishing Corporation, Norwood, New Jersey.

Saracho, O.N., & Spodek, B. (1983). 'The Preparation of Teachers for Bilingual Bicultural Early Childhood Classes', in O.N. Saracho and B. Spodek (eds.). Understanding the Multicultural Experience in Early Childhood Education.

Saracho, O.N., & Spodek, B. (1981). 'The Teachers' Cognitive Styles and Their Educational Implications', Educational Forum, 45 (2), 153-159.

Wilson, M.S., & Fox, B.J. (1982). 'Computer-Administered Bilingual Language Assessment and Intervention', Exceptional Children, 49 (2), 145-149.

Chapter Six

'THE DARK CASTLE' — AN ADVENTURE IN FRENCH

Peter Saunders, Inner London Education Authority

The story of the development of 'The Dark Castle' is in itself rather like an adventure game. A whole unknown area lay ahead of the writers at the outset, the eventual goal was by no means clear and along the way all sorts of questions had to be answered, decisions taken on a trial and error basis and strategies devised to negotiate the problems which arose. The present title is, then, no accident. A slightly anecdotal resumé of how the program came about will put the dual adventure in context before going on to describe in more detail the thinking behind it, the facilities of the program and some observations on its use. It is hoped that in describing the project a number of points will be raised which could be relevant to thinking in general about the use of computers in language study.

In December 1981 the Computing Inspectorate of the Inner London Education Authority organised a short course to promote the idea of computing across the curriculum. Already in their short history in schools, computers had acquired the reputation of being only for the maths and physics departments, and this course was aimed at dispelling that idea by introducing teachers from humanities subjects to micros, making them aware of what sort of things these machines could do and encouraging them to think about what use could be made of the new resource in their disciplines. Among those invited to the course were three languages advisory teachers, all total computer naives.

Our initial uninformed impression was that computers could probably only handle drill-and-practice exercises which, if well-written, are perfectly alright for certain purposes and for some students, but are hardly what is needed in schools today, where communicative methodology has shifted

69

the emphasis away from this type of skill. Uppermost in our minds was the need to think in terms of programs that could actually help in the real conditions of the classroom, most urgently in the area of fourth- and fifth-year French classes, where numbers of pupils and staffing often lead to widely mixed-ability groups working for different examinations. An introduction to the 'Eliza' program prompted the thought that perhaps we could develop something along those lines to simulate a conversation for our pupils - maybe practising the sort of questions and answers that they have to deal with in the examinations. Was this the answer? Our optimism was short-lived as we soon realised that using a reading/writing program to simulate that most aural/oral of conventions, the conversation, would scarcely set the language-teaching profession on fire with enthusiasm!

As we struggled to get used to thinking in terms of what we could make micros do for us (and we were repeatedly encouraged not to be limited by any restrictions in the machines' abilities that we might imagine existed), we were worried by two basic problems: our RML 380Z machines' lack of an accented character-set, and the standard of accuracy in the average pupil's written French. The prospects of working solely in upper-case, where accents can be omitted, or in unaccented, and therefore incorrect, lower-case were both unacceptable, and the vagaries of many pupils' spelling and grammar might prove too much for any machine. Fortunately, at this point we were shown the original 'Colossal Cave' adventure just as another example of what a micro can do. After spending many hours fighting with the tunnels, dwarfs, caverns and other hazards, it occurred to us that something similar could provide a great stimulus for reading in a foreign language; rather than having to type in commands about where to go and what to do, pupils could have multiple-choice options at each stage. Although this means that 'The Dark Castle' is not an adventure in the purest sense, it does allow the readers to exercise a degree of control over how the story unfolds while avoiding the need for them to input anything but the number of their chosen option. We were assured that a character-set with accents could be created and that some form of dictionary could be incorporated so that help could be sought when problems with understanding the text arose. The decision was taken to pursue the idea and, as suggested above, we set out into the unknown to write a story and invent a new type of learning resource, on the understanding that a programmer could certainly make it all work for us. An act of faith as far as naives were concerned, but one that should be adopted by any other non-computerates who have a good idea and access to a programmer.

After further thought about the potential uses of such a program, it became clear it really could be an extremely valuable resource with which to service an important area of language study. Extended narrative reading is a very difficult thing to 'teach' to a class, since every reader has different needs and difficulties and it is anyhow essentially an individual activity. By providing a focus for reading whereby a small group of pupils could work together, with readily-available support, on tackling a story whose format and content would, hopefully, engage them, we would at least be making the reading of a foreign language a more realistic and enjoyable exercise than is traditionally available. In addition, the program would provide yet another alternative in language classes that are already often organised around a variety of activities, and would enable teachers to send off a group to work independently for the best reasons. Our decision to develop an adventure program seemed thoroughly justified.

Work began on two fronts; the complete adventure was written in the form of a 360 page branching-story with one starting-point, one ending and an enormous number of possible routes between, and a clear, accented character-set was created. This was done using the graphics facility of the 380Z so that letters much larger and clearer than the standard matrix allows could be produced. The story takes readers from a picnic in the countryside through a forest full of tortuous paths, crossroads and junctions, by boat, bridge or twisting tunnels into the eponymous castle. Here they find their way around a bewildering series of staircases, rooms and corridors, occasionally encountering the strange inhabitants of the castle until they find themselves in a maze which eventually leads them to the denouement. The pages of text vary in length from a single sentence to a short paragraph and alternate descriptions of places and happenings with opportunities for the readers to choose between various courses of action with unknown consequences. In some cases there are loops in the story where readers have to learn by their mistakes in order to

71

progress, but there are no disasters along the way and perseverance guarantees reaching the end.

As decisions began to be made about various aspects of the story and the program, ideas about the educational issues involved became more evident and concrete. Four main aims were recognised which had already begun to govern our thinking and which were subsequently kept in mind as work progressed:

1. to motivate reading by providing an interesting stimulus and allowing a degree of control over the story
2. to support pupils' reading by helping them to keep going when they have problems, thus ensuring progress
3. to promote accuracy by encouraging group discussion and reference to the program's dictionary
4. not least, to show that reading a foreign language can lead to enjoyment and satisfaction

The first of these points has already been covered in passing, but it also links with the second in that the instant reference to the dictionary allows the use of enough language to develop an interesting story without being shackled by the limited vocabulary and understanding of the target pupils. Although the language level is not comparable to that found in the sort of realia which pupils have to deal with for general comprehension at this stage of their studies, it is certainly higher than many could cope with in a reader. The dictionary is described in more detail later, but it can be noted here that as well as helping readers to keep going, it also encourages them to be careful as it requires no effort or skill to check or find out the meaning of a word or phrase. In practice the ease of using the dictionary and the discussion in the group have meant that they <u>do</u> tend to read accurately and <u>do</u> bother to work out what things mean rather than guessing wildly. These considerations of motivation, support and accuracy are all part of realising the fourth, and perhaps ultimately most important, aim listed above.

Classroom experience has shown that the suggested group size of three to five pupils is ideal since it allows all of them to see clearly, to contribute what they can to discussions and to take turns at handling the keyboard. They need no previous experience of computers at all and the program is controlled completely by single-key commands, all of which are displayed at the bottom of the screen at all times.

'The Dark Castle' has a 'save' facility which allows pupils to keep their position at the end of a session and to resume at a later date. This was felt to be essential where time on the micro is limited, and also ensures that those who are progressing slowly are not penalised. There are also several points in the story where the computer selects randomly the direction in which to continue, so the adventure is not likely to follow the same course if restarted from the beginning.

As stated before, the main aim of the dictionary is to give immediate help with any problems in the text and to enable the pupils to keep going. It was expressly not our intention to give references which would require the application of any rules, paradigms or analysis of structures; such assistance might well be appropriate in the context of another program with a different purpose, but here we were concerned with on-the-spot help so if, for example, readers look up a verb form such as 'choisissez', they are shown that it belongs with its subject 'vous' and that they mean 'you choose', as distinct from being told that the word is the second person plural form of the verb 'choisir'.

The procedure for looking up a word is very simple: having decided which word is causing a problem, the readers place a cursor under it and press the 'F' key to make the micro find the reference on the disk; in the space of a few seconds the word and any others that belong with it are underlined and a translation is given at the bottom of the screen. Any number of words can be looked up on a page. The system works in the following way: every word in the story is allocated a number and the dictionary contains a translation related to those numbers. Words which stand alone and have a simple one-to-one reference, e.g. 'soudain' has the number 199 and the dictionary has 199 meaning 'suddenly'; 'derrière' has the number 81 and the meaning 'behind'. Words which belong together in context are simply allocated the same number as each other, and so the dictionary views them all as the same entry. This allows the compiler to make sure that nouns are shown, where appropriate, with their articles or that verbs are linked with their subjects. Thus both words of 'le chateau' have the number 14, so both would be underlined if either was looked up and the meaning 'the castle' given. A whole phrase that makes up a unit of meaning and which it would be impracticable to subdivide can be grouped together, e.g. every word in 'qu'est-ce que vous decidez de faire?' has the number 270, so whichever word is looked up the whole is shown to belong together and is translated as such. Where an adjective separates a noun from its article, the noun and the article can be given the same number and the adjective another, so that in 'une grande porte', 'une' and 'porte' have the number 45, and 'grande' has 75. This also allows all other occurrences of 'grande' (and 'grand', 'grands', 'grandes') throughout the story to share the same entry in the dictionary, provided they have the meaning 'big' or 'large'. Where they occur with a different meaning they have a separate entry, e.g. 'les grandes vacances' has the number 192 and the reference 'the summer holidays'. Similarly, verbs which have more than one meaning have separate entries; the opening words of the story are 'Vous passez les grandes vacances ...'; 'vous passez' is translated as 'you are spending'; in 'Vous passez devant une pancarte ...' they are linked with 'devant' and translated as 'you go past'. Many more examples could be given to show how different groupings of words can be treated, but perhaps enough has been shown already to indicate how the compiler has the opportunity to divide up the text into the units of meaning which are felt to be appropriate to the context and to the readers' needs.

There is, of course, no guarantee that pupils will not make some mistakes in their reading by assuming that they understand something when in fact they do not, but this is true of all readers at all levels, and in practice it has been noticeable that they tend to look up a lot rather than too little. The amount of accurate reading done in the groups seen so far has far outweighed the odd error. It has also been evident that as they progress through the story they tend to look up less words as they gain the confidence to make sense of the text. A fair number of words and phrases are re-used during the course of the story, and this naturally helps pupils to speed up as they get used to the recurrent words and structures.

A final comment on the use of the dictionary reveals a pleasing feature of how it works. The necessity of picking out with the cursor the words which are causing problems means that the pupils need to be very specific about which words they look up first. A good example was seen in a class faced with the sentence 'Vous offrez du pain au pigeon.' Not, perhaps, a particularly difficult sentence, but there was enough there to create a problem for the pupils in question (average fourth-years). The initial reaction was, 'Let's look up everything', but they had to pick somewhere to start and in fact went straight to the word they really did not know, namely 'offrez'. As soon as they saw 'you offer' on the screen, the rest fell into place - 'Oh! "You offer some bread to the pigeon" - let's go on.' Solving the one real problem gave them the confidence to make sense of what they already partly knew.

Earlier in this chapter it was mentioned that the suitability of 'The Dark Castle' for use in mixed-ability groups would be one of its virtues. One such arrangement into which it fitted ideally was observed in a school during the trial stage of its development. A teacher had a fifth-year group of very varied abilities for a long session on a Friday afternoon; the class was split into four - one group with the French assistants, another with a teacher who helped out regularly if she was free, a third group working on their own at the computer, leaving the class-teacher to give intensive help to the remaining group with some difficult written work. This sort of arrangement would clearly not always be possible, but on this occasion it meant that all the pupils spent the lesson working hard at various activities and with the maximum help. Even where such a good division of the class is not possible, the option of having groups of four or five pupils working independently at reading with the help of the micro could be a valuable asset to the teacher.

In conclusion it is worth mentioning a few observations that have come out of seeing the program in use, discussing it with other teachers and reflecting on lessons learnt from the development process. Firstly, in case the impression has been given that the author feels 'The Dark Castle' to be a wonderful panacea, it should be made clear that this is not so. The adventure has weaknesses which would be avoided or eliminated were another one to be written or a rewrite of this one made possible: the story is too long for comfort and could profitably have more exciting elements introduced; it takes too long at the start before the first set of options is reached; the ending has been criticised by some users as a let-down (obviously a very subjective matter), but the point is taken that perhaps a variety of endings would make for more interest; a few teachers have doubted the wisdom of having pupils conduct all their discussions around the adventure in English, but more have agreed that they are already working quite hard enough without requiring the additional and restrictive burden of working in French (enough to kill the exercise for some pupils); some have said that it would be better if there were graphics to illustrate parts of the story - again this is a matter both of taste and of priorities. In a different context, graphics might be desirable, but the aim of 'The Dark Castle' was to provide reading material in a way that it would work on the imagination, as 'The Colossal Cave' had done so vividly in the first place. To add graphics would both lessen the imaginative element and mean that the capabilities of the machine were starting to dictate the use to which they are put, which is surely to be avoided.

These reservations apart, it is generally felt that producing 'The Dark Castle' was a thoroughly worthwhile project. As a first attempt at showing how a micro can be used as a tool for tackling a text and helping readers to overcome problems, it has opened up to many teachers the possibilities of using computers in languages and a number of variations and spin-offs have already been suggested. There is a great appeal in the idea of a shorter story and a program equipped with a routine to store each page that is read by a given group so that at the end of the adventure they could receive a print-out of their own unique story. The principle employed by the dictionary to reference words in a text to some form of help at the bottom of the screen has been seen as a potentially useful aid in teaching slow mother-tongue learners in primary schools. The avoidance of traditional dictionaries or glossaries, combined with the clarity of the monitor image, has already been shown to enable partially-sighted pupils to read with greater ease.

No claim is made that pupils will necessarily 'learn' a great deal in the long run from a session at 'The Dark Castle' or that it instantly transforms them into better readers, but it does afford them the opportunity to achieve more thorough reading than they might otherwise and to experience reading as something enjoyable rather than as an unrewarding task. The spin-offs may or may not eventually prove to be worth pursuing, but a number of teachers with different preoccupations within languages have at least seen that computers need not be limited to testing and drills. It would be encouraging to think that in the future ideas would continue to develop around imaginative applications of this new resource and that the program described here might have been instrumental in helping to demonstrate what can be done in this field.

Chapter Seven

A MICROCOMPUTER GAME IN FRENCH CULTURE AND CIVILIZATION

Betje Black Klier, Ph.D. University of Texas-Austin

How do people learn? Theories range widely – overlapping, supporting or contradicting each other. The question of what people like about computers may be as unanswerable as "How do people learn?" or may bring forth many suggested theories.

> When we try to understand various motivating events (a grade, a smile, a tinfoil star, a trip to Spain), we should expect them to be psychologically complex, with some features that are "extrinsic" and some that are "intrinsic", some "integrative" and some "instrumental." Moreover, when we are searching for how the events help a student or hinder him, we should look beyond the realm of language itself, or even cross-culture experience, and try to relate the events to patterns that pervade the entire personality (Stevick, 1976, p. 49).

From Stevick's description of the complex nature of motivation, one might conclude that, in the case of students and microcomputers, it could be useful in curriculum development to move ahead and to pair person to machine and evaluate the results. Papert (in Taylor, 1980) advises that "If you are interested in learning how learning happens, you should start by looking at success stories" (p. 198).

This success story describes the creation and implementation of a microcomputer game called POKER PARI. The game serves as an event of team competition in the state French contest, the Texas French Symposium.

Each spring the Texas French Symposium assembles approximately 1500 participants for a two-day contest among students from state-supported and private high schools. They convene to compete individually in such events as poetry and prose recitation, or in groups performing dramatic interpretations. The keen competition often motivates students both to prepare themselves to perform in front of live judges and to continue to study French and return for subsequent competitions. However, finding a host school and a sufficient number of qualified judges has become increasingly difficult. At times students complain about unfair judging or disorganization since schedules cannot be perfectly controlled, especially when these contests rely on unpaid volunteers as judges.

One approach to solving some of these problems without giving up the benefits of the Symposium could be to create a new event which (1) gave students the responsibility and independence to prepare, (2) did not require more French-speaking judges, (3) could be controlled to fit a predictable schedule, and (4) would be perceived by participants as "fair" and impartial.

When the board of directors of the French Symposium identified these criteria, I was a member of the board and a graduate student studying instructional design for computers. Foreign language teaching and CAI constantly polarized and strained both my schedule and my priorities. Integration of these fields and interests became both useful and necessary.

In <u>Megatrends</u>, John Naisbitt renames and redefines man's eternal dichotomy as "high tech/high touch". What philosophers dub Yin/Yang, literary scholars classicism/romanticism and poets "l'ordre et l'aventure" becomes a "balance of the material wonders of technology with the spiritual demands of our human nature" (Naisbitt, 1984, p.35). Foreign language teaching provided me the high touch to balance the high tech of computing. Even within the discipline of language teaching, "l'ordre" of grammar studies can be balanced by "l'aventure" of culture and civilization.

Many years of teaching gifted students in mixed-ability groups ("mainstreaming") at various levels suggested to me that sequential organization of the knowledge structure, "l'ordre" of the language's grammar, could be fortuitously complemented with "l'aventure" of random civilization lessons. In addition to providing an intellectual balance, a practical advantage is served, for although grammar lessons vary according to level (most secondary instructors teach several), multi-level enrichment activities appeal to and instruct all.

Even the chronological order of traditional history classes unnecessarily constrains the cultural adventure especially in a mixed level French class where many examined the "Merovingians last Autumn". Random selection of topics imitates travelling - it is difficult to travel in chronological order!

Over the years my report topics, slides, postcards etc. had grown into an enormous collection which was organized alphabetically, chronologically, by subject, and into multiple choice questions. Because students seemed to regard as a treat any activity dealing with culture and civilization, this collection suddenly appeared to be the data necessary for a game.

Given the task of creating a new Symposium event (fair and without more judges), I met in 1981 with five students to discuss an event which would exploit some of the game elements of teenage culture: card game, quiz shows, video games, and computers. People tended to avoid pronouncing the original name, IL or ELLE after the Fench equivalent of animal, vegetable or mineral. Instead POKER PARI was chosen. This homophone PARI plays on PARIS plus the French word "bet" well known in the expression "pari-mutuel". Poker contributed the method of establishing a hand, although no other poker conventions emerged. POKER PARI, acceptable and pronounceable even by nonlinguists, would offer points for correct answers which were selected by a single keystroke to multiple-choice culture and civilization questions. The computer's capabilities were considered: storage capacity was exploited to bank questions, random capacity to select questions, and mathematical accuracy to keep score. The computer would be our ideal volunteer, the fair and impartial judge!

The number of topics (14) in POKER PARI was chosen before the specific topics had been defined. From the game of poker came the option of discarding two cards. Thirteen topics correspond to a deck of cards - Ace through ten, plus Jack, Queen, and King. Using the fourteenth, Joker, to represent a wild card, permitted subsuming any uncategorizable items. Therefore language and civilization questions would be divided into fourteen topics of discrete questions which did not refer to any other screen. The computer could randomly select seven topics and present the player with the corresponding questions one at a time. Each game would be fresh and different, generated just for the player. There is no time limit on answering although this is easy to implement on most microcomputers. Students providing input suggested that the focus would not be on the content if time stress were added. Racing against the clock obscures the importance of knowledge.

The curricular organization in delineating topics proceeded from the topic covered to the larger topics into which they grouped themselves. After establishing the topics, new questions were generated to replace or supplement those already gathered. It became apparent that topical item analysis could be valuable to achieve balance and representation. This analysis could be useful in carrying stated values into practical application.

Not only do topics facilitate the learner's attempts to assimilate the input, the student and teacher are guided in study by having a framework into which to sort the material and verify the thoroughness of their efforts. Some schools even chose to divide topics among specialists who learned everything about a topic.

The topics

"Card"	Topic Number	Topic Name
	01	Grammar, Elementary
	02	Grammar, Advanced
	03	Vocabulary, Elementary
	04	Vocabulary, Advanced
	05	History, Government, and Education
	06	Literature (Authors and Their Works)
	07	France (Geography, Cities, Provinces, and products)
	08	Monuments and Masterpieces
	09	Outstanding Persons and Their Works (Artist, Musicians, Scientists, Inventors, etc.)
	10	Francophone Countries
Jack	11	Paris
Queen	12	Quotes, Proverbs, and Idioms
King	13	Kings, Queens, and Castles
Joker	14	Wild Card: Anything Goes

To announce the game, a bleu-blanc-rouge POKER PARI is dressed up in a flashing white theatre marquis. Jay Snyder, one of my French students, programmed the graphics. A quick upward scale, to tell the player that the game is loaded and ready to play, is followed by the option of instructions or a hand. Few choose the instructions after the first or second experience.

Because an original game was our goal, no attempt was made to adhere to all of the conventions of "traditional CAI", the CAI which grew out of programmed learning transferred to mainframe computers. Although this learning style had strongly appealed to a narrow band of highly motivated linguistically adept students, POKER PARI represents rethinking the experience of a secondary student interacting with the kind of computer that beeps and flashes communications from a desk top. Goals were to entertain, to teach, and to motivate - not to conform!

The poker convention of discarding and randomly replacing two topics had been a suggestion of some of the advanced French students who met in the summer of 1981 to help design the game. They felt this made the experience more "gamey", but also more "lifelike" because at times one simply chooses not to deal with certain issues.

To provide even more student control, another choice built into the game structure, in addition to the opportunity to discard up to two topics, was an EASY-HARD option. For each topic, a choice was offered between an EASY (5 points) or a HARD (8 points) question. Easy questions generally cover content in a typical first year book with one or two answer possibilities easily eliminated. Hard questions frequently come from higher level content and have less easily discounted distractors, but the distinction is not always clear since decentralized American education fosters wide variations in content among different levels. A simple French "(incorrecte)" appeared for wrong answers, whereas a correct answer prompted a flashing message:

BRAVO!
5 (8) points

The total score is presented at the end of the game. Students frequently compare scores. When they begin to score the maximum of 56, the goal changes to a "roll", several perfect scores in a row.

At our formal contests, a <u>round</u> consisted of seven "cards" or topics, but the number of rounds per <u>game</u> would have to be decided based on the number of students, the availability of computers, and time variables. The game was designed to be played individually or by a school team.

The game element which has subsequently been the most controversial among adults who have not observed students playing is not "flagging" or electronically marking questions which have appeared. This simple but powerful routine enchanted early CAI writers who were computerizing programmed texts. It surprised the students that a teacher would tolerate having a question reappear in the same game. Situations can be observed to illustrate the advantage of this clear departure from the usual CAI which would have removed from the question bank those which had been answered correctly and would have recycled those missed. Potential recurrence caused students to direct their learning attention to remembering questions which they had already answered correctly. Knowing that the questions will not recur sends a message that learning what one sees on the screen is futile since it's too late for those points which are so important to students. What if a question recurs? Freebies are fun. Do you remember playing <u>Monopoly</u>, passing Go and collecting $200? On-going learning pays off! Consider the difference between the attention one directs to new names in a limited accountability receiving line compared to a dinner party where introductions occur frequently.

Having to type my name at the beginning of a program always annoys me. Students feel this unwillingness to share something so personal before ascertaining that they will like the experience and succeed. No name is required in POKER PARI although a file for top scores would be motivating now that computers typically have larger memories. On the other hand, the student gradually commits himself by making choices which influence the hand he soon holds.

Besides the choices about computer routines which deviate from traditional pedagogy, for motivational reasons POKER PARI also deviates from foreign language pedagogy by asking some of the questions in English.

High school and college students who are beginning to study a language often know little grammar but have learned about the culture in other contexts or can choose to accelerate their studies in English. A senior who studies 3 years of Spanish before switching to French should have learned about France in world history, geography, and even English literature classes. The English questions serve to pique his interest and to build his confidence. A game entirely in French would turn away underconfident beginners, who often get "hooked" and play for long periods. Years of mainstreaming gifted students through all levels of French classes suggests to me the usefulness of encouraging motivated students to pursue independently learning in their native language until · they are advanced enough to switch to the target language. BRAVO flashes invariably (without changing reinforcement) because the student garners points. His accuracy controls the intermittant nature of his reinforcement.

The potential of blatant or subtle humor exists among the rote or ordinary questions and the blinking bravos and standard format questions. The routine of hand, questions, score does not vary, but elements of simple or sophisticated humor in the answers season the game intermittently. Students chuckle over identifying "ELLE A MAL AUX DENTS."

1.   SHE HAS BAD BREATH.
2.   SHE CURSES FREQUENTLY.
3.   SHE HAS A TOOTHACHE.
4.   SHE HAS DIRTY TEETH.

Two explanations have been given by students. First it is funny that something as serious as a school computer would mention "bad breath," and second, the juxtaposition of a serious adult word, "frequently," to the word "curses". Teenagers find this incongruity amusing although dissecting humor generally destroys it. Do you see humor in this question? "SI VOUS AVEZ MAL AUX CHEVEUX," you have

1.   A HEADACHE
2.   A BAD HAIRCUT
3.   BOWED LEGS
4.   A HANGOVER

For the more sophisticated, please consider this: "Voltaire: TOUTES LES GENERALISATIONS SONT FAUSSES"

1.   ET RAISONNABLES.
2.   SAUF LES MIENNES.
3.   SOUS MICROSCOPE.
4.   Y COMPRIS CELLE-CI.

When a French audience pilot-tested the game, this question especially amused them: NUL N'EST PROPHÈTE

1. À ROME
2. EN SON PAYS
3. SANS ARGENT
4. QUI FINIT BIEN

After developing the game, only the choice of implementation remained. Students' suggestions to compete together influenced the decision to structure a team competition. Research supports the effectiveness of a cooperative learning environment. Johnson, Johnson, Nelson, Skon (in Jernstedt, 1983) concluded that cooperative goal orientation (where student's performance depends on the performance of the entire group) is significantly better than individualistic performance in individual academic achievement and productivity. The strong conclusion (Jernstedt, 11983) states:

> For all age groups and for all subject matters studied the effect (of evaluating the individual by the group's performance) is so strong that it overwhelms other potential mediating variables (p.99).

The fact that the computer did not know and did not care who provided the answers made some potential negative effects of group play moot, i.e. as long as someone knew the answer, all shared success. In subsequent interviews, students said they did not feel like failures if they missed a question or guessed wrongly. Their two partners obviously did not know either, and besides, they were considering the next question. Students unanimously declared that playing as a team was more fun.

Although students compete as teams in sports events, most academic contests (band, speech, math) pit competitors against an abstract standard or against each other. Students said specifically they wanted to work together – to prepare and to compete <u>with</u> their friends <u>against</u> other schools. To keep advanced students from monopolizing the event, and also to promote continuity from year to year, each team was required to have a first year student among its top three members.

Although some of the files were stored on a DEC10 during developmental efforts, the game itself was developed on a 48K Apple II Plus using only upper case letters. (The release of 2Es coincided with the publication of the game after almost two years of pilots and revisions.) Text for the questions is run in text mode, thus avoiding the "bleeding" of

85

combining graphics and text.

Since the game is software driven, no knowledge of computers was necessary to play nor did knowledge of computers or programming influence scores in any way. Three students who had "never seen a computer up close" were the first winning team. By putting 5 desks with computers facing outward in a circle (pentagon) 15 students can compete at the same time. As recently as 1983, when the competition site was in West Texas, we had to borrow computers and bring them along on the school buses.

In addition to the on-going student input during the game development, some formal research was conducted over the period of the development of the game and the implementation of the event. Of long-term value in other contexts (but little interest here) will be data documenting the growth in availability of micros in homes and schools from 1981 through 1985. All students who played in teams filled out questionnaires. I personally interviewed all winning students the first three years.

Early formal surveys may be summarized:
1. Students felt motivated to prepare for the contest by four factors:
    a.   objectivity of judging
    b.   possibility of getting easy questions,
    c.   potential of avoiding topics not desired,
    d.   novelty of activity.
2. Focusing on the task of earning points for their teams, students quickly learned to:
    a.   turn on microcomputer,
    b.   insert the diskette,
    c.   touch "return" key for entering data.
3. Evaluating the "social factor," students said playing in a team:
    a.   intensified their feelings of success;
    b.   helped them remember answers which they associated with experiences with team members;
    c.   made it more fun.
4. Students asked to play "unofficially" after their game scores had been posted because they wanted to see if they could achieve a higher score.

Much software could be improved by weeding out many elements of CAI which are present because they have always been present. "Social" or collaborative software can be highly motivating. Students can contribute fresh insight to software development. Watching students play and listening to their discussions gives us the kind of information psychologists devote their lives to eliciting.

A harmonious synthesis of "l'ordre et

l'aventure" can be achieved with high touch high tech.

References

Jernstedt, G.C. Computer Enhanced Collaborative Learning: a New Technology for Education. T.H.E. Journal, May 1983, pp.98-101.
Naisbitt, J. Megatrends. New York, New York: Warner Books, 1984, passim.
Stevick, E.W. Memory Meaning and Methods: Some Psychological Perspective on Language Learning. Rowley, Massachusetts: Newbury House Publishers, Inc., 1976, 49.
Taylor, R.P. (Ed.) The Computer in the School: Tutor, Tool, Tutee. New York: Teachers College Press, 1980.
*POKER PARI (French), POKER LISTO (Spanish version with Dr. Barbara Gonzalez Pino) and POKER PARAT (with Anna Thompson) are available from Gessler Publishing Co., N.Y., N.Y.

Chapter Eight

DEVELOPMENT OF A CHARACTER SET AND INITIAL TEACHING
PROGRAMS FOR MODERN HEBREW

M. West, Department of Applied Acoustics, University
of Salford

1.   Introduction

Hebrew presents some challenging problems for the
software engineer. The characters are fairly ornate
in the most popular print styles and run from right
to left! They have different sizes and can have
appendages above or below the line of type. The
vowels, which are essential for the beginner, are
dots and dashes appearing mostly beneath the letters
though occasionally above them. (1)

This chapter describes the development of a
character set using a 16 x 16 matrix initially for
the BBC microcomputer. The letters produced are not
over stylised and resemble those used in standard
print in both religious and secular texts. They have
been widely praised for their clarity and
readability.

The overriding philosophy behind the character
design and generation was simplicity. Hebrew can be
quite daunting to the beginner because of the
graphical complexity of the characters and the vowels
and the many other markings used. All such markings
which do not have any substantial phonetic
contribution have been discarded. The Hebrew
characters are stored in terms of ASCII equivalents
which in turn correspond to keyboard characters
chosen on the basis of their phonetic similarity to
the Hebrew character. This makes the word processing
software easy to use for the beginner and will
ultimately allow the inclusion of a speech
synthesiser.

The introductory educational software packages
which use the Hebrew character generator are
described with specific reference to the problems
associated with the presentation of Hebrew and
English text on one screen.

The development of a simple Hebrew word

processor based on the same Hebrew character generator is described with the aid of pieces of code in BBC Basic.

2. Character Selection

The objective of this implementation was to produce a simplified easy to read Hebrew. Any pointing relating to stresses or defunct Ashkenazi usage was removed. A character is considered to be a <u>single</u> Hebrew symbol which relates to a <u>single</u> phoneme. This is a very useful definition for a computer implementation since it allows a phonetic choice of ASCII keyboard characters which is easily remembered. In addition it permits an easy extension of the Hebrew character generator to a Hebrew speech synthesiser. One exception has been made to this rule to avoid the need for extra vowel positioning software and this is the final chaf, ך , with the vowel ָ , which has been made into a separate character 'chafa', ָך

The list of characters and their ASCII equivalents are shown in Figure 8.1. The one to one correspondence of a Hebrew character with an ASCII character has required the use of a number of characters which do not have phonetic meaning, for example, X (א),] (ו), J (ע), C (שׁ), W (שׂ) together with most of the special function keys. This could have been avoided by the use of combinations of two ASCII characters, which is a particularly attractive approach for dealing with those Hebrew characters which are phonetically similar, for example ב ו; כ ק; ט ת; ס שׂ.

Such a scheme could include final letters which are phonetically identical to non-final counterparts. The characters with a final version are listed below.

כ	ך
מ	ם
נ	ן
פ	ף
צ	ץ

Using dual ASCII character representations though attractive for phonetic usage and therefore for synthesis would be very cumbersome for educational and word processing use and was therefore abandoned.

Some of the Hebrew characters in Figure 8.1 are graphically very similar though phonetically different. These are

בּ	ב
ו	נ
ה	ח
כּ	כ
הּ	ה
פּ	פ
שׁ	שׂ

Figure 8.1: The Letters and their ASCII Equivalents

These graphical similarities would allow some data storage economy since only a base character and a modification to it would be needed in each case. The saving in storage would be offset by increased complexity and has therefore not been used.

3.   **Character Design**

The characters were designed by hand on a grid arrangement allowing for the differing letter sizes (see Figure 8.2).

Figure 8.2: Grid Layout for Letter and Vowel Design

f_{00}	f_{01}	f_{02}	f_{03}
f_{10}	f_{11}	f_{12}	f_{13}
f_{20}	X,Y f_{21}	X+1,Y f_{22}	f_{23}
f_{30}	X,Y+1 f_{31}	X+1,Y+1 f_{32}	f_{33}
f_{40}	X,Y+2 f_{41}	X+1,Y+2 f_{42}	f_{43}
f_{50}	f_{51}	f_{52}	f_{53}

The letters can be fitted into two size categories
Single size (8 x 16) נ י ז ו ו ג
Double size (16 x 16)

ס מ כ פ ט ח ה ה ד ב ב א

ת שׁ שׂ ר ק צ פ פ ע ס

The final nun ן goes in the single size category, and
the other final letters which go below the line, ך ,
ן, ף , ץ go in the double size category. ק and ל
(which is the only letter which goes above the line)
are also in the double size category. The letters are
placed in the frame against the right hand edge
(except ן , י , ד , ר which have a gap of one or two
squares from the right hand edge) and are designed so
that they end at least two squares from the left hand
edge. This technique avoids the need for spacing the
characters when they are printed on the screen, the
frame design providing an automatic spacing. If all
the letters had a blank space of precisely two
squares on the left of the frame the printed
characters would be evenly spaced. Unfortunately
this was not possible because it would have required
distortions of the letter shapes rendering them less

readable. In a number of cases a larger number of blank squares on the left was used to ensure a balanced letter shape. In one case, the shin, ש , only one blank space remained on the left because of the complexity of the letter (see Figure 8.3).

Figure 8.3: Design of the Letter Shin showing the single Blank Square on the Left Hand Side

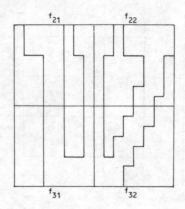

In general however the deviations from the two blank space norm are small and the printed text has a spacing which is quite acceptable.

4.   Character Generating Algorithm

The single and double size scheme not only has the above advantage of providing automatic spacing it is also very simple to implement on the computer. The scheme to be described is for the BBC microcomputer but can easily be adapted to any other microcomputer. Each letter is 'set up' in a subroutine which contains a separate call to a routine to print it. Taking Alef, א , as an example the routine for this letter (subscripted "f" replacing real code) is

```
DEF PROCALEF
VDU 23, f21, 16, 24, 28, 30, 15, 7, 7, 13
        f22, 31, 31, 6, 6, 140, 216, 240
        f31, 12, 12, 12, 12, 12, 31, 31, 31
        f32, 228, 240, 120, 60, 30, 15, 7, 3, 1
PROCHC2
```

```
VT = 0: OT = 0
ENDPROC
```

The data in the VDU command is broken down into the data for each 8 x 8 frame which is labelled with a frame code f_{21} to f_{32}. The design procedure is well documented and character design software to speed up the process is available. (2)

The frame codes are redefined for each letter called since there are insufficient codes available for all the Hebrew letters and vowels. The routine PROCHC2 prints up the defined letter on a double frame. The routine is

```
DEF PROCHC2
X = X-2
PRINTTAB (X,Y); CHR$(f_{21}); TAB(X+1,Y);CHR$(f_{22})
PRINTTAB (X,Y+1);CHR$(f_{31}); TAB(X+1,Y+1);CHR$(f_{32})
ENDPROC
```

The co-ordinates X,Y refer to the top <u>left</u> of the character being printed, the Y co-ordinate increases down the page (Figure 8.4). Before the procedure can be operated the X-co-ordinate must be <u>decremented by two</u> units from its previous value to allow space for printing this two frame character. This procedure allows the characters to be printed on the screen from right to left.

Figure 8.4: Vowels and their ASCII Equivalents

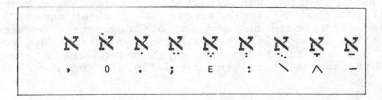

For a single size letter ony two frames f_{22} and f_{32} need be 'set up'. The printing routine for the single size letters, PROCHC1 decrements the co-ordinate X by one and only prints frames f_{22} and f_{32}.

Because there are only six cases where the letter goes below the line and one (ך) where it goes above the line it is not worthwhile to produce additional printing subroutines. The required extra PRINTTAB statement for frame f_{42} (f_{41} for ק), where the letter goes below the line or frame f_{11} for ל where the letter goes above the line, is included in the appropriate letter subroutine.

5. Vowel Selection

The vowels available in the system are the smallest set which are phonetically meaningful. All modifications to vowels which indicate subtleties of stress have been omitted. As with the letters a single ASCII keyboard character has been used for each vowel. This is justifiable because Sefardi Hebrew vowels are nearly all a single phonetic sound and difficulties due to diphthongs which would require two characters to represent them can be avoided. Unlike the letters the keyboard equivalents of the vowels have been chosen mostly on a non phonetic basis. This was done to make it easy to use the system as a typewriter. Some of the ASCII punctuation marks are identical to the actual Hebrew vowel symbol; · , − , : and other chosen symbols bear some resemblance to the Hebrew vowel; ∧ to ⊤ and ╲to ·. . The vowels ∵ and ˙א were assigned the nearest phonetic ASCII character (E and O respectively). The remaining vowel ·· is almost the same as ∵ in Sefardi Hebrew although in some dialects it is closer to a diphthong. The symbol ; was arbitrarily assigned to this vowel.

The vowels used and their ASCII equivalents are shown in Figure 8.4.

All vowels except ˙א are placed beneath a Hebrew character. Sometimes there is no vowel required at all. The absence of a vowel must be indicated here by a symbol, which was arbitrarily chosen as a comma (,), so that a simple scheme using alternate ASCII characters could be used for discriminating between letters and vowels. The exception to this occurs for ‏ל and all final letters which never take a vowel (This is consistent with our definition of ‏ה).

6. Vowel Design

The vowel shapes are sufficiently simple not to present any design problems. The main difficulty is ensuring that the vowel is printed in exactly the correct location below its Hebrew letter. This location must be very precise otherwise the vowels appear confusing and do not relate properly to the letter above.

All the vowel shapes will fit easily into a single frame and it would appear simplest to design them centrally within one frame and then arrange to adjust the X,Y co-ordinates of that frame to place it beneath the appropriate letter. Unfortunately this is not possible with the simple printing scheme used for the letters which is based on <u>integer</u> values of the co-ordinates X and Y. The BBC micrcomputer does have facilities for printing at the graphics cursor which would permit more accurate positioning of the vowel. This scheme was not however used since the procedure adopted was to be capable of implementation on all microcomputers.

Positioning of the vowel can only be achieved with an integer co-ordinate system by designing different versions of each vowel within one or two (adjacent) frames. The chosen designs must cover all the required positions for any Hebrew letter. In order to cut down the enormous number of designs required for one vowel four types were identified which were set by the letter above (five types in the case of ×).

Let us just consider the four types of vowel design used for all vowels except × :

Type 0. This applies to all double frame letters except פ , ר, ד . The vowel is positioned so that it appears centrally beneath all the above letters and requires two frames for the design (f_{41}, f_{42}) (see Figure 8.5 (0)). The subroutine for the vowel has VDU commands defining the contents of the two frames. The character representing the merged frames is then printed at location with co-ordiantes X, Y+2.

```
DEF PROCE
VDU 23, f₄₁, 0, 0, 1, 1, 0, 0, 0, 0,
    f₄₂, 0, 0, 152, 152, 0, 96, 96, 0
    E$ = CRS$(f₄₁) + CHR$(f₄₂)
    PRINTTAB(X,Y+2);E$
ENDPROC
```

Type 1. This is used with ז ג נ and פ . For the ז ג נ , which are single frame letters, the vowel uses only one frame for the design (f_{42}) (See Figure 8.5(1)) and appears centrally beneath these letters in a similar manner to the type 0 vowel design. In the case of פ , which is a double frame letter the design may be used provided the frame is moved one space right. This is achieved with the variable VK which is set to 1 in the routine for פ but to zero in the routines for ז ג נ . VK is added to the X co-ordinate in the PRINT statement for the vowel.

Type 2. The vowels are placed beneath the right hand stem for each of the letters ו , י , ד , ר . Like type 1 vowels only one frame is required (f_{42}) but this time the vowel is moved as far <u>right</u> as possible and drawn right up to the right hand edge of the frame. (See Figure 8.5(2)).

Figure 8.5: Designs for Vowel ◌ֱ   (Similarly for −, T, ː, ‥, .)

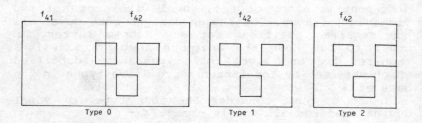

A difficulty arises here with the vowel ◌ֱ which fills the complete frame (f_{42}) in the type 1 case. (Figure 8.6(1)). Movement to the right would mean that a part of the vowel would spill over into the previous vowel's left hand frame. This would spoil the clarity of the two vowels which would lose the clear relationship to the letters above them. A design using an extra frame (f_{52}) <u>below</u> the above frame (f_{42}) was used (see Figure 8.6(2)) to overcome the difficulty.

Figure 8.6: Designs for Vowel ◌ֱ

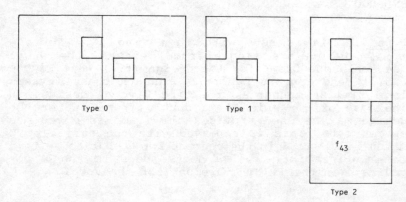

We can now see why the letters ר ד were
designed so that the right hand edge of their stems
was two squares from the right hand edge of the
frame. The vowels in the type 2 design will now
appear exactly centrally beneath the stems of these
letters. In the case of י the separation between the
stem and the frame edge was made one square instead
of two. This effectively moves all the vowels a small
distance left. This is often done in printed texts
and improves the clarity of the relationship of the
vowel to the י because of its small size and also
because it ends some distance from the bottoms of the
other letters. The use of the extra space on the
right hand sides of the above characters does spoil
the evenness of the character spacing a little and on
the ד and ר the overall character width is slightly
reduced. In order to preserve the even spacing all
the letters would have to be designed to finish two
spaces from the right hand edge of the frame, the
consequent loss of definition would not be
acceptable. The extra spacing on the right of the
above letters does not noticeably affect the
presentation.

The letters ד and ר are double size characters
and the co-ordinate X will therefore need to be
incremented by one unit before the vowel is printed.
This is done using the variable V which is set to 1
in the routines for ד and ר and zeroed in the
routines for י and ו . V is added to the X co-
ordinate in the PRINT statement for the vowel.

We can now consider the five types of design
used only for the vowel אָ .

Type 0 is for all the double frame letters except
שׁ and שׂ . The vowel is drawn as a square close to
the bottom right hand corner of frame f_{11} which is
immediately above the top left of the letter (see
Figure 8.7(0)).

Type 1 is for all the single frame letters except
ה which do not take any vowels, that is for נ ,
ג , ז , י , ו . This is similar to type 0 except that
frame f_{12} is used. A little experiment was needed to
find the best position for the vowel in the frame.
The small space on the right of the י and ו places
the square closer to these letters than would
otherwise be the case so improving the presentation
of the letter-vowel combination.

Figure 8.7: Designs for Vowel X

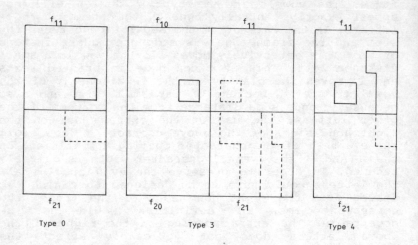

Type 0   Type 3   Type 4

Type 2 is only for ּשׂ and places the vowel over the left hand stem of the letter. This is very similar to type 1 but a slightly different positioning of the square in frame f_{11} is required to ensure the vowel appears above the left hand stem of the ּשׂ

Type 3 is only for ּשׂ   In printed texts only a single dot is shown above the left hand stem. This would however be difficult to read for the beginner. A design almost the same as type 1 with the square in the bottom right hand corner of the frame was used. This time however frame f_{10} was chosen which is to the left of frame f_{11} and f_{21} (see Figure 8.7(3)). In order to prevent the vowel being overwritten by the next letter the co-ordinate X must be decremented by one unit after the vowel has been printed at the end of the routine.

Type 4 is for ך . This is also similar to type 1 in that frame f_{11} is. used. For ך this frame contains the part of the letter which goes above the line, which must be included with the vowel if it is not to be lost when the vowel is printed (Figure 8.7(4)).

A summary table of the vowel designs used is

shown in Figure 8.8.

Figure 8.8: Table of Vowel Designs

Vowel	ASCII	Subroutines	
-	-	A, Al, A2, A3	
ָ	^	AS, AS1, AS2, AS3	
ֳ	\	00, 001, 002, 003	
:	:	ER, ER1, ER2, ER3	VT
ֲ	E·	E, E1, E2, E3	
..	EY	EY, EY1, EY2, EY3	
.	EE	EE, EE1, EE2, EE3	
ֹx	0	0, 01, 02, 03, 04	OT
blank	,	NOVOW	

For VT = 1, VK set to 1 for ק otherwise 0
For VT = 2, V set to 1 for ו ,ןotherwise 0
The fourth design (indexed 3) for each vowel is used
only for the shin and is very similar to type 0.

7. **Software for Vowel Selection**
Each subroutine for a given letter has two variables
set in its last line, VT and OT, the values
corresponding respectively to the above two sets of
vowel design types. In addition variable VK is set to
1 in the routine for ק and variable V is set to 1 in
the routines for ו and ן , elsewhere V and VK are
set to zero. The above variables are then passed
directly to the vowel routine which is activated
immediately after the preceding letter so that the
correct vowel design is selected.

8. **Generating a Line of Hebrew Text from an ASCII String**
The subroutines for each of the letters in Figure 8.1
and the vowels in Figure 8.4 are listed sequentially
each one starting at a known line number. Any ASCII
character corresponding to a letter will generate a
GOTO command to the correct line for the start of the
appropriate subroutine when that character is input
as LE$ to the routine PROCLETTER(LE$). A similar
procedure is used for an ASCII character
corresponding to a vowel. Here the appropriate
routine is PROCVOWEL(VD$) where VD$ is the ASCII
character. The two routines PROCLETTER and PROCVOWEL
have built in protection against spurious ASCII
characters including vowel characters when a letter

99

is expected, and letter characters when a vowel is expected. PROCLETTER and PROCVOWEL are essentially look-up routines for conversion of the ASCII character to the line number of the letter or vowel printing routine. The look-up is done for each character to avoid storing the look-up tables in arrays, storage being at a premium because of the large amount of data held in the letter and vowel printing routines.

The conversion routine for the ASCII string ST$ is

```
DEF PROCHEBSTR(ST$)
K = LEN(ST$)
DE$ = "LETTER"
for  I = 1 to K
     C$ = MID$(ST$, I, 1)
     IF DE$ = "LETTER" THEN PROCLETTER(C$)
     ELSE PROCVOWEL(CS)
     DE$ = "VOWEL"
     RESTORE *
     FOR LO = 1 to 11
     READ TE$
     IF C$ = TE$ THEN DE$ = "LETTER"
     NEXT
*    DATA @, > , < , *, U, } , { , m, n, f, j
NEXT
```

The string is assumed to start with a letter. If the letter is a blank, a punctuation mark, ‎ג‎ , ‎ה‎ , ‎ה‎ , ‎ם‎ , ‎ן‎ , ‎ף‎ , or ‎ץ‎ a letter is expected as the next character.

Providing the starting co-ordinates X, Y of the string are known the above routine will print the Hebrew string from the input ASCII string ST$. This may alternatively be input at the keyboard or from a data statement. In theory then, provided a graphic character mode (4 or 5) is being used, the above routines could be added to any program and used to generate Hebrew text. This is precisely what has been done in the educational programs described below. Unfortunately the available memory for additional program lines is small unless a second processor is used.

9.   **Educational Programs**

A package of programs using the above Hebrew text generator has been produced as an introduction to the Hebrew language. The first program, which uses four colour graphics in the large character mode (5), introduces the letters and vowels of Hebrew presented singly with English phonetic equivalents. Similar introductions to Hebrew are available in text book form but tests in a school have shown that the animation and colour of the computer presentation is preferred by children.

The second program is a 'singalong' where there is a computer musical accompaniment to the text appearing on the screen. By using delays at the end of each line sychronisation between the text and the music can be achieved.

The third program is for teaching Hebrew vocabulary and is similar to vocabulary programs available for other languages but it has some interesting added features. In the learning phase a page of Hebrew words with their English translations is presented. The pupil is then given a single Hebrew word from the page and asked for the translation. A correct response is congratulated in Hebrew together with a few bars of Hava Nagila. An incorrect response is noted and a request made for another attempt - all in Hebrew of course! If repeated incorrect or very stupid responses are made the program produces an appropriate retort, once again in Hebrew.

10. **A Simple Hebrew Word Processor**
A straightforward modification of the ASCII string converter routine PROCHEBSTR will permit characters to be typed in at the keyboard and the Hebrew equivalent to appear on the screen. The routine for accepting and converting keyboard characters is given below.

```
      DEF PROCTYPE
      X = 39: Y = 4   LV$ =" " : DE$ = "LETTER"
*     PRINTTAB(2,1) ; "LETTER            "
      VT = 0: OT = 0 : V = 0 : VK = 0
      IF Y>26 THEN X = 39 : Y = 4 : CLS
      IF X<3 THEN PROCNEWLIN
      IF X>39 THEN PROCBAKLIN
      LE$ = GET$
      PROCLETTER(LE$)
      LV$ = LV$ + LE$
      RESTORE **
      DE$ = "VOWEL"
      FOR LO = 1 TO 11
      IF LE$ = TE$ THEN DE$ = "LETTER"
      NEXT
**    DATA @,> ,< , *, U,} ,{ , m, n, f, j
      IF DE$ = "LETTER" GOTO *
```

```
        PRINTTAB(2,1) ; "VOWEL
        VD$ = GET$
        PROCVOWEL(VD$)
        LV$ = LV$ + VD$
        GOTO *
ENDPROC
```

The routines PROCLETTER AND PROCVOWEL as explained earlier are protected against the input of spurious characters. They ignore the character and execute GOTO *. The ASCII string is accumulated in the string LV$.

The end of a line is detected when the co-ordinate X goes less than 3 as we print the characters from right to left. Before we can commence typing characters for the next line we must shift the first letters of the word broken by the edge of the screen page onto the next line. This is done by splitting the ASCII string into two strings one on the left of the blank character @ (on the Hebrew right of @) STL$, and the other on the right of the blank (on the Hebrew left of @) STRI$. The original line is then erased and the shortened line reprinted using PROCHEBSTR(STL$). The other string is printed at the beginning of the next line using PROCHEBSTR(STRI$). The X and Y co-ordinates are now correctly set to accept more characters input from the keyboard. The routine for performing the above line change is

```
        DEF PROCNEWLIN
        ILI = ILI + 1
        K = LEN(LV$)
        K1 = 0
        K1 = K1 + 1
        LER$ = MID$(LV$, K1, 1)
        IF LER$ < > "@" GOTO *
        STL$ = LEFT$(LV$, K1-1)
        STRI$ = RIGHT$(LV$, K-K1)
        FOR IN =-1 TO 3
           FOR XIN = 0 TO 39
           PRINTTAB(XIN, Y + IN) ; " "
           NEXT
           NEXT
        X = 39 :   PROCHEBSTR(STL$)
        X = 39 :   Y = Y + 4 :   IF Y > 26 PROCNPG
        PROCHEBSTR(STRI$)

        TL$(ILI) = STL$
        LV$ = STRI$
        ENDPROC
```

The above routine requires a minor modification to make allowance for the last character on the line being a blank (@) when only a return to the beginning of the next line is needed. The routine PROCNPG clears the screen and resets X and Y ready for a new screen page. In addition it includes facilities for a fast screen dump to a printer.

Deletion of incorrect Hebrew text can be achieved using the "£" key which is recognised as a Hebrew letter in the routine PROCLETTER. A single frame blank character is printed at co-ordinates X-1, Y. The £ character is added to the ASCII string LV$ containing all the other ASCII characters, which correspond to Hebrew letters. If we wish to delete the whole of the current line and part of the previous one routine PROCBAKLIN must be used which reduces the co-ordinate Y to Y-4 and the line number ILI to ILI-1. The £ characters make the ASCII strings unnecessarily long and slow up the line change procedure above. A routine to clean up the strings may be included at the beginning of PROCNEWLIN to remove all the £ characters and the ASCII characters to which they refer.

Other minor refinements include a cursor for the Hebrew characters and a flashing cursor to cue input for a 'LETTER' or a 'VOWEL'. Editing on a screen page is done by first locating the line to be edited using the cursor keys (↑↓) each operation altering the line number, ILI, by one. Once the left hand end of the line has been located the text on that line may then be deleted in the usual way using the "£" character. New text may then be inserted but no facilities are available for going beyond the end of the line since this would involve adjusting the position of all subsequent stored text.

A much more sophisticated Hebrew word processor could only be developed on a microcomputer with substantially more memory and a faster execution time for commands relating to the screen graphics. The next generation of microcomputers will certainly have these capabilities.

References

Levy, H. Hebrew for All 3rd Edition, 4th Impression, revised, 1964. Novello and Company, London

McGreggor J. and Watt A. The BBC Micro Book, Basic, Sound and Graphics. Addison-Wesley, 1983, p.278.

Chapter Nine

COMPUTER-BASED INSTRUCTION IN HINDI (1)

Tej K. Bhatia, Syracuse University, New York

Introduction
The importance and need for teaching non-western
languages in North America and Great Britain has been
stressed time and again in journals, reports and
books (for details, see the recent report of the
President's Commission on Foreign Languages and
International Studies (1979), Atkins and Craft
(1983), Houlton and Willey (1983), and Hainline and
Jogia (1984)). Because of the undisputed role of
these languages in promoting universal literacy and
providing bilingual education, along with the lack of
trained teachers of non-western languages and of
economic resources, the need for teaching non-
western languages by computers, preferably by
microcomputers, is greater than ever before. This is
especially true of Hindi, which in addition to
ranking among the five most widely spoken languages
in the world, serves as an ethnic language for Asian
Indians settled in North America, Great Britain and
other Western countries. Therefore, the role of Hindi
in providing bilingual education for children of
Asian Indians can hardly be underestimated. For these
reasons, as educators in North America and outside
North America prepare to complement their classroom
instruction in Hindi with computer-based pedagogy,
they encounter a scarcity of programs. This problem
is especially serious for computer-based pedagogy on
microcomputers.
       The aim of this chapter is to fill this
important gap by way of presenting the salient
features of computer-based Hindi pedagogy on PLATO
IV. In addition to this specific goal, the chapter
aims at achieving the following three general goals:
(1) to present a model example for developing
sophisticated Hindi teaching courses on microcomputers; (2) to indicate the scope of computer-

based language pedagogy; and (3) to exemplify the development of more satisfactory and efficient testing procedures which could not be realized in non-computer-based pedagogy. Before I proceed to achieve these goals, a brief description of PLATO as a computer-controlled teaching system is in order.

PLATO IV: A COMPUTER-CONTROLLED TEACHING SYSTEM

PLATO IV, an abbreviation for Programmed Logic for Automated Teaching Operation, is an economically feasible, large-scale, computer-controlled teaching system. The more advanced stage of PLATO III is currently in operation at the University of Illinois. More than just another laboratory curiosity, it is presently being employed in twenty fields, from astronomy to the medical sciences. Foreign language teaching includes both western languages (such as English as a second language, French, German, Italian, Latin, Russian, Spanish) and non-western languages (such as Chinese, Hindi, Hebrew, Japanese, Arabic and Swahili).

PLATO IV Configuration
The PLATO system consists of a central computer and several hundred terminals through which students communicate with the computer. Each terminal has an inherent memory, a plasma display panel, and an attached keyboard. The display panel is an 8½-inch square of glass containing a 512 x 512 matrix display. Any individual dot can be selectively lighted. The keyboard looks like that of an electric typewriter with the addition of some functional keys such as NEXT, BACK, HELP, DATA, the pressing of which allows the student to branch to a designated section of a lesson. Watching the display on the panel, the student communicates with the computer mainly through the keyboard. Four types of additional equipment are available: an audio device permitting random access to messages recorded on a disk, a touch panel attachment enabling the student to respond by touching the display screen instead of typing, a slide selector allowing a microfiche to be rear-projected and as superimposed on the panel, and an external input capable of interfacing with other machines. Terminals are connected by telephone wires to a CDC CYBER 73 computer with two central processors.
    A specially designed program language, called

TUTOR can be quickly learned by people who have no expert knowledge of computers (see Sherwood 1974). The software system has the ability to interact with students, asking questions and correcting their errors. It can tell them what word contained the error and what type of error (spelling or otherwise) was made. Responding within a fraction of a second, the computer can force students to review areas of difficulty. In addition, it can record their responses, generate questions, and examine responses to those questions.

GOALS AND THE HISTORY OF THE COMPUTER-BASED HINDI TEACHING PROJECT

The project for computer-based Hindi teaching (henceforth, CBHT) currently being developed at the University of Illinois can be divided into experimental, developmental and final stages. The experimental work, initiated by the author of this chapter under the supervision of Professor Y. Kachru in 1973, entered its developmental stage as the result of the joint effort with Dr. Cecil Nelson and others. Currently, it is being used to teach Hindi as a second language and at the same time being subjected to rigorous editing, supplementation and testing procedures. During the last two stages, technical development was jointly carried out by Dr. R. Hart and myself.

The main goals set for the project have been:

1. to identify potential areas of Hindi and Sanskrit language courses where computer-based pedagogy could efficiently supplement the non-computer-based teaching;
2. to provide individualized instruction, especially at the early stages (such as script-learning), so as to make classroom instruction more efficient and economical by eliminating problems of non-synchronic learning;
3. to supplement non-computer-based Hindi teaching with additional lessons in grammar, cultural background, vocabulary, and other topics, and
4. to provide for instant review of basic material for advanced students.

Despite the claims made by several independent computer groups in India and outside India, it is the only program of its kind which can teach the Devanagari script (henceforth Nagari) as well as the

Hindi language with the aid of a computer. To date, all other attempts to teach Hindi do not go beyond generating the Nagari script on computers. (2)

General Design and Organization

When a student signs on for the lessons, the computer asks his name. After that the student is presented with an index page on the screen. The index page contains a table of contents and a list of lessons. The student can thereon choose a lesson to study by typing an appropriate number corresponding to the lesson of his choice. Each individual lesson also has a table of contents listing sections of the lesson. The concept of sequencing, which involves selection, grading, presentation and testing, has gone into the planning of our lessons on PLATO.

The lessons programmed are followed by exercises. An attempt has been made to make some exercises generative in nature. In other words, some exercises randomly select questions out of a set of given questions and present them to the student so that whenever he signs his name, he comes across a new quiz. Built into these exercises is an option for a student to review his material in case he is not prepared for a quiz.

Creation and Teaching of the Devanagari Script

In developing a computer-based Hindi teaching course, our first and foremost task was to create the Nagari script on PLATO IV. The Nagari script is used to write several Indic languages including Sanskrit, Nepali and Marathi in addition to Hindi, and is ranked one of the most scientific scripts, if not the only scientific script, among the existing writing systems of natural languages. This is primarily for the following two reasons: one, the arrangement of its graphemes is sensitive to the point and manner of articulation of the sound denoted by a grapheme; and two, the script in itself is largely phonetic in nature, i.e. a word is written the way it is pronounced and each grapheme essentially denotes one sound. In spite of its scientific and phonetic merits, programming the script was not free from problems, as the main basis of the hardware and software of our existing computer systems is the Roman script. From the reference point of the Roman script, the Nagari script exhibits the following specific properties:

1.   The script is non-linear in nature. Although it
      is written from left to right like Roman, a
      vowel in a word is written as super or
      subscript. For example, syllables such as tu and
      te are written something like u̱ and ṯ ,
      respectively, in Nagari.
2.   Unlike Roman which is alphabetic, the Nagari
      script is syllabic in nature, that is, Nagari
      contains a short vowel a̱ in addition to the
      corresponding consonant symbol of Roman.
      Consequently, every consonant manifests itself
      in two shapes termed full consonant and half
      consonant. The half consonants, like their
      Roman counterparts, do not contain the inherent
      short vowel and are derived by using three
      distinct graphemic strategies: (i) consonants
      having a right hand vertical stroke (e.g. kha,
      ga) often drop the vertical stroke to yield half
      consonants (e.g. ख़ kh, ⌐ g); (ii) consonants
      not having right hand stroke indicate lack of a̱,
      concatenating with the subscript known as Viram
      or Halant, (denoted by a symbol ⌣); and (iii)
      complete amalgamation, e.g. क ka, + ष sha
      yields क्ष ksha.
3.   Each vowel has two symbols termed main and matra
      vowels. The matra forms are used only to attach
      a vowel symbol to a preceding consonant symbol.
      The main vowel forms are used in all other
      phonetic environments. For the long back vowel
      u, the main and the matra forms are ऊ, and ॖ ,
      respectively. Therefore, the word, ut is
      written as ऊत (not ुत); whereas tu is तू (not
      तॖ) .
4.   There is no upper and lower case distinction in
      Nagari.
5.   Being a phonetic script, Nagari has more symbols
      than Roman - at least ninety.

      These idiosyncratic properties of the script,
together with the complexity of graphemic shapes,
posed a serious challenge for programming Nagari on
PLATO. The strict limitations of character set space
called for many crucial decisions in the course of
programming, often forcing us to decide between
traditional pedagogical practice and alternative
methods that would accommodate the characters within
the limited space of the PLATO keyboard.
      Therefore, our problems were primarily three:
one, to program each character in an adequate manner;
two, to overcome the inadequacies of graphemic
representation of the Nagari script resulting from

108

algorithmic properties of the machine; and, three, to achieve efficiency and to improve performance in writing the Nagari script on PLATO in terms of speed and graphic precision. Perhaps it should be added that given the traditional sequencing of syllabic and non-syllabic characters, it would have been practically impossible to program the Nagari script on PLATO. However, all three problems have been solved and a new system was devised as the result of the careful structural analysis of the Nagari graphemes and the successful exploitation of options available at each point on PLATO. The following discussion will clarify this point further.

In order to solve the first problem, all the characters of Nagari were designed individually on an 8 x 16 grid on PLATO as shown in Figure 9.1.

Figure 9.1

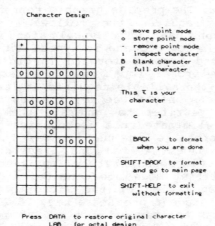

Character Design

```
+    move point mode
o    store point mode
-    remove point mode
ı    inspect character
B    blank character
F    full character

This ऋ is your
     character

  c    ɔ

BACK      to format
   when you are done

SHIFT-BACK  to format
   and go to main page

SHIFT-HELP  to exit
   without formatting
```

Press DATA to restore original character
     LAB for octal design

Information specifying various character images is stored in a system supported database called a "character set". Execution of an appropriate "charset" command causes this image information to be transmitted to a read/write memory in the user's terminal called the <u>regular font</u> which contains the standard Roman characters available at all times on PLATO. Each character slot in the alternate font is associated with a particular key (upper or lower case); when the terminal is in <u>altfont mode</u>. A key press causes the associated altfont character to appear. A special key called <u>FONT</u> toggles back and

109

forth between altfont and regular modes.

Considerable space-saving within charset was achieved by deriving full consonants ending with right-hand vertical strokes from their corresponding half-consonant form. For example, the consonant ta in our program is composed of two character images: त which occupies altfont t and T which occupies altfont slot 1. The production of त ta on PLATO involves a half backspace to get proper positioning of T relative to त .

The problems of spacing and speed caused by a wide variety of factors such as the insertion of the right-hand vertical stroke and the non-linear nature of Nagari, were resolved by making use of microtable, a standard PLATO database feature which allows the author to specify a one-to-one mapping from key caps to sequences of character codes. Consider, for example, the writing of the Nagari syllable tu. In the syllable, the matra vowel is assigned to the altfont slot u. The precise graphic representation of the syllable requires the following steps after typing the consonant. The vowel sign is moved $1\frac{1}{2}$ spaces back, is lowered and is typed. Afterwards, the cursor is moved $\frac{1}{2}$ space forward in order to resume typing at the proper location. In other words, the generation of the syllable requires at least nine key strokes, whereas only three key strokes are required on a Hindi typewriter to generate the syllable in question. To eliminate this uneconomical process, we specified microtable in such a way that pressing altfont t produces त ta; and pressing altfont u produces ु u, appropriately positioned. Keys pressed in altfont mode are considered distinct and have their own region of the microtable. In other words, when a student presses a key, PLATO intercepts and substitutes the sequence of key strokes assigned by the microtable. Thus, using microtable and other such features enabled us to solve the last two types of problems for programming Nagari on PLATO. For more details on these problems, see Bhatia (1974), Kachru, Nelson and Hart(1981); and for a detailed description of microtables, see Sherwood (1974).

Keyboard Design

Based on two distinct approaches, a number of Hindi keyboards have been proposed for computer users in the past two decades. The first approach which faithfully borrows the Nagari typewriter keyboard yields a complex, slow and uneconomical keyboard, whereas the second approach, relying exclusively on the structural analysis of Nagari graphemes renders a much simpler, but a totally unrealistic keyboard. In spite of their engineering ingenuity, keyboards based on the latter approach failed to gain any acceptability because they advocate sacrificing the traditional nature of the Nagari script as a reward for a simpler keyboard . (For details, see Bhatia (1974).)

The keyboard devised for PLATO users represents an ideal compromise between the two approaches. It attempts to achieve the simplicity of the structural approach without compromising or sacrificing the traditional nature of Nagari. In addition, unlike the Nagari typewriter keyboard, it presupposes that users of the Hindi keyboard on PLATO have some familiarity with the Roman keyboard. Also, at no time does it overlook the fact that designing the alphabet is primarily a programming task, while a keyboard design presents a problem in human factors.

To maximize learning the accurate performance and to minimize frustration on the part of a learner, a set of two types of principles - general and specific - went into the design of our Nagari keyboard. The general principles are as follows:

1. Keys should be assigned to symbols so that the key has some visual or phonetic mnemonic value.
2. Symbols perceived as basic and/or frequent by the users should be produced simply, ideally by one key stroke.
3. Symbols perceived as derived (or complex) either structurally or linguistically (aspiration, vowel length etc.) may be produced with a sequence of strokes.
4. The derived symbol should be constructed by exploiting general and simple construction rules.

The specific principles are sensitive to the linguistic properties of Nagari and refer to mnemonic rules of the following type:

1. Unaspirated consonants and short matra vowels are considered basic and are assigned the equivalent non-capital Roman key position.
2. Aspirated consonants are treated as derived consonants and they occupy the SHIFT (capital) unaspirated consonant keys.
3. Half consonants are derived from the full consonants and constructed by means of a key called MICRO. While the SHIFT key on PLATO, as

on typewriters, must be held down while the following key is struck, the MICRO key is only tapped.

4. Like aspirated consonants, the SHIFT key is employed to derive long vowels – main as well as matra vowels. The MICRO key is reserved for less frequent matra vowels. For example, MICRO u (yields) उ u; MICRO SHIFT u ऊ , u; u ु (matra u) and SHIFT u ू (long matra u).

The keyboard thus developed for our Hindi teaching course is shown in Figure 9.2. Although other intricate details of our keyboard system are beyond the scope of this chapter, it should be stressed that even with careful design and planning, the Hindi keyboard is sufficiently complex to require some special instruction in the form of an on-line keyboard lesson (Figure 9.3).

Teaching of the Hindi Language

The computer-based teaching of the Hindi language includes lessons dealing with script phonetics, grammar, conversations and vocabulary. The list and contents of these lessons can be obtained from the language learning laboratory of the University of Illinois. Therefore, I will not detail them here. Instead, I will offer briefly some remarks on the design of these lessons which will further explain to some extent the strategies which have gone into the teaching of the various aspects (phonetics, grammar, etc.) of the language on one hand and will reveal some interesting properties of the course on the other.

The general learning hierarchy which has been built into the teaching of the Nagari script is presented in the following chart:

```
┌──────────────────────────────────────┐
│   Graphemes – Sound Association        │
└──────────────────┬───────────────────┘
    ┌──────────────┴────────────────┐
    │ Identify main letters in       │
    │ written and spoken form        │
    └──────────────┬────────────────┘
    ┌──────────────┴────────────────┐
    │ Identify secondary letters in  │
    │ written and spoken form        │
    └──────────────┬────────────────┘
    ┌──────────────┴────────────────┐
    │ Identify similar-looking main and │
    │ secondary letters in written form │
    └──────────────┬────────────────┘
        ┌──────────┴─────────────────┐
        │ Write, read and listen to words │
        │ with main and secondary letters │
        └────────────────────────────┘
```

Figure 9.2

HINDI KEYBOARD

क	ka	k	ख	kha	K				ा	ā	A	श्र	śra	1c
ग	ga	g	घ	gha	G	ि	i	i	ी	ī	I	त्र	tra	1C
च	ća	c	छ	ćha	C	ु	u	u	ू	ū	U	द्य	dhya	1d
ज	ja	j	झ	jha	J	े	e	w		ai	W	ह्म	hma	1h
ट	ta	◆	ठ	tha	◆+	ो	o	o	ौ	au	O	ज्य	jya	1J
ड	da	-	ढ	dha	◆-	ृ	ri	R			/	क्ष	kśa	1k
ण	ṇa	N										द्ध	ddha	1H
त	ta	t	थ	tha	T	अ	a	◆a	आ	ā	◆A	त्त	tta	1L
द	da	d	ध	dha	D	इ	i	◆i	ई	ī	◆I	ट्र	tra	1V
न	na	n				उ	u	◆u	ऊ	ū	◆U			
प	pa	p	फ	pha	P	ए	e	◆e	ऐ	ai	◆E	◆ = MICRO		
ब	ba	b	भ	bha	B	ओ	o	◆o	औ	au	◆O	1 = SUPER		
म	ma	m				ऋ	ri	◆r				↑ = SHIFT		
य	ya	y												
र	ra	r				ॄ	ru	=	ॡ	rū	)	◆ moves		
ल	la	l					ra	f	,	ra	F	diacritics		
व	va	v										halfspace		
श	śa	z				:	aspir	H				left		
ष	ṣa	Z					nasal	x						
स	sa	s					nasal	M				MICRO gives		
ह	ha	h				.	arabic	X				half		
ञ	ny	-				ॱ	stop	q				consonant		
ङ	ng	◆												

press NEXT for exercise

Figure 9.3

HINDI KEYSET: Index of exercises

a. Introduction

b. Consonants
c. More consonants
d. Aspirated consonants
e. Review of single consonants

f. Half-consonants
g. Forms of <u>ra</u>
h. Forms of <u>ru</u>
i. Consonant compounds

j. Vowels
k. <u>Matra</u> forms of short vowels
l. <u>Matra</u> forms of long vowels
m. Review of <u>matra</u> forms
n. Initial forms of vowels
o. The vowel <u>ri</u>
p. Review of vowels

q. Diacritics

r. Numerals

s. Erasing letters
t. Spacing of attached symbols

Type the letter of the topic you want, or
SHIFT-BACK → index of Hindi lessons ⟩

113

On the student screen, lessons on the Nagari script introduce graphemes in small sets, teaching the students to type the graphemes and master the order of strokes and sound, as shown in Figure 9.4.

Most of the lessons dealing with vocabulary, conversations and phonetics are interphased with an audio unit. The audio unit uses magnetic recording on a flexible-plastic disk of 15 inches in diameter. One half second is the average time required for the disk to begin playing after receiving a command. Most of the lessons are recorded on this disk and students can listen to a lexical item, sentence or isolated sound used in the lessons. For example, the lesson on Hindi phonetics incorporates individual sound segments such as retroflex or voiced aspirated sounds. In going through this lesson, students cannot only listen to the pronunciation but are also required to successfully distinguish them in quizzes (see Figure 9.5). They can indicate their choice by touching the item or by typing the appropriate number.

The vocabulary lesson is designed to help students with new words encountered in a lesson. This lesson contains several drills. Each drill is offered in the student's choice of three formats. For example, our Hindi course offers translation of written Hindi into English, translation of written English into Hindi, and dictation, i.e. audio Hindi into written Hindi. Full keyboard typing help is constantly available for each drill (see Figure 9.6). The key-LAB replays the audio message. The HELP-key provides an immediate access to answers.

The grammar and exercise sections are not rigidly separated. The grammar lessons include such topics as verb forms, tenses, negation, question and answering systems, plural formations, oblique cases, etc. Drills often follow the explanation of a grammatical point. This lesson embodies substitution, transformation, fill-in-blanks and translation exercises. Figures 9.7 and 9.8 present a sample of a grammar and exercise lesson, respectively.

One of the most important and unique aspects of computer-based pedagogy on PLATO is that it allows each student to advance at his own pace and to learn at the time he chooses. It makes judgments on the student's response and corrects mistakes before he goes on to compound similar errors. A correct answer is shown to the student usually when a student fails to correct his answer twice. It can also tell a student about the nature of his error, i.e. whether the mistake is a spelling mistake or a grammatical

Figure 9.4

Now let's review all the consonants.

क	ka	k	स	kha	K
ग	ga	g	घ	gha	G
च	ća	c	छ	ćha	C
ज	ja	j	झ	jha	J
ट	ta	+	ठ	tha	↑+
ड	ḍa	-	ढ	ḍha	↑-
ण	ṇa	N			
त	ta	t	थ	tha	T
द	da	d	ध	dha	D
न	na	n			
प	pa	p	फ	pha	P
ब	ba	b	भ	bha	B
म	ma	m			
य	ya	y			
र	ra	r			
ल	la	l			
व	va	v			
स	sa	s			
ह	ha	h			

Practice by typing the Hindi consonants
at the left:

भ   ≫   (8)

press BACK to return to index

Figure 9.5

unit: phonetics   disc: hindiwords
exercise type 2   item 12
now contrasting 1-syllable words   25 to go

Exercise 2   type/touch the item you hear

Touch the item, or type 1 for LEFT, 2 for RIGHT

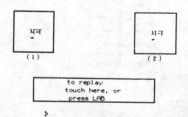

(1)   (2)

to replay
touch here, or
press LAB

≫

BACK → index; SHIFT-BACK → index of lessons

Figure 9.6

```
item  9                                    Dictation
  8 to do                                  drill 4

audio disc:
"hindi vocab"              >
                                आदमी
```

क	ka	k	ख	kha	K				ा	ā	A	श्र śra 1c
ग	ga	g	घ	gha	G	ि	i	i	ी	ī	I	त्र tra 1C
च	ća	c	छ	ćha	C	ु	u	u	ू	ū	U	द्न्य dnya 1d
ज	ja	j	झ	jha	J	े	e	w	ै	ai	W	ह्म hma 1h
ट	ta	+	ठ	tha	++	ो	o	o	ौ	au	O	ज्य jya 1J
ड	da	-	ढ	dha	+-	ृ	ri	R				क्ष kśa 1k
ण	na	N										द्ध ddha 1H
त	ta	t	थ	tha	T	अ	a	+a	आ	ā	+A	त्त tta 1L
द	da	d	ध	dha	D	इ	i	+i	ई	ī	+I	
न	na	n				उ	u	+u	ऊ	ū	+U	
प	pa	p	फ	pha	P	ए	e	+e	ऐ	ai	+E	◆ = MICRO
ब	ba	b	भ	bha	B	ओ	o	+o	औ	au	+O	1 = SUPER
म	ma	m				ऋ	ri	+r				↑ = SHIFT
य	ya	y										
र	ra	r					ru	=		rū	)	◆ moves
ल	la	l					ra	f	,	ra	F	diacritics
व	va	v				_	dra	(				halfspace
श	śa	z										left
ष	sa	Z				:	aspir	H				
स	sa	s				˙	nasal	x				MICRO gives
ह	ha	h				~	nasal	M				half
ञ	ny	+				.	arabic	X				consonant
ङ	ng	*				,	stop	q				

press BACK for index; HELP for answer; LAB for audio

Figure 9.7

Exercise c: Questions and answers
             (36 items)

You will see a picture, and be asked a
question about it. Answer the question.
Example:

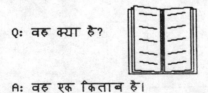

Q: वह क्या है?

A: वह एक किताब है।

NEXT → begin exercise

Figure 9.8

unit 2   item 11
exercise g   13 to go

Substitute the indicated subject-phrase in
this sentence:

प्रकाश बाज़ार से आ रहा है।

मेरा दोस्त

≫ मेरा दोस्त बाज़ार से आ रहा है।

SHIFT: aspirate consonants;   long vowels
MICRO: half-consonants;   initial vowel forms
SUPER: compound consonants
✦ : position diacritic half-space left

ट ✦   ण N   ऋ =   ´ f   ˎ q   ʹ x
ड -   त्र z   ॠ +=   F   : X   ˗ M
ठ +✦   ष Z   ˎ R
ढ +-

DATA → grammar; HELP → see answer
BACK → index of parts; SHIFT-HELP → instructions
SHIFT-DATA → full keyboard; ANS → skip item

Figure 9.9

गणतंत्र दिवस
२६ जनवरी, दिल्ली में

रमेश: मौन, नमस्ते ।

मौन: नमस्ते रमेश भाई । क्या हाल-चाल है ।

रमेश: सब ठीक है । अरे , आप अभी तक तैयार नहीं हैं ?
       चलना है कि नहीं ?

मौन: कहाँ ? अरे हाँ, मैं तो भूल ही गया था कि आज २६
       जनवरी है और हमें उत्सव देखने जाना है । मैं अभी तैयार
       हो जाता हूँ । इस बीच आप मुझे इसके बारे में बताते
       जाइये ।

रमेश: २६ जनवरी को गणतंत्र दिवस कहते है । यह तो भारत का
       सबसे बड़ा राष्ट्रीय त्यौहार है । इसका संबंध हमारी

117

one. Furthermore, PLATO can keep a record of a student's performance which is automatically updated each time he finishes a lesson; a class average and a warning are given if his performance is poor. Readjustment takes place after the student retakes a quiz.

The enormous amount of data gathered from a student's performance record makes the testing procedures truly objective and realizable, the data gathered on every aspect of each student's language learning process, each vocabulary item and every grammatical point provide an opportunity to test various theories of learning and, at the same time, to measure the student's language gain, maintenance and attrition in a truly exhaustive, objective and systematic manner. Needless to say, even under the most ideal conditions no human instructor can maintain such an exhaustive record of a student's performance. Also, the tests at the University of Illinois show that graphic display and animation on PLATO increase the pace of learning (see Alpert and Bitzer (1970)).

Conclusion

Although most of the technical and methodological problems have been solved and encouraging results have been registered in the form of student evaluation, the project is still in the developmental stage. Perhaps it should be added that even in its advanced stages, it will never be able to replace a human instructor; the only thing it can do is successfully exploit the complementary abilities of man and machine and present an excellent model for developing computer-based pedagogy on micro-computers.

Notes

1. This paper is a revised version of my two earlier works, Bhatia (1980, 1981). The author wishes to express his sincere thanks to CHum for permitting him to make use of his published article.

2. In the context of computer-based generation of the Nagari, it is noteworthy that two Hindi writer programs are available for personal computers. A sample of the Nagari text generated by the MacIntosh program is shown in Figure 9.9.

The other program called HINDIWRITER is a program that enables the user to compose texts in Romanized Hindi on the video display of an IBM

Figure 9.10

| Paper Flowers | कागज़ के फूल |
| Usha Priyamvada | उषा प्रियंवदा |

Gopal stirred. He suddenly realized that he had spent practically the whole day sitting and reading in the library. He put back the newspaper, stretched his limbs, and started down the steps. His hand touched his pocket where he had put the paper on which he had jotted down a few addresses of jobs available. He knew it would be useless, but he took them down anyway. Now he let out a deep breath, almost a sigh. Gopal refused to think about the job anymore. He wanted to go home and have a cup of tea. It was evening, but he could see the last slice of sun sinking behind the broken mosque. The street was crowded with people going home after the day's work. He thought he saw a man who still worked in the same office, but he passed Gopal without looking at him. Gopal tried to convince himself that it wasn't deliberate.

गोपाल उठा। उसने सहसा जाना कि उसने सारा दिन लाइब्रेरी में बैठकर पढ़ते हुए बिता दिया है। उसने अख़बार वापस रख दिया, हाथ और कंधों को झटका दिया और नीचे जाने लगा। उसका हाथ जेब पर गया जहाँ कि उसने कुछ नौकरियों के पते लिखकर डाल लिए थे। वह जानता था कि यह व्यर्थ है, फिर भी उसने पते लिख लिए। अब उसने लम्बी साँस ली, एक आह की तरह। गोपाल नौकरी के बारे में नहीं सोचना चाहता था। वह घर जाकर एक प्याला चाय पीना चाहता था। शाम हो गई थी, और टूटी मस्जिद के पीछे सुरज का आख़िरी टुकड़ा डूब रहा था। सड़क पर सारे दिन के बाद घर जाने वालों की भीड़ थी। उसे लगा कि उसने अपने एक पुराने सहयोगी को देखा, जो अब भी उसी दफ़्तर में काम करता है, पर वह गोपाल पर नज़र डाले बिना चलता गया। गोपाल ने अपने को समझाने की कोशिश की कि ऐसा अनायास ही हुआ है।

Figure 9.11

आदरणीय महोदय,

टी.सी.एम. डाटा प्रॉडक्टस का द्विभाषीय आकलन यंत्र सिट्पार्थ आपका स्वागत करता है।
भारत में मेरा आगमन हिन्दी भाषीय लोगों के लिए हुआ है। मैं हिन्दी और अँग्रेजी दोनों भाषायें लिखना, पढ़ना जानता हूँ तथा दोनों में काम कर सकता हूँ। हिन्दी भाषा से इतना प्यार है कि मैं हिन्दी को छोटे और बड़े दोनों अक्षरों में लिख सकता हूँ।
संगणन के अनगिनत लाभों के अलावा मुझे देवनागरी शब्द के संसाधक के रूप में भी प्रयोग किया जा सकता है।
मेरा एक भाई टी.सी.एम. में तमिल भाषा भी सीख रहा है। आशा है वह जल्द ही आपके समक्ष उपस्थित होगा।

आपका प्रिय

सिट्पार्थ

Personal Computer and then print them in Nagari script on an NEC dot matrix printer as shown in Figure 9.10.

A sample print out of DCM products' Siddharth "India's First Multilingual Computing and Word Processing System" is given in Figure 9.11.

Bibliography

Alpert, I. and Bitzer, L. (1970) "Advances in Computer-Based Education", Science, 167, 1582-90.

Atkins, Madeleine and Craft, Maurice, (1983) Training Teachers of Ethnic Minority Community Languages, School of Education, University of Nottingham, England.

Bhatia, Tej K. (1974) "The Problems of Programming Devanagari Script on PLATO IV and a Proposal for a Revised Hindi Keyboard", Language, Literature and Sciety: Occasional Papers, 1, Center for Southeast Asian Studies, Northern Illinois University, 52-64.

Bhatia, Tej K. (1980) "Computer-Based Hindi Pedagogy", CHum, 14:3, 181-186.

Bhatia, Tej K. (1981) "Computer-Based Pedagogy of Non-Western Languages", Intus News, Stellenbosch Unviersity, 5:2, 67-73.

Hainline, Douglas and Jogia, Vijay. (1984) "Microcomputer Support for Bilingualism".

Houlton, David and Willey, Richard. (1983) Supporting Children's Bilingualism, Longman for Schools Council.

Kachru, Yamuna, Nelson, Cecil and Hart, Robert. (1981) "Computer-Based Instruction in Elementary Hindi", Studies in Language Learning, 3, 54-73.

President's Commission on Foreign Language and International Studies: Background Papers and Studies; (1979) U.S. Government Printing Office, Washington, D.C.

Sherwood, Bruce A. (1974) The TUTOR Language, Computer-Based Education Research Laboratory, University of Illinois, Urbana.

Chapter Ten

CALL FOR RUSSIAN AND OTHER EUROPEAN LANGUAGES

J. Ian Press, Queen Mary College, University of London

Introduction

Change creates crisis. With a few exceptions, it is only in the last few years that teachers of foreign languages have grown aware of the potential advantages to them of the new technology. The pioneers, using minicomputers or mainframes, spent untold hours on problems of the past such as alternative character sets. Of the newcomers, some have joined the pioneers, others are coasting along, somewhat confused, somewhat after the fashion of fellow travellers; yet others, confident of their methodology, have decided to 'wait and see' - either the misuse of the language laboratory has chastened them, or they are apprehensive, caught in mid-career and hoping it will all go away. The new technology will not go away; in fact, it has already been here for far longer than many of us laymen suspected. The surface has hardly been scratched; there is a need for experimentation, discussion and collaboration. The accumulated experience of EFL/ESL teachers, and the pressure of circumstances, will help teachers of foreign languages to create a valuable and relevant learning tool. In this Chapter I wish to argue why we must persevere with CALL and to survey the scene as it affects foreign languages, in particular Russian. I look at the creation of character sets on the most widely used microcomputer in British education, the BBC 'B', draw the strands together, and conclude with an appendix listing a Russian character set.

Why CALL?

An intellectually irrelevant justification is the need for overworked teachers to be assisted by the patient micro in the performance of repetitive and remedial tasks. This releases the teacher for more

121

creative work and benefits the student, particularly the less strong one, who is thus relieved of the anxiety of performance in class. A less irrelevant justification would be that, through play and the acquisition of keyboard skills, the computer may well improve and even create motivation. Native speakers of majority languages feel little need to learn other languages - and the simple <u>need</u> to master another linguistic code in order to achieve communication is often the key to learning another language.

Computers are often portrayed as 'scientific instruments', irrelevant to the non-numerate (an absurd term often used to refer to themselves by Arts specialists). But computers manipulate data. And learning a language is learning about the manipulation of data too - sounds, forms, words, sentences, meanings. Of these the middle three are already to a greater or lesser extent implemented in CALL; the first is on its way, and doubtless the fifth eventually also. This role has already been exploited on an academic level; now it is being exploited, through CALL, on the language-learning level. If we leave aside self-contained packages, authoring packages, games and adventures, of which more below, then multilingual word-processing with its sophisticated editing and text-manipulation facilities now widely and inexpensively available on microcomputers, greatly increases the skills with which an Arts student will graduate.

Needless to say, a good deal of basic training has to be done first: familiarisation of teachers and students with keyboards, different types of monitors, interactive use of video and the language laboratory, where to keep the machines and how to maintain security. And how to find the time to train people, in a situation where until recently much of the work has been done through sheer enthusiasm.

A General Survey

CALL allows a student to work alone or in a small group. The situation where <u>each</u> student has a micro is still very rare; but group work has advantages as a relaxed compromise between keeping one's problems to oneself and having to face the whole class with them.

Nothing will ever replace the competent, gifted teacher; but the computer is, surprisingly, a type of liberation. The students can proceed at their own pace. Some constraints - examinations, tests - will remain (and with good reason). However, for once the emphasis will be on the student's needs.

Few students and teachers will have the inclination or time to learn how computers work, so a prime concern, to which the software writers have given particular attention (either because the packages have been written by language teachers or by language teachers in collaboration with professional analysts/programmers) has been to spare the user any need to know how it works. It is, incidentally, important to bear in mind that 'writing computer programs' is a task requiring clear and logical reasoning, based on pencil, paper and eraser - these are the analysis and design stages. Only when that is done do we take up the coding in the most appropriate computer language: most often, due to its current wide use in the British Isles, BBC BASIC with its valuable facility to incorporate 6502 assembly language. In this way the naive user (as he or she is often called) is 'talked through' the package, so that only good advance planning, careful attention, and patience are required once the threshold of familiarisation, the crisis of change, has been overcome. Here I would like to run through a few of the Russian software packages which are available for the BBC 'B' microcomputer. Details are given in the appendix.

On the remedial or presentation side, there exist packages which allow revision of, testing in, or browsing through grammatical forms. Parts of the paradigms of selected verbs can be presented on screen almost instantaneously, verb lists can be gone through, or a student can set up his or her own test parameters. An advantage is that they are ready-made; we simply take delivery and run them. As with the other types of CALL package, the student has the motivation and fun of rivalling the machine - such programs may work best when a small group of students works, as an informal peer group, together.

A problem with the above packages is that they have to be good, to compensate for their inflexibility. Different from them are authoring packages or languages, though they do usually come with a demonstration or two. Such packages typically have a routine to create tests and one to do tests; an editing facility is a must (typing errors without fail slip in during the creation of tests); and an option to print out all or parts of a test can be an advantage.

Particular success has been achieved here with, first, packages offering great versatility in the type of exercises which may be created and, secondly, packages which allow the teacher to create sentences or passages with gaps of one sort or another: the omission of significant parts of words, of part of the text, or the whole text.

An example of the first type would be Questionmaster. Of the second type would be Gapkit and Storyboard. (See Appendix Two at the end of this Chapter.)

Questionmaster permits the creation of almost any type of test, providing the answer can be put into one line and that there are no more than forty questions (far too many anyway!). The teacher can incorporate an introduction and help notes into the file, the answers if appropriate can be placed in order of preference, comments may accompany them, and some flexibility is allowed over misspelling. And, if attention falters and the teacher inputs errors, then the test can be edited.

The Gapkit type of package is very much aimed at practice in morphology and word formation, though knowledge of syntax and attention to context is developed too. Again, an introduction and/or help notes may be available, then a passage or series of sentences is typed in by the teacher, who leaves gaps in words by, for example, enclosing the letters to be omitted in slanting lines. The number of letters in the gaps may be concealed by the user of selected dummy characters, say, an asterisk. The student is presented with a series of gaps to fill, aided or not by clues, which the teacher may also include in the file. Such gap-filling tests are invaluable in their forcing us to put words into their grammatical context - very testing for languages with 'lots of grammar', like Russian.

Constrained like gapping tests, but offering considerable potential for variation, are the Storyboard type tests, technically known as 'clozentropy exercises'. On its simplest, but very useful level, a passage is displayed to the student, then erased (leaving dashes representing the erased letters). The passage is then reconstructed by the student. It is clearly a useful test of memory, of context, and of grammatical knowledge particularly in, again, synthetic languages like Russian. Help is available, here as in the other types, in the chance to be given the first letter of the next word, the whole next word, or to see the text again. There is a cost in that your score is reduced! Minor variations allow one to see the text at the beginning of the test for a few seconds or not at all (!), and to type in any word or follow a specific order. We may choose how frequently words will be omitted - the gaps will then be numbered and we may select which gap to attempt. Other packages are being developed where, for example, a few titles and selected words in a text will be displayed, and the student will have to match the text to one of the titles. Or the text may be jumbled, and recreated by the student. Possibilities exist also for the exploitation of word substitution. These tests cater, to varying extents, for crucial aspects in the teaching and learning of languages: constructions are explained through help notes, are drilled, and the written language is presented. The student is only under stress insofar as he creates it himself - none of the anxiety apparently created by arcade games. All the attention is devoted to leading the student to a 'winning' situation - not to defeat, as in many games. We dip into CALL to learn, as with books.

Straightforward language games are indeed possible: quizzes, Hangman, and so on. Still in the future are foreign-languages simulations: packages where the student can learn through asking questions and taking decisions. Here there is the potential of negotiating mazes or adventures in foreign languages, using more and more sophisticated parsing so that the enquiries are not in a pidgin-type Russian or Spanish. On the linguistic side, one might seek the various cases of a certain Russian noun, follow the plot of a famous novel, or simply tackle a straightforward fantasy adventure. All of these will force the student, without realizing it, to read and understand text, and to communicate. These possibilities are explored elsewhere in this book.

The computer, then, does free us - it is not big brother (unless we abuse it by excessive networking, reducing the possibilities for individualisation of tuition). It informs us, it depends upon us, appearing only as intelligent as we choose it to be, e.g., by our choosing gap frequency, size of gap, how much text to set the context before the gaps start, and so on. Knowledge of grammatical structure can allow analysts more and more precisely to locate individual words according to their grammatical function: verbal particles and consonantal mutations in the Celtic languages, object pronouns in Romance languages, functional sentence perspective in Slavonic languages, morphological endings. Much of this can be done now, by relatively inexperienced analysts, on the basis of a fixed and only partly representative corpus. A full implementation, with the appropriate data-bank, would be another matter, though feasible given time and a big enough team.

Word processing is of considerable importance. For foreign languages the need is for extra characters. The best systems, say, from Compucorp or IBM, are relatively expensive and not generally accessible. In order that everyone can manipulate text, it is an excellent idea to set up a few inexpensive microcomputers with their perfectly adequate WP packages. The ease with which spellings can be checked; text updated, deleted, inserted, and corrected; and bibliographies updated without wastage of paper, is a revelation.

For CALL purposes we need on-screen display of special characters, and the option of a print-out is desirable. Until recently this has not been generally available. Below I look at three implementations for the BBC, each of which can be used at least with perhaps the most commonly used printer for such systems, the Epson FX80 (or a compatible machine).

First, Coventry (Lanchester) Polytechnic has released Rustext for Russian and Unitext for French, German and Spanish. This is essentially a cloze exercise package, but it allows simple word processing of text up to eighty-eight lines long. The combination of English and one of Russian, French, German or Spanish is possible. The English/Russian combination is particularly valuable, since one may switch between alphabet by pressing the TAB key. The only disadvantages, once familiarisation has been achieved, would appear to be the rather narrow page, which can be overcome at some cost to user friendliness, and, easily overcome, the wide line spacing. It should be remembered, though, that this is a teaching package, and a clear presentation is an advantage. It, or other WP packages, can relatively simply be used for inter-line translation exercises.

Secondly, there are the two most widely used WP packages for the BBC, both of them of a very high standard: Wordwise (Plus) and VIEW. The former allows user-defined characters, but will not display them on the screen. VIEW has had language add-ons prepared by Coventry for French, German, Spanish and Russian. Uniview, for the first three, is excellent, involving only the sacrifice of certain little-used characters. The drawback to Rusview is that, though both alphabets can be displayed on the screen, only one can be printed out. This situation has, however, changed in that a proper English/Russian toggle VIEW is now available from 3SL. Returning to Coventry, a very valuable add-on, prepared at my request, is

Viewkey, which allows one to design one's own keyboard from a repertoire of screen and printing characters held in the add-on. The program is so clearly written as to allow the person with special needs to replace all or part of the supplied repertoire with her own characters (more on this in the following section).

The latest package available is Lingo, a straightforward word processor which displays and prints out the characters of all the European languages, plus 99 IPA (phonetic) symbols and a set of English italics. Four type scripts are available too. With an 80-column screen and up to 23 lines per page, this is outstandingly useful for course notes and handouts.

All these WP packages, with their multilingual facilities, offer to the language teacher and student immediate inexpensive access to the advantages of text manipulation.

Keyboards and Characters

Of considerable importance is compatibility of keyboards. The data used to design each character should be allocated to the same key. For foreign languages using the Roman alphabet, the red function keys on the BBC can be used for this purpose. The same goes, for a restricted upper-case alphabet, for Russian - my first effort! For Russian proper, however, we need to redesign the keyboard and it has to be accepted that the Soviet keyboard is preferable. This is what Coventry and 3SL have done; 3SL even have engraved keys displaying Roman and Cyrillic, while most of us have to do with sticky labels and memory. A short-term drawback here is that the Soviet keyboard is totally alien to the QWERTY one and, while this should not be a problem for word processing, for CALL, where the students have enough to do tackling the grammatical structure of the language, it may represent an unwelcome extra burden. To this end David Adshead of the University of Birmingham designed two slightly different keyboards for the Carsondale packages, based, partly, on the shape of the individual characters. For Questionmaster, Gapkit and Copywrite/Clozewrite there is a keyboard, designed by me, based largely on phonetic criteria. One of the Carsondale keyboards is used on Lingo. Which of these two is 'better' is a vacuous problem. Experience with my own design suggests that it is very successful for CALL purposes and for people who know the QWERTY keyboard, but have little

Russian.
It is as follows:

```
#   $   %   &

(Ъ  ъ   Ь   ь)                              Я  Э

Q   W   E   R   T   Y   U   I   O   P   @   (   £

Ч   Ё   Е   Р   Т   ъ/ы  у  И   О   П   ь   Ш   Щ
                    (Ы)

A   S   D   F   G   H   J   K   L   )

А   С   Д   Ф   Г   Х   Й   К   Л   Ю


Z   X   C   V   B   N   M

З   Ж   Ц   В   Б   Н   М
```

In parentheses is the adaptation for a 66-character Russian Cyrillic.

One might propose a gradual transition to the Soviet keyboard once students are beyond the beginners stage and the demands of an extra skill no longer apply. It will not be a case of 'unlearning' anything, because of the proximity of the CALL keyboard to a keyboard they will know, or ought to know, anyway.

Let us look at the definition of characters on the BBC, using a relatively unsophisticated technique. There are far more professional techniques, some of them closely guarded secrets, but to go deeper would demand too much space and defeat the object of this chapter. I outline this here because, though it is a relatively trivial exercise, it does afford some insights into the working of the microprocessor - and it is exciting to see one's own creations coming up on screen.

The BBC has eight screen modes, 0-7. Mode 7, the default mode is excellent since it uses up so little memory. Unfortunately it cannot be used for characters which we have designed ourselves, and so we choose Mode 6, the nearest equivalent in character and screen shape. The memory problem will be a thing of the past once screen memory no longer eats into the read/write memory (RAM, usually referred to as Random Access Memory).

First, the paperwork: which characters are needed? This does bear thinking about - French needs rather more than one might expect. Our real concern here, however, is Russian, and a little thought will

128

reveal that, if we restrict ourselves to upper case, and use the Roman keyboard, then we need only define twenty-two characters to have a full Russian Cyrillic alphabet. An absolutely full Russian Cyrillic will demand sixty-six, though if we omit heading in upper case sixty-three will do (as in mine for the authoring packages, but not for the adventures I have done).

Secondly, defining the characters. This can take some getting used to, but once in full flow everything goes very quickly and, if we use hexadecimal numbers (based on 16) instead of decimal (based on 10), it is not only easier but also invaluable if we want to go further in our understanding of computers. We can save ourselves all the hassle by using a character generation program, but a little hard work helps the understanding. We are going also to want to input the characters just as if we were typing - by a single keystroke. Below we shall see how this can be done, using either the QWERTY keyboard or the red keys.

Characters on the BBC are defined on an 8 x 8 matrix - good enough, though rather difficult for the most intricate characters (Russian is mercifully rather angular). We can imagine that each of the sixty-four squares is a tiny switch; when it is off, it remains part of the background, when it is on, we have a part of a character. Since the micro works in binary arithmetic (based on 2, i.e. 0, 1), when a switch is on it has the value '1', and when off it has the value '0'. If now we see the matrix as a series of eight horizontal rows, then starting from the right, each square has a different decimal value. If, on the other hand, we use hexadecimal arithmetic (based on 16, i.e. 0 to 9, then A to F), we can split the matrix vertically into two sets of four columns, each set offering a count between O and F - we then simply put the two results side-by-side. Thus:

```
128 64 32 16  8  4  2  1 : Decimal
 &8 &4 &2 &1 &8 &4 &2 &1 : Hexadecimal

  0  0  1  1  1  1  0  0  =  60 or &3B
  0  1  1  0  0  1  1  0  = 102 or &66
  0  1  1  0  0  1  1  0  = 102 or &66
  0  1  1  1  1  1  1  0  = 126 or &7E
  0  1  1  0  0  1  1  0  = 102 or &66
  0  1  1  0  0  1  1  0  = 102 or &66
  0  1  1  0  0  1  1  0  = 102 or &66
  0  0  0  0  0  0  0  0  =   0
```

Convince yourself that the hexadecimal numbers (identified by '&') really do correspond to the decimal by multiplying the first component by sixteen, then adding on the decimal value of the second component.

Looking carefully, we see a capital 'A'. The sequence of totals, decimal or hexadecimal, each number separated by a comma and preceded by some extra information, will be keyed into the micro just like that. Anything coming 'below the line' will be defined on the bottom line of the matrix.

The Appendix contains a possible set of character definitions for a complete Russian Cyrillic alphabet. The actual shapes are a matter of aesthetic judgement, irrelevant to the program; what matters to the program and the user is where we put them.

If we only want upper-case Russian, and that we want to put the characters on the red keys, there is no further problem. Given the limitations, this is an excellent solution, since it gives us Roman and Cyrillic without any complex analysis. The definitions will be slotted into the program by placing them within, for BBC BASIC, a PROCEDURE, taking care to set Mode 6 beforehand, or as a SUBROUTINE, in which case the mode can be set within the subroutine. The procedure or the subroutine will be placed after the end of the dynamic part of the program, but be called from within the program. Since program lines are numbered, we simply given the procedure or subroutine suitably large line numbers, say 10000, and 'call' them by 'PROCcharacters' or 'GOSUB 10000'. The procedure is delimited by the lines 'DEF PROCcharacters' and 'ENDPROC', and the subroutine by line 10000 and 'RETURN' (sending us back to the instruction after 'GOSUB 10000'). The beginning of the subroutine seems rather anonymous and unfriendly, so we can slip in a REMark line, ignored by the computer, e.g. '9990 REM Russian characters'. Thus, if '1111' indicates any line within the dynamic part of the program:

```
(i)    1111 MODE 6 : PROCcharacters
       ...... (rest of program)
       10000 DEF PROCcharacters
       ...... (character definitions, etc.)
       10??? ENDPROC
(ii)   1111 GOSUB 10000
       ...... (rest of program)
       9990 REM Russian characters
       10000 MODE 6
```

```
...... (character definitions, etc.)
10???  RETURN
```

Now we can complete the definitions and locate them on the red keys or elsewhere. Begging a host of questions, we may say that all the letters of the Roman alphabet have a code (an ASCII code, where ASCII stands for 'American Standard Code for Information Exchange'). The codes for A̲ to Z̲ are '65' to '90', and those for a̲ to z̲ '97' to '122̲'. On the BBC ASCII codes 224 to 255 (a total of thirty-two) are reserved for user-defined characters. So we can easily assign our twenty-two upper-case characters to codes 224-245. The full statement to achieve this, using my version of upper-case Cyrillic - (if our ordering is alphabetic), is:

```
1111 VDU23,224,62,50,48,60,50,50,60,0
```

Here VDU23 is the code to reprogram a screen character; it is immediately followed by a comma, then the code, then another comma and the eight character-defining numbers, each separated by a comma.
Now we must assign each character to a red function or 'f' key. To do this we precede each block of ten, or less, definitions, with a call to the micro's operating system. This takes the form '*FX' plus a number or numbers. There are four such calls: *FX225, *FX226, *FX227, *FX228. The first places up to ten definitions on the red keys themselves, the second on them with the SHIFT key held down, the third on them with the CTRL (CONTROL) key held down, and the fourth on them with both held down. So the simplest program will require the first three. The call to the operating system is concluded by inputting the code of the first location, so *FX225,224 will start the location on red key 'f0'. Thus:

```
(1111 DEF PROCcharacters - if appropriate)
1111 *FX225,224
1111 VDU23,224,62,50,48,60,50,50,60,0
.... (plus 9 more definitions)
1111 *FX226,234
1111 VDU23,234,.... (10 definitions)
1111 *FX227,244
1111 VDU23,244,.... (2 more definitions)
1111 ENDPROC or 1111 RETURN
```

Appropriately slotted into a program, this will

131

give a full upper-case Russian Cyrillic.

What if we need more than the maximum thirty-two characters? The immediate solution here is to redefine certain of the keys which we are unlikely to need: the curly brackets, the ratio sign, the 'tilde', the pound sign, the 'circumflex' and the 'underline' (ASCII codes 95, 123-126, 94-95). We must, of course, ask ourselves if these symbols are not important in the rest of the program. If not, then we proceed by stealing memory from elsewhere in the micro to store them, as only thirty-two characters can be user-defined without complication. The redefinition in itself is straightforward: we simply slot in the ASCII code for the symbol where 224-255 would go. The appropriation of memory requires a short 'header' or 'loader' program which is executed before the main program - it steals space in readiness for the extra characters. Here is such a program: (1)

```
10 REM**Russian Cyrillic Loader - 63 chars**
20 *FX20,2
30 ?&369 = &9
40 ?&36A = &A
50 PAGE = &1900
60 CHAIN "RUSSIAN"
```

Here *FX20 explodes the character set, paving the way for us to redefine characters. The '2' clears two pages of memory for us - we need access to two, since 94-95 belong to one, and 96, 123-126 to another. The other characters within these ranges we leave alone. In the next two lines we address locations &369 and &36A in the micro - these are the memory addresses for the fonts for codes 65-94 and 96-127, and we place them in pages &9 and &A of the memory. Line 50 gives the default setting for the start of the BASIC program area (using a disc drive), and line 60 LOADs and RUNs (i.e. sets going) the main program. Using this procedure we can provide ourselves with a 63-character Russian Cyrillic, though we will have to write a toggle (a switch to alternate between Roman and Cyrillic) if we wish to retain both alphabets.

None of the above applies to the printout, for which, if a dot-matrix printer is used, the characters have to be specially defined! There is no space here to go into this in detail, and the range of printer types makes it a futile exercise. With the BBC, however, one most often uses the EPSON FX80 or an FX80-compatible printer, and the acquisition of the data may be summarised very simply. As for inputting the data into the program, that is another story. The matrix is as follows - note that the count line is vertical:

```
0 0 0 1 0 1 0 1 0 0 0    128  or &8
0 0 0 0 0 1 0 0 0 0 0    64   or &4
0 1 0 1 0 1 0 1 0 1 0    32   or &2
0 1 0 0 0 1 0 0 0 1 0    16   or &1
0 1 0 1 0 1 0 1 0 1 0    8    or &8
0 0 0 0 0 1 0 0 0 0 0    4    or &4
0 0 0 1 0 1 0 1 0 0 0    2    or &2
0 0 0 0 0 0 0 0 0 0 0    1    or &1
0 0 0 0 0 0 0 0 0 0 0    Left blank
```

Adjacent 1's are not allowed on the horizontals, so the raw data will be, for Russian upper-case Φ:

0,56,0,170,0,254,0,170,0,56,0

For the BBC the whole line is introduced by VDU, then a '1' precedes each number, and the first number is '139' if the character rests on the line, '11' if it descends below it. Thus:

VDU1,139,1,0,1,56,1,0,1,170,1,0,1,254,1,0,
1,170,1,0,1,56,1,0

No more on that here!

Conclusion

CALL is still in the experimental stage. We do not know precisely what its value will be, though the interest of students and teachers makes it very probable that its role will be considerable. Demonstrations more often than not seem to fail; everyone needs bullying to 'have a go'. Later, however, one learns that teachers and students have been surreptitiously using the micros singly or in groups, and getting pleasure and profit out of the experience.

The more experimentation with programs such as the ones mentioned, the more feedback to the writers, and the more ideas for new programs, the better. Not many people will have the inclination or the time to investigate the workings of the microprocessor - many people who have got involved are amazed at how they manage to find the time. Perhaps the layman who has seen how straightforward the definition of characters can be will now feel more confident of exploring ADC (analysis - design - coding). I might justify the professionally trivial examples I have given by saying that I have yet to see such a description in a manual! In any case, it should be clear that a minimal knowledge of the keyboard, and an ability to follow simple instructions on the screen, are all that is required.

The communication of information using the latest technology is a field in which Arts-based people have a greater role to play than they may have imagined.

Notes

1. S.Smith, 'Relocating Character Definitions', BEEBUG, vol. 3, no.1 (1984), p.29. This short piece provided the source for the ideas.

Appendix 1: A Full Russian Screen Alphabet - 66 Characters

The 'loader' given above would need adapting: '*FX20,3.' instead of '*FX20,2', and the addition of ?&368 = &8'. Note that '*FX225', etc. are not needed because we are not using the red keys, and that the data are given in the form of a subroutine.

```
10000 REM**TOTAL RUSSIAN CYRILLIC**
10010 REM**IN ALPHABETICAL ORDER**
10020 REM**UPPER CASE FIRST**
10030 REM**@J. IAN PRESS, MAY 1984**
10040 MODE6
10050 VDU23,65,60,102,102,126,102,102,102,0
10060 VDU23,66,62,50,48,60,50,50,60,0
10070 VDU23,86,124,102,102,124,102,102,124,0
10080 VDU23,71,126,98,96,96,96,96,96,0
10090 VDU23,68,62,62,22,22,22,54,127,99,0
10100 VDU23,69,126,96,96,124,96,96,126,0
10110 VDU23,87,36,126,96,124,96,96,126,0
10120 VDU23,88,107,107,42,62,42,107,107,0
10130 VDU23,90,60,102,6,28,6,102,60,0
10140 VDU23,73,102,102,110,126,118,102,102,0
10150 VDU23,74,20,107,99,103,111,123,115,0
10160 VDU23,75,102,108,120,112,120,108,102,0
10170 VDU23,76,30,22,22,22,22,22,54,0
10180 VDU23,77,99,119,127,107,107,99,99,0
10190 VDU23,78,102,102,102,126,102,102,102,0
10200 VDU23,79,60,102,102,102,102,102,60,0
10210 VDU23,80,126,102,102,102,102,102,102,0
10220 VDU23,82,60,102,102,124,96,96,96,0
10230 VDU23,83,60,102,96,96,96,102,60,0
```

```
10240 VDU23,84,126,24,24,24,24,24,24,0
10250 VDU23,85,102,102,102,126,6,6,126,0
10260 VDU23,70,28,8,127,99,127,8,28,0
10270 VDU23,72,102,102,60,24,60,102,102,0
10280 VDU23,67,102,102,102,102,102,102,126,6
10290 VDU23,81,102,102,102,126,6,6,6,0
10300 VDU23,123,107,107,107,107,107,107,127,0
10310 VDU23,96,107,107,107,107,107,107,127,3
10320 VDU23,89,98,98,98,98,122,106,122,0
10330 VDU23,35,112,112,48,48,62,54,62,0
10340 VDU23,37,48,48,48,48,62,54,62,0
10350 VDU23,124,60,62,6,62,6,62,60,0
10360 VDU23,125,55,53,53,61,53,53,55,0
10370 VDU23,126,62,102,102,126,54,102,102,0
10380 REM**END OF UPPER CASE**

10390 VDU23,97,0,0,60,6,62,102,62,0
10400 VDU23,98,2,30,48,60,50,50,28,0
10410 VDU23,118,0,0,124,108,120,108,124,0
10420 VDU23,103,0,0,62,50,48,48,48,0
10430 VDU23,100,0,0,62,22,22,54,62,54
10440 VDU23,101,0,0,60,102,126,96,60,0
10450 VDU23,119,0,36,60,102,126,96,60,0
10460 VDU23,120,0,0,107,107,62,107,107,0
10470 VDU23,122,0,0,62,38,28,38,62,0
10480 VDU23,105,0,0,102,102,110,118,102,0
10490 VDU23,106,0,24,0,102,110,118,102,0
10500 VDU23,107,0,0,54,54,60,54,54,0
10510 VDU23,108,0,0,30,22,22,54,54,0
10520 VDU23,109,0,0,99,119,107,107,107,0
10530 VDU23,110,0,0,54,54,62,54,54,0
10540 VDU23,111,0,0,60,102,102,102,60,0
10550 VDU23,112,0,0,62,54,54,54,54,0
10560 VDU23,114,0,0,62,54,54,62,48,48
10570 VDU23,115,0,0,60,102,96,102,60,0
10580 VDU23,116,0,0,126,24,24,24,24,0
10590 VDU23,117,0,0,54,54,54,62,6,62
10600 VDU23,102,0,28,8,62,42,62,8,28
10610 VDU23,104,0,0,102,60,24,60,102,0
10620 VDU23,99,0,0,102,102,102,102,126,6
10630 VDU23,113,0,0,54,54,62,6,6,0
10640 VDU23,91,0,0,107,107,107,107,127,0
10650 VDU23,95,0,0,107,107,107,107,127,3
10660 VDU23,121,0,0,98,98,122,106,122,0
10670 VDU23,36,0,0,56,24,30,26,30,0
10680 VDU23,38,0,0,24,24,30,26,30,0
10690 VDU23,64,0,0,24,24,30,26,30,0
10700 VDU23,92,0,0,60,6,62,6,60,0
10710 VDU23,93,0,0,55,53,61,53,55,0
10720 VDU23,94,0,0,30,54,30,54,54,0
10730 REM**END OF LOWER CASE**
```

```
10740 REM**SOFT SIGN DOUBLES**
10750 REM**UNDER & AND @**
10760 REM**REMOVE ASCII 38 OR 64**
10770 REM**IF FELT SUPERFLUOUS!**
10780 REM**AND GET RID OF THESE REMS!**
10790 RETURN
```

Appendix 2: Russian Software (and Hardware)

CAMSOFT: Questionmaster, Gapkit, Copywrite/Cloze-write (also available for almost all European languages, plus some IPA). 10, Wheatfield Close, Maidenhead, Berks SL6 3PS.

CARSONDALE: Russian Irregular Verbs, and the cloze test package Rusfill (also French and some German). 44 Kingsway, Stoke-on-Trent, Staffs. ST4 1JH.

COVENTRY (LANCHESTER) POLYTECHNIC: Rustext, Rusgap, RusView, Viewkey (also French, German, Spanish). Dept. of Language Studies, Priory Street, Coventry, CV1 5FB.

D.A.HULL: Lingo (also Rustext – Lingo restricted to Russian, Helpwrite for the disabled; Lingo co-authored by D.A. Hull with J.I. Press and D. Adshead). 20, Heath Park Avenue, Halifax, HX1 2PP.

WIDA SOFTWARE: Russkiy vybor, russkiye slova (vocabulary and multiple choice tests; also a very wide range of language educational software), 2, Nicholas Gardens, London, W5 5HY.

3SL: Acorn USSR-East Europe distributor – Russian BBC and VIEW word processor with Russian/English toggle. Brook House, 513, Crewe Road, Wheelock, Sandbach, Cheshire, CW11 0DX

LocheeSoft, 5, Inverary Terrace, Dundee, DD3 6BS (mainly French and German).

Chapter Eleven

COMPUTER-BASED INSTRUCTION AS A SUPPLEMENT TO A MODERN FRENCH CURRICULUM

Theodore E.D. Braun, Professor of French, Department of Languages and Literature, University of Delaware, USA
George W. Mulford, ICAI Specialist, Office of Computer-Based Instruction, University of Delaware, USA.

When Computer-Assisted Instruction came to first-year French at the University of Delaware, it came not as a supplement to the existing materials, but as part of a radical restructuring of the entire curriculum.

Gone from the curriculum are the grammar drills that formed the basis of our old methodology; gone is our reliance on textbooks and our assignment of so many pages to "cover" as homework; gone, too, is the language laboratory with its mindless repetitions of forms and its drills on obscure points of grammar. These traditional elements of learning have been replaced by an integrated course featuring active learning of oral French in the classroom, an inductive (indirect) acquisition of the most important grammatical principles of the language, a writing laboratory/workshop, and a computer classroom utilizing two large programs designed by the authors. Before we discuss these programs (or "lessons"), we would like to describe the organization of the curriculum and show how each part contributes to the whole.

1.   CLASSROOM WORK

The linchpin of the curriculum is, of course, the classroom. Here the students meet for 40 or more hours of instruction, 3 hours a week for about 14 weeks. Our approach is language acquisition through the acquisition of vocabulary in meaningful contexts (1). To this end we use, for the most of the semester, a modified version of Total Physical Response (2). One of our modifications has been the development of vocabulary lists of words that are in fact the most commonly used in the French language -

oral and written, formal, informal, and colloquial. For the first quarter or so of the semester, students do not speak: they internalize the vocabulary and syntax by acting out commands (e.g. Touche ton nez. Place le coeur (en papier) dans la boîte. Lève-toi; va à la porte en sautant; ouvre la porte; sors. Pierre, mets-toi à gauche de Marie et devant Jean-Paul). Sometimes commands are humorous (Tire la langue, Touche l'oreille gauche avec le pied droit). Two interesting results of this process are that students' listening comprehension is noticeably superior to that of students taught with audio-lingual methods, and that our students' pronunciation - even without formal instruction and drills later on - is at least as good as that of their audio-lingually-trained colleagues.

Among the classroom aids used is a colorform set of a house, including furniture and a stereotypical family. This material is introduced at about the time that students are encouraged to speak. Once the vocabulary and structures have been mastered (judged by the students' ability to respond to commands like "placez la table dans la salle à manger, à droite et près de la porte"), the class is divided into groups of two or three students who give each other commands. The teacher circulates around, making sure that the work is satisfactory, encouraging the students, offering ideas and suggestions, and so forth. Corrections are kept to the minimum, praise is offered for all comprehensible communications ("Le garçon monter escalier" is comprehensible; later in the semester this type of error would be corrected, but at this point it's more important that the student speak meaningfully than that what he says be grammatically accurate: as with the child learning his native language, grammatical accuracy is acquired gradually). Students are usually surprised - even amazed! - at their ability to communicate in French so early in their studies, and find the transition to oral expression exciting.

For much of the rest of the semester, vocabulary and structure continue to be introduced through TPR methods, and small-group activities (which reduce the embarrassment some feel when called on to "perform" before a group of 25 to 35 of their fellows) continue in the classroom. In addition, role-playing activities, scenarios developed by the students, and other techniques are used to stimulate conversations at an elementary level. Gillian Taylor's <u>Conversations Situations</u> (Longmans) has proven to be a useful aid in the classroom.

In this short time, students master a basic stock of adverbs, prepositions, articles, and conjunctions, along with a noun-adjective vocabulary of some 400-500 words. Grammatical points acquired include the basic syntax of French, the relative pronouns <u>qui</u> and <u>que</u>, negation, and interrogation by intonation. More importantly, students acquire rather than learn these things: they integrate the language into their own patterns of thought, and can use it, in simplified form, in various contexts.

2. ACTIVITIES OUTSIDE THE CLASSROOM

Some material is judged best learned outside the classroom. Instructors see two areas where outside study can be most effective in complementing classroom work: vocabulary and verb conjugations. At their discretion, some of the staff assign occasional written exercises (e.g. appropriate passages from <u>Conversations Situations</u>); but all require attendance at the writing workshop and the computer classroom. Both have been designed primarily as vehicles for review rather than as alternative teaching tools: primary learning and acquisition are the work of the classroom. And since classwork is overwhelmingly oral, it is in the writing workshop and at the terminal that students begin to master the difficult art of writing in French (3).

A. <u>The Writing Workshop</u>
The language laboratory has been replaced by a kind of writing workshop scheduled in the same room, and at the same hours, formerly reserved for lab work. A typical session might begin with a teacher commenting on a projection. The vocabulary and structures mastered in class are reviewed and introduced in a new context. The comments, in the form of a brief story or narrative, are repeated. Students are encouraged to ask questions to ensure that they understand the material, and the teacher asks them questions to check their comprehension. After another retelling of the narrative, they reconstitute the text, bit by bit. In this way, they acquire a firm grasp of the specific subject matter of the lesson, and their general knowledge is reinforced. Obviously their aural comprehension is developed as a by-product of the workshop experience.
At this point, they are distributed a quiz which typically includes, early in the semester, some key

words and expressions useful for describing a projection they have discussed. Later in the semester, quizzes include other exercises: Cloze dictations, Cloze texts, responses to questions, completion of a story, etc. Students' reaction to this writing laboratory has been positive, compared to their almost universal rejection of the traditional language laboratory, and the results have been rewarding: they feel confident in their writing skills, and are in fact reasonably competent.

B. The Computer Classroom

As indicated above, the computer classroom is used as a vehicle for review; attendance is a standard homework assignment. Students have access to terminals at several public sites, the largest of which is open virtually around the clock. They can use the terminals on a drop-in basis or, if they prefer, they can schedule a specific time. The terminals are linked to a Control Data Cyber(R) 174 supporting the PLATO(R) system.

There are two distinct programs (or "lessons") used in conjunction with this curriculum: one on vocabulary, the other on verb forms.

1. The Vocabulary Lesson

Our vocabulary lesson calls on as many of the senses as possible: sight, hearing, and touch. In fact, students choose to study their word lists by using one or more of three formats; a picture format, an audio format, and a word-arrangement format. All three formats insist on correct spelling; the picture and word-arrangement formats emphasize dictionary-entry forms (infinitives, singular forms of nouns, masculine singular forms of adjectives), whereas the audio format requires conjugated forms of verbs, both singular and plural forms of nouns, and all forms of adjectives.

There is extensive, but not complete, overlap among the words in a given vocabulary assigment which can be studied using each one of the three formats. The current database includes 599 words divided into 24 "lists"; of these, 29% overall can be studied using the picture format and 60% using the audio format. Any word can be drilled using the word arrangement format. In practice, a frequent student choice is the picture format (which is quick) followed by the word-arrangement format. When a student has demonstrated mastery of a word in one format, it is removed from the list and will not appear in subsequent study using another format.

a. <u>The Picture Format</u>. For the picture format, some 175 illustrations were made by a student computer-graphics buff. (Technically, these are character graphics, each using 18 characters 16 dots high and 8 dots wide, so that the whole image occupies a square grid of 48 x 48 pixels.) Each illustrates a French word. For concrete nouns, this was uncomplicated; for adjectives, a contrasting pair could often be used, with the non-applicable half of the pair crossed out. For verbs, a cartoon version of Rodin's thinker was used, with a "balloon" containing the substance of his thought: a person performing the illustrated action. Figure 11.1 shows the representation of descendre. The student response is completion of a short sentence with the target word. On request, the program will show the student the English equivalent of the target word; we use one of the PLATO keyboard's function keys for this. Another key, labelled "HELP", produces the target word itself, one letter for each keypress.

Words the student misses (and words where the HELP key was used) are placed in a queue for review three items later.

b. <u>The Audio Format</u>. The audio format is equally straightforward from the student's point of view. Each word is presented in two sentences. The entire sentence appears on the screen with the target word left out, while the sentence is played over the student's headphones. The student must type in the missing word. As in the picture format, the HELP key displays the answer one letter at a time; another function key allows the student to hear the sentence again.

A third and a fourth sentence illustrating the target word are used only for remediation: that is, the student who gets the word right in the first two times never sees these two extra sentences, but they become part of the exercise for students who make mistakes on the first two sentences containing the target word.

The implementation of this design involved the most costly of our development processes. First, a script of over 1400 natural-sounding short sentences was produced. Each sentence was designed to illustrate its target word without introducing any

Figure 11.1: The vocabulary lesson, picture format:
illustrating a verb. Graphics by Mark Baum.

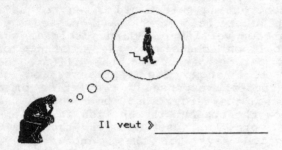

LIST #5	ACTIVE

    11   words to study with pictures
     6   words left to study
     6   answered correctly on the first try

Il veut ⟩ _____

Answer this question, or press:
        DATA for English,
        HELP for one letter at a time,
        SHIFT-BACK for picture format index.

vocabulary from later in the semester (so of course the shape of the entire semester's curriculum was constrained once the recording was made). Where possible, the four sentences for a given word used a variety of inflected forms and syntactic patterns. Next, the sentences were recorded using native speakers (one male and one female voice, alternating). The direct supervision of this process by the authors assured a lifelike delivery; in several cases, awkward sentences were screened out and altered at this stage. Next, a series of master disks for the delivery device (the Instavox random-access audio device by EIS Corporation of Urbana, Illinois) was prepared, and each sentence was identified as an audio fragment and assigned a message number. At the same time, the messages were entered into the program's database and double-checked against the recorded versions. Last, the recordings were transferred to a second device, the cassette-based Spiritus by Fowler Corporation of California, and a second table of message addresses was created in a format that that machine found congenial.

The completed audio material is housed in the language laboratory and may be requested from the lab supervisor when the device is used; we shall return to the logistical aspects of delivering computer-driven audio materials in this way.

c.   The Word-arrangement Format. Since it proved impossible, even given a climate of imaginative collaboration between designers and artists, to produce an unambiguous graphic representation of more than a third of the words in the database, and since sheer constraints of time limited the number of sentences that could be recorded, a flexible third alternative was needed to allow students to drill any word at all. A "flash-card" scheme would have suited the purpose, but would encourage students' natural tendency to make simple single-word associations between French and English, and worse, to use English words as a mnemonic for French words. It seemed to us that the preponderance of opinion in the language-teaching profession favored all possible effort to build a network of associations entirely within the target language. Balanced against this was a recognition that students overwhelmingly prefer learning tools that are no more complex or time-consuming than need requires.

Our response to this dilemma was to borrow

elements of a design by University of Delaware psychologist John P. McLaughlin, who tested short-term memory by having subjects arrange a group of English words on the computer screen and then attempt to recall the entire group of words. Professor McLaughlin found that the best recall of words occurred in subjects whose spatial arrangement was motivated semantically: those who grouped like words in clusters, or represented semantic relations by spatial relationships, or imagined a narrative that could be read left-to-right in their arrangement of the words given. These mnemonic strategies seemed quite reasonable to us as a way to give students, within a fairly simple instructional context, a tool to encourage mental processing of French words.

The drill design as we originally conceived it presented students with a nearly-empty screen; in the top centre, a "well" out of which French words could be drawn, one by one, until a screenful (in practice, sixteen words) was present. Students could place a word anywhere on the screen by touching the word, then touching the desired spot. Words once placed could be moved any number of times by touching them again. Once the words had been arranged, students were to be faced with a screen upon which a straight line of the appropriate length represented each place where they had placed a word; they were to use that arrangement of blanks as a memory aid, and to type all the words, one after the other.

In consonance with the normal development process for computer-based instructional materials at the University of Delaware, this design was subjected to group discussion, then to pilot student use, with a revision and re-thinking each time. The final version after two revisions gives the students much more support for the recall process. The lesson stands as an example of how a clever, but unworkable, initial design can evolve into a useful teaching tool given careful review and trial use.

In the final version, each screenful of words appears three times. The first time, the words appear one after the other, and the student places them at will. (Figure 11.2 shows a completed screen.) The second screen uses that placement but the spaces formerly occupied by the French words are now occupied by their English equivalents, as in Figure 11.3. Students type in the French words one by one, and each French word as typed replaces its English equivalent. Then the words go away again, and a third screen (shown in Figure 11.4) appears, with a line under the space each French word should occupy.

Figure 11.2: The vocabulary lesson, word arrangement
format: the student has made an initial placement of
one whole screenful of words

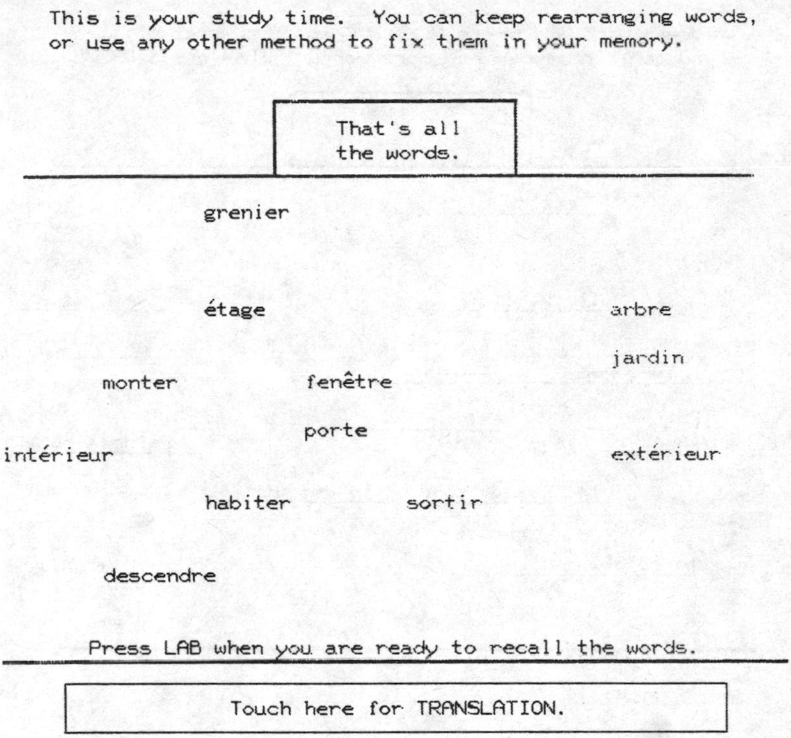

This is your study time. You can keep rearranging words,
or use any other method to fix them in your memory.

```
                        ┌─────────────────┐
                        │ That's all      │
                        │ the words.      │
────────────────────────┴─────────────────┴──────────────────

            grenier


                étage                        arbre

                                             jardin
        monter          fenêtre

                        porte
    intérieur                                extérieur

                habiter         sortir


        descendre

        Press LAB when you are ready to recall the words.
─────────────────────────────────────────────────────────────
    ┌────────────────────────────────────────────────────┐
    │          Touch here for TRANSLATION.               │
    └────────────────────────────────────────────────────┘
```

Figure 11.3: The vocabulary lesson, word-arrangement format: the student is about to begin replacing English words with French ones.

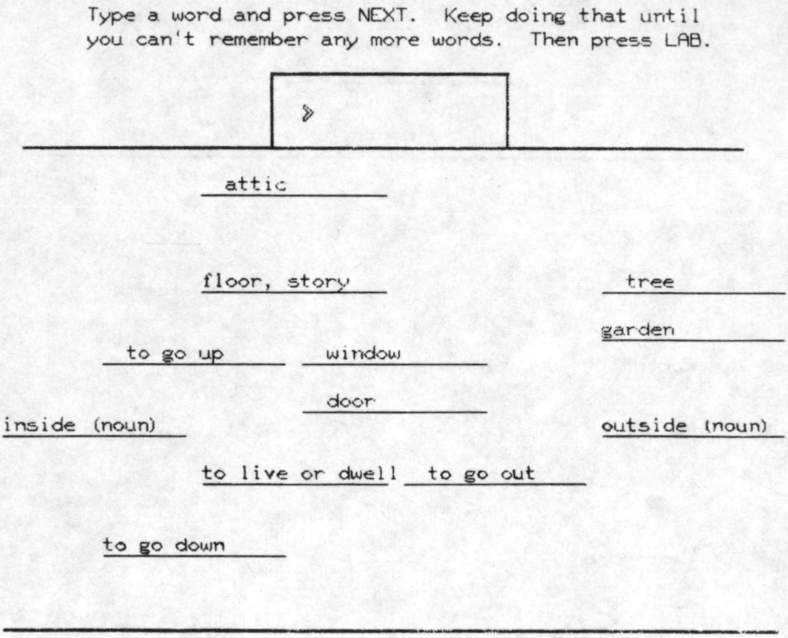

Type a word and press NEXT. Keep doing that until you can't remember any more words. Then press LAB.

≫

attic

floor, story   tree

garden

to go up   window

door

inside (noun)   outside (noun)

to live or dwell   to go out

to go down

Figure 11.4: The vocabulary lesson, word-arrangement format: now the student must remember the French words, with their first letters and spatial arrangement as clues.

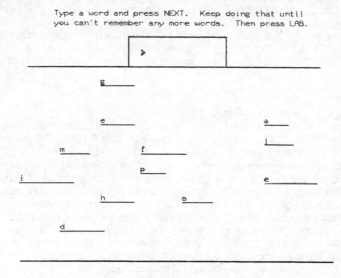

Students must remember and type the words (in any order). However, the initial letter of every French word is shown at the outset, occupying the first letter space of the corresponding line.

A function key allows the student to terminate the exercise without remembering all the words; at that point, a list of the words not successfully recalled is displayed, and those words are put back in the eligible "pool" for subsequent drill.

d. Features Common to All Three Formats. On beginning a session, a student is given the opportunity to take a quiz on the words in the appropriate "list". Two days after completing a list, a student may again take a quiz and compare the score to the earlier one. (This apparent "frill", even though it is completely optional, does not result in "mastery" of a list for record-keeping purposes, and does not generate any score seen by the instructor, has met with considerable student approbation.) Even after completion of a list, a record of problem words is kept, and those words are merged as "review words"

147

with the ones the student is given to study in subsequent sessions. Before beginning study, the student sees a list of all the words to be included in the current session, with English translations available. Since most instructors do not hand out a word list with English translations, a frequent student use of this page is to call up each translation in turn and write it down – an activity not within the purpose of the authors, but which they are more than willing to condone if students find it useful.

e. **Results of Student Use**
The most promising of three formats, from our point of view, was the audio format. Not only does it support a meaningful context for words (if only a context of one sentence), but it allows the student to hear the French as well. Compared to a traditional language-lab exercise, the computer-driven random-access audio exercise has manifest advantages: students control the pace, see each sentence as it is read (without having to find their place in a workbook), hear sentences repeated any number of times with no awkward or lengthy search process, have immediate access to help up to and including the entire answer, and receive immediate correction when their answer is wrong. Most important, the program reacts to the students' error history by presenting extra material (new sentences containing the target word) when needed for remediation, whereas the student who is proceeding successfully is able to complete the session without ever seeing half the available material.

In a fair trial against straight text materials, however, the audio materials have not held their own in obtaining student preference – that is, given the requirement that they must study the words and the choice of using the audio device or going without it, students have by and large chosen to go without it. Data reflecting student use for the eighteen month period ending in October 1984 show that of 26,204 choices of a format for study, students elected to use the word arrangement format 72% of the time, the picture format 25%, and the audio format 3%. The breakdown of time spent studying is similar: of the total 6,228 hours spent in the lesson package, 35% was spent in the quizzes or on the initial page listing the words for study, 55% was spent with the word arrangement format, 9% with the picture format, and 2% using the audio device.

To explain this disinclination of our students to use the study method we prefer, we can observe that it is less convenient for students to use the audio materials than to use the other lessons. The single terminal connected to an audio device is located in a room adjacent to the language lab, and the headphones and disks are stored by the language lab director. Any use of the device requires checking out the materials and bringing them back, which can represent a few minutes' overhead (whereas the average time-in-lesson is nine minutes). Then again, because each word is embedded in sentences read aloud, work with the audio device is slower than work which involves ony silent reading of single words.

The low average usage masks the fact, however, that a few individual students, having taken the trouble to get started with the audio materials, use them intensively and report great satisfaction with them.

Our intent was to compare the two audio devices; both have proved satisfactory. The Spiritus takes slightly longer to find a sentence, but its standard cassette tapes are handier to duplicate and store than the EIS's bulky 15" disks. We have not seen enough usage to assess the reliability of the Spiritus, but the EIS device is holding up well with very little maintenance.

Students' reaction to the computer classroom has been very positive, and there is a high correlation between success in the course and regular completion of work on the computer. Correspondingly, students who have not kept up to date at the terminal have done poorly. A comparison of the 77 students in a class who spent the greatest number of hours at the terminal with the 16 who spent the least time shows this clearly. Half of the students in the first group (40 of 77) were judged as doing excellent work in an oral examination at the end of the semester (4), whereas no students in the second group (0 of 16) did excellent work on the oral exam. Nearly 80% (61 of 77) of the first group did good or excellent work on the oral exam, against only 38% (6 of 16) in the second group. Only four students in the first group of 77 (5%) did poor or failing work, compared with five of the second group of 16 (31%) whose performance was judged poor or failing.

It is not clear, of course, whether it is mainly the good students who work at the terminal, or whether students who complete their computer exercises do better for having done that work; but it is clear that the students who do not perform well are likely not to have studied at the computer terminal and that those who do perform well have studied there.

2. **The Verb Lesson**

Our second lesson drills verb forms. Since it has been designed for use at all levels, from beginners to very advanced students, we have decided to make it as flexible as possible in terms of verbs and forms to be drilled, and as adaptable to the needs of the individual teacher and the individual student as possible. We felt, at the outset, a temptation to generate a context around each verb as it was drilled; this approach has been successfully demonstrated by Henry W. Decker and Thomas Rice (5). In order to accommodate drill of many tenses through many semesters, however, the contexts allowed for each verb would have to be quite varied, and selectively applied as meaning shifted: a sentence that is apt in the imperfect may be awkward in the passé composé. For the subjunctive, there must be an appropriate main verb and subordinating conjunction, and variety in these would be dearly bought in terms of semantic complexity. Further, there is some evidence that students focus on the question at hand to the exclusion of context when the context provides no clues to the solution of the immediate challenge (6). We therefore elected to keep the program, in that regard, simple by presenting each verb form as a discreet item. The bulk of our effort went, instead, into diagnostic and tutorial routines to individualize the lesson and make it suitable as a teaching tool (especially for remediation) as well as a reviewing vehicle.

The permanent database of the program contains all possible regular endings of the French verb system and a tree structure describing the regular derivation of stems. The program uses this knowledge to allow the instructor (or the instructor's surrogate) to enter verbs with a minimum amount of typing: a verb like parler can be entered in the infinitive form alone. The instructor can establish an arbitrary number of chapters (up to 60) with an arbitrary number of verbs in each; each chapter can be assigned one or two tenses. (Other verb drills we have seen allow mixing more than two tenses in an exercise; in students we have observed, this creates many mistakes which are mere artifacts of an unrealistic drill environment.) For each chapter, the instructor can specify a mastery level in terms of a minimum number of forms the student must see and a minimum percentage of answers right on the first try.

The "page" on which the drill is presented is shown in Figure 11.5. The midscreen area is reserved for diagnostic messages issued in response to various student mistakes and for the displays called up by the HELP key.

Possible diagnoses include analysis of the stem, the ending, and any morphophonemic changes (like the "e" in mangeons). Because the program has rules for the regular derivation of stems, forms incorrectly derived by following the rules (like *je devoirai or *je sentis, present indicative) can be diagnosed as such. We have taken particular pains to spot confusions between verbs (forms of aller appearing in the conjugation of avoir, for instance); as data from student use accumulate, we should be able to predict which such confusions in fact occur, and so reduce the amount of searching the program needs to do. Accent mark errors are pointed out to the student only if the form is otherwise correct.

The HELP key produces a menu of tutorial displays from which the student may elect to see the principal parts of the target verb, its stems in the target tense, its endings in the target tense, or the rules for deriving forms in the target tense. These rules, for the student who finds such things helpful, essentially account for the morphology of the French verb system. At the conclusion of each "rules" explanation, the student can enter a verb to use as an example; the program will then derive the forms of that verb in the target tense, reiterating each derivation rule as it is applied, in an animated display.

Like our vocabulary lesson, the verb lesson assumes that immediate correction of mistakes should be followed by review of the forms in question, both later in the same session and during subsequent sessions. Forms the student misses are presented twice more after a lapse of two or three "innocent" items. A record is kept from session to session and opportunity is given to review the previous session's problem forms.

III **CONCLUSION**

The methodology of our classes is based on acquisition of the skills of communication in the target language. The computer programs designed to

Figure 11.5: The Verb Lesson

| Verb: | venir |
| Tense: | present subjunctive |

elles ⟩

TOUCH HERE
FOR
TRANSLATION

Type the correct form, then press NEXT.

Press HELP for more information about this problem
or SHIFT-BACK for more choices.

You must do 12 more forms.
You have 81% correct; you need to have 85%.

accompany this work are, as will not have escaped the reader, discreet-point drills. The vocabulary lesson encourages the formation of associations between the French words and images, imaginary contexts, and whole-sentence contexts, but it presents and tracks words individually; explanations and screen instructions are in English, and English equivalents of the words are readily available at all times. The verb lesson concentrates on morphology and the paradigm.

We seen no contradiction between that methodology and those materials. Students studying alone are cut off from the environment in which acquisition proceeds efficiently; their independent work is most profitably devoted to learning tasks which build confidence and assure mastery of detail. Conversely, the classroom is emphatically not the place for learning the things that are best learned using our computer lessons. As long as students and teachers alike place some value on recall of individual vocabulary items, correct spelling, and correct conjugation of verbs, there will be a need for tools to further the development of these skills. We have found the computer, with its ability to offer the student immediately whatever information meets the needs of the moment and its willingness to remember errors and keep reminding the student of troublesome forms, an ideal tool for this kind of work.

This is not to say that efforts to extend the range of computer learning tools are misguided. A number of possible avenues leading toward a richer, more meaningful sort of computer exercise deserve careful exploration. As a first modest step, the treatment of whole passages can be contemplated. We will soon make available to our students a program which makes a Cloze exercise of a passage, with the same sorts of information-gathering tools, helpful analysis of errors, and tracking of problematic items that are offered by the two programs described above.

Numerous projects are investigating, in various forms, the possibility of simulating a situation in the target language and allowing the student, by assuming a role, to change the course of events. The idea is a very good one; but such programs will need careful thought and long development if they are to approach the intensity of interaction the student can achieve in a relatively simple drill environment. They will also require much more effort on the developers' part for each hour of student contact, whereas our work so far has concentrated on materials which could grow rapidly, by simple addition of items to the database, to offer appropriate instruction for a whole semester or (in the case of the verb lesson) an entire curriculum. As far as the students are concerned, our experience tends to suggest that they value above all simplicity, speed, and clarity of focus; as our programs grow more complex, these humble virtues had best be kept in sight.

Notes

1. The vocabulary is derived from the list provided by Jean-Guy Savard and Jack Richards in their book, Les Indices d'utilité du vocabulaire fondamental français (Quebec: Les Presses de l'Université Laval, 1970).
2. TPR is described by its originator, psychologist James J. Asher, in his Learning Another Language Through Actions: The Complete Teacher's Guidebook. Third Printing (Los Gatos, California: Sky Oaks Productions, 1981).
3. The curriculum described here has been developed by a team led primarily by Theodore Braun and his colleague, Deborah Coen. Ms. Coen has been largely responsible for the gradual development, after much experimentation, of the writing laboratory.

4. For this oral examination students are expected to be able to do the following tasks:

Fr 101 Examen Final Oral
   Tu dois être capable de ...
   1. saluer un français (bonjour, comment ça va, etc.)
   2. parler de toi-même (age, profession, études universitaires, amis, camarades, interets, profession future)
   3. parler de ta famille (père, mère, frères, soeurs, animaux domestiques)
   4. parler de ta maison, ton appartement, ou ta chambre a l'université
   5. parler de la vie universitaire (une semaine typique dans ta vie, les cours, les repas, les examens, les professeurs, tes passetemps favoris, le weekend)
   6. décrire la femme (ou l'homme) idéal(e) pour toi (apparence, personnalité)
   7. decrire tes vêtements (ou les vêtements d'une autre personne)
   8. donner des directions en ville
   9. commander un repas dans un restaurant
   10. mettre la table
   11. interroger un(e) camarade sur ses préférences personelles
   12. parler d'une ville (les magasines, les rues, les endroits interessants)
   13. décrire une ferme
   14. parler des moyens de transport
   15. parler de tes projets pour les vacances
   16. poser les mêmes questions au professeur.

5. "Generative CAI for Foreign Languages", *Proceedings of the National Educational Computing Conference* (1979), 326-328.
6. Carol Hosenfeld, "Learning about Learning", *Foreign Language Annals* 9 (April 1976), 117-129.

Chapter Twelve

PROFORMA - AN AUTHOR LANGUAGE FOR TEACHERS

John Collette, University of Waikato, New Zealand

An author language for computer aided learning was developed in the French Department of the University of Waikato, and is now in regular use in several departments there, major users being Maths, Computer Science, Education, Management Studies, and of course French. It is used in two other universities, one in New Zealand, the other in Britain, in two Teachers' Colleges and some schools in New Zealand, and by the Australian Army.

The program in which the author language is implemented has become a generally available work-horse at Waikato for those aspects of CAL work which do not require specialised programming. It is ideal for work in almost any discipline where an uncomplicated tutorial mode of student-machine interaction is required - where a typical sequence of activities includes presenting material, explaining details, giving examples, checking understanding, and offering opportunities for practice.

The Origins of Proforma
The first version of the program to bear the name Proforma had its origins in a program designed to teach French pronouns. Other programs available to French students had been, and still are, an important element of our teaching resources, offering useful learning, practice, and revision materials in French tenses, vocabulary, general comprehension, etc. but they have the major limitations of being repetitive - the same sequence of events for each verb, each item of vocabulary, or each paragraph - and of having taken a long time to plan, write, and debug. Their mode of operation cannot be altered without major changes to the programs. Other verbs, other vocabulary or other paragraphs can be entered into

155

the data files, but the programs always handle them in the same way.

An area not covered by our earlier programs was that of French pronouns, a topic of such variety and complexity that the repetitive nature of earlier programs would be inappropriate and inadequate. Nearly every type of pronoun would need handling in a different way, but clearly a separate program for each type would be too time-consuming to accept as a reasonable plan of campaign. A new type of program was needed, one which would be flexible enough to cope with the intricacies of all types of French pronouns, and to allow easier control of output at each phase of presentation than was possible in the other programs.

Those programs already contained subroutines dealing with recurring needs in screen formatting - titles, reverse video, framing part of the screen, and so on, and these were assembled to form the basis of the new system. But there had to be a method of invoking such features with ease, depending on the immediate context, rather than having them built rigidly into an inevitable, always identical sequence. While the best method of invoking these formatting features was being sought, progress was made on an initial draft of the contents of the pronouns study units - which pronouns, in what order, how many examples, what form of questions, and so on. The program soon grew to an uncomfortable size, and all the specifically French material was moved out of the program into data files - with hindsight, the obvious place for it to be. The contents of a file would be read into the program, a line at a time, as needed. The data files also held the key to the problem of how to invoke subroutines as needed. They would contain a system of signals by which the various subroutines could be invoked exactly when and only when they were needed. A convention was established that any line beginning with   was to be interpreted by the program as a command line. The following word was a command to invoke a particular feature. Any further details needed for each type of command would be entered as required. Thus if the file contained " TITLE Interrogative Pronouns", then the latter two words would appear in large letters centred on the screen. The original set of commands was TITLE, PAGE, JUMP, HIGHLIGHT, BOX, MOVE, and QUESTION, but since then the program has grown to include over twenty commands.

It was soon realised that something much more useful was taking shape than a program to teach

French pronouns. Since all the French was not in the program but in the data files, it could easily be exchanged for material on some other aspect of French grammar. The files could contain German, or Spanish, or ... any language not requiring a special script. Or they could be in English, and be used to teach maths, physics, engineering, road safety, even computing. A CAL system with considerable potential was emerging.

All that was some years ago, the program is still alive and well, with student uses which can now be counted in their thousands per year over the campus as a whole. And yes, French students are still regularly using the units on French pronouns.

As soon as it became apparent that the program had a far greater potential than just to teach French, and that other users might be interested, two things were necessary. The first was to give it a name, and I called it Proforma (it seemed like a good idea at the time!). The second has been much more difficult to achieve. If the program was to be used with speed and ease, by people who should be protected from all its bugs and quirks and foibles, then it had to be refined, thoroughly tested, and fully documented, all of them seemingly never-ending tasks. Reasonable limits to the program needed to be defined, and a balance obtained between power of the program and its ease of use. My colleagues are busy people who would not be interested in a program if it took them a week to learn how to use it. But a day might be possible, and this was taken as a rough guideline in subsequent stages of development. Only those features were considered which could be implemented in such a way that someone not versed in computer science could readily use them. In its present shape it would admittedly be quite an undertaking for a beginner in computing to attempt to learn to use Proforma in a day, but Education students, practically beginners, have produced attractive and useful study units within a twelve-hour course.

The Proforma program was written to run on a DEC PDP-11/70 (RSTS), and later converted to run on a VAX-11/780(VMS). Subsequent versions have been written to run on a POLY microcomputer (manufactured in New Zealand, and designed specifically for educational purposes), and the BBC microcomputer. More are in the pipeline. For each machine we have to accept that it cannot fully implement certain features which another can. A more positive way of looking at it is to say that each machine has particular strengths, and to attempt to make the most of them. (A good example is the multiple screens of the POLY, which work like transparencies on an overhead projector when you place on top of another.)

Proforma's Main Features

This is not the place for a detailed specification of the Proforma commands and of the various additional arguments most of them can take to specify user's exact intentions. It is hoped, however, that a brief summary will give some idea of the power of the program, and especially of its ease of use. Most command words will be mentioned; that they can nearly all be abbreviated to their initial letter is a great time saver when files are being created. This description will not distinguish between versions of the program for each type of machine, except where certain machine-specific details are of particular interest. There is no guarantee, therefore, that any feature as described here will actually behave in the manner stated on a given type of machine. It will do so, however, on at least one of the types of machine mentioned.

The following outline will be divided into three parts, to describe in turn the organisation of a set of study units, certain aspects of a single unit, and finally the features available for each screen load.

A Set of Study Units

We need to distinguish between a contents file and a study file. The first offers students a set of subject headings from which they make their choice by entering 1, 2, 3 etc. The selected unit is then screened. At the end of a study file the program returns students to the list of contents from which the selection was made, to make a further selection or to exit from the program. Only the first file - the initial list of contents seen by students - must be given a particular name. On opening, Proforma always looks for a file called PROFILE. All other file names are user-determined, consisting of two parts, a prefix and a number. There must be a command line in Profile which passes to the program the prefix needed for identification of study files. Such a line might read CONTENTS MATHS. If there are, say, ten study units in the set, and no other contents files, then those ten must be called MATHS1, MATHS2, etc., and a student must be offered ten numbered titles to choose from when Profile is screened. If, for example, Unit 5 is selected, then the program concatenates the prefix and the student choice to obtain the name of the file required: MATHS + 5 = MATHS5. Files may be contents files in their turn, each containing their own contents command with its prefix. They might be STATS, ARITH, ALGEB, GEOM, CALC, etc. With a sequence of nodes and branches, a subject can be sub-divided down through several levels.

A Study Unit within a Set
Normally students proceed in a linear fashion through a unit, but there are several other possible study routes. Each study unit is divided into screenloads of material, with as much or as little material on each screen as the user decides. For convenience they will be referred to as pages. The command line which divides one page from another is < PAGE (or < P). It causes the message "Type a space, or H for Help" to appear at the foot of the screen, and the program waits for a response before continuing. Entering "H" produces another message: "B=Back: F=Forwards: P=Page: E=Exit this unit". Further messages appear as needed: "Back how many pages?" "Forward how many pages?" or "Which page do you want to go to?" With "E" one goes directly back to the contents list from which the present study unit was selected. Apart from the special keys mentioned, any other key will get the next page, though in fact the message gives the impression that it has to be a space bar.

A student is therefore free to move at will around a unit – to go back over material, to skip over material already covered in an earlier study session, and so on. This can sometimes produce strange results, and students should be warned of the dangers of excessive use of the movement options. For example, a diagram may be 'stored' at one point in a unit for a later 'recall', to screen the same diagram a second time. If a student jumps over the 'store' point, and then comes to the 'recall' point, there will be no diagram in memory. Less serious is that colour and background settings may be skipped over, and the screen appearance may then be other than what was intended. Question numbering and scoring stands up fairly well to this type of thing, however. If a student tries questions 1 to 4, and then goes back to repeat the last two, the question numbering will show 5 and 6. When the fifth question is attempted, it will be this student's seventh, and will be headed "Question 7".

The user (teacher, not student) has the option of preventing free movement within a unit if this is preferred. There is a command < SCAN, and it is normally set at ON. The command < SCAN OFF prevents free movement, and only the next page will then be available. SCAN ON can be used to re-enable free movement at any time.

It is also possible to include a type of branching within a unit on the basis of scores, whereby high, middle or low scorers may follow different routes through a unit. Text occurring between the commands EXTRA 80 and EXTRA 0, for example, will be seen only by students whose score is over 80%. They are doing well, and can probably cope with extension work. Text between EXTRA 40 and EXTRA 0, for example, will be seen only by students scoring below 40%. This is where remedial work can be placed - more explanation and/or extra practice for those who need it.

A Page within a Study Unit

The following features enable material to be arranged in such a way as to assist understanding, learning, and remembering. One can draw a student's attention to underlying structures or to particular details of material in various ways, and obtain an aesthetically pleasing screen appearance.

< TITLE prints text in large letters, centrally on the screen. < SUBTITLE also uses large letters, left justified.

< JUMP x,y places the cursor at row x, column y. If only x is entered, the cursor goes to the left-hand end of that row. One of the annoying differences between machines is that some give coordinates for a point on the screen as column/row, others as row/column. In Proforma it is always row/column. I believe that this more accurately reflects how we interpret text and particular points within a text. The line is the larger unit, the word or character the smaller, so we define the line first.

< HIGHLIGHT sets into reverse video any text on the following line which is enclosed thus . < HIGHLIGHT n invokes the highlight command over n consecutive lines of text. < HIGHLIGHT colour1, colour2 specifies particular colours for the background and printing respectively in a highlighted word or phrase, irrespective of currently set main background and text colours. For language teaching purposes, I have found the highlight command an excellent way of drawing

attention to a word or phrase.
< FLASH causes any text which is enclosed
thus on the following line to flash. < FLASH n
invokes the flash command over n lines.

< BOX and a small set of numbers draws a
rectangular frame on the screen in the required
position and of the stated dimensions. The box can be
divided into any number of vertical panels and
horizontal zones of specified dimensions. The colour
of the box can be set. < BOX is a major tool for
screen organisation. I use it frequently, not just
for presenting summaries in a clear format, but also,
for example, to separate French text from
accompanying English commentary or vice versa.

Colour

All references to colours in commands are by their
names in plain English - red, green, blue, etc. This
seems preferable to having to remember a set of
numbers. It could be argued that numbers are shorter,
but any of the command references CAN be abbreviated
to one letter, upper or lower case. The < COLOUR
command, plus additional arguments, is used to set
the main text colour and to arrange for insertions in
other colours. The < BACKGROUND command sets the
background colour for the whole screen or for part of
the screen, depending on the arguments supplied.

Graphics

The graphics feature available in Proforma range from
merely drawing a box as described above through to
fairly detailed pictures. In general there are three
clearly discernible levels of complexity.

1. Chunky graphics

In this feature it has been made easy for a user to
produce simple diagrams which are built up, in place,
a character at a time. The pieces needed to construct
such shapes are organised into a quickly learned and
easily remembered system. The command to invoke this
feature is < GRAPHICS n, where n is the number of
screen lines involved. The graphics segments are
< enclosed > in the usual way, to separate the
graphics entry from the remainder of the line(s). A
different colour can be specified for the graphics
elements. This command works well in all versions,
and can produce quite impressive diagrams with little
effort. There is a mediaeval castle I am particularly

161

proud of! The command works at whatever position on the screen the running text happens to have reached, without the user having to work out the number of the line(s) at which the graphics are needed.

2.   Graphics from 'line descriptions'

In this second type of graphics, points on the screen are linked by lines to produce a drawing. The central item in this type of command is the line description, a series of pairs of row/column coordinates. These diagrams need to be drawn on squared paper beforehand unless you are very good at visualising screen positions in terms of row and column values. In all Proforma commands which involve screen coordinates the top left corner is used as the absolute base point to determine the position of text and graphics. I still find it difficult to accept that, on some machines, you count down from the top to determine text position, but up from the bottom of the screen to determine graphics positions. Proforma is at least consistent - one base point for everything.

The RELATIVE base point is then determined, to express the distance in rows and columns from the absolute base point. The entries in the line description express the distance of each point of the diagram down from and to the right of the relative base point. The great advantage gained from having a relative base point is fully realised when we wish to repeat a diagram at another point on the screen. All we have to change is the relative base point. The line description, and they can become quite lengthy and error-prone expressions, merely has to be repeated as it stands (actually not even that on the POLY, where a line description can be STOREd at its first use and RECALLed later on). Further arguments deal with colour and the number of "line clusters" in a diagram - the number of separate entries needed to construct the final figure, or the number of times the pencil would be lifted from the page in an ordinary drawing.

3.   Coloured areas

Any enclosed area as defined by a line description can be filled with a selected colour. This feature has been fully implemented on the POLY machine, and that version is described here. The line description for an area to be filled is a set of row/column coordinates, to be entered in a clock-wise direction around the area. The following parameters can then be assigned: colour, pattern, density, border, and store/recall.

Colour needs no further comment. A pattern argument is used to address individual pixels in such a way that attractive effects of rippling, patterning, zig-zagging, etc., appear in the coloured patch. A jungle of mind-boggling complications has been reduced to a small set of plain English command words: DOTS, VERTICAL, +DIAGONAL (up to the right) and -DIAGONAL (down to the right). They can be abbreviated to D, V, +, and -. Each pattern is available in three densities, controlling the ratio of foreground colour to background colour in a patterned patch. BORDER is invoked by the presence of 'B' in the command line, and the filled, patterned area is enclosed by a continuous line. Without 'B', no such line is drawn. With a series of < FILL commands, I have constructed a very useful map of France, and reasonable landscape scenes on which to base questions and vocabulary exercises.

It is the area of graphics that there are the widest differences between what can be achieved with various machines, and in which the conversion of Proforma from one machine to another is most time-consuming. The problems of program size and available memory have also been considerable. Various solutions have been attempted and compromises adopted. We need not go into details here, but the attempted solutions include using machine code, dividing the program into parts and using CHAIN, and of course the standard procedures of using short variable names, as many local and shared variables as possible, no REM lines, and as few line numbers as possible. It was considerations of space which led to the selection of MODE 7 for the first BBC version of Proforma, and this has placed some constraints on the quality of graphics which can be produced in the program. Even so, I have been agreeably surprised with what can be done in graphics on a screen where only about 75 points can be addressed in each direction. If high quality graphics are essential for a particular part of a unit, one can always make use of the < PROGRAM command to chain to any other program, written in any mode, use that program, and then return to the original point in the Proforma study unit.

Movement
Two commands relate to movement: < MOVE, which is

used to move words of phrases on the screen, and < ANIMATE, for movement of diagrams. In < MOVE, eight directions are available, using the arguments UP, DOWN, RIGHT, LEFT, or any pair of vertical and horizontal arguments for a diagonal movement. Direction words can be abbreviated to one letter. For example < MOVE x,y,text,R,z will move "text" from row x, column y, z columns to the right. A set of linked moves is also possible. With this command an entirely new dimension is possible in the manipulation of language for teaching purposes. I have made much use of it to show not only how a pronoun may replace a noun in a sentence, but also how, as a pronoun, it may well occupy a different position in the sentence. < ANIMATE is an extension of graphics, involving the repeated printing and deletion of a diagram at a sequence of positions on the screen.

Additional features for use with < MOVE and < ANIMATE are PACE, which controls the rate of movement, TRACE, in which the image is NOT deleted as the movement is made, and by which some really spectacular visual effects can be achieved, and WAIT, which determines whether the move occurs at once, as soon as the object is screened, or whether it waits for a key to be pressed before taking off.

Sound

Nothing has been done in Proforma to make it easier for the user to obtain Star Wars sound effects. What has been done is to convert one set of symbols (frequencies and micro-seconds) into another set, the new set being instantly recognisable and usable by musicians. They can ask for a note by name, and set its length by means of notation (no pun intended) with which they are familiar. The tempo of a whole piece of music can be changed by adjusting a single argument.

Questions and answers

Some of the features available in Proforma are applicable to any type of question. The number of tries allowed is normally one, but it can be changed to any value for any question. A header "QUESTION n" normally appears, as does a brief, randomly selected, program-supplied comment on a right answer or a wrong answer. Either or both can be suppressed. User-supplied comments on answers to questions are optional. Colours can be set for various parts of questions, these settings applying to all subsequent questions. Other features are specific to particular types of question, there being five main categories.

OPEN, with one or more stored correct answers. The student's answer must exactly match a stored answer, apart from built-in punctuation, case, and spacing tolerances.
KEYED, where the stored answer must be contained within the student's answer.
MULTIPLE CHOICE, with an option of fixed format for the suggested answers or a randomly arranged presentation.
CALCULATION, in which numerical values are different each time the program runs, but lie within a user-defined range.
SELECTION, a multiple choice variety of CALCULATION, in which all alternative answers bear a user-defined relationship to the correct answer. (The correct answer may require the product of variables A and B. Suggested answers may feature their sum, their difference, etc.)

In the last two categories, the user may define not only the range of values produced by the program, but also the size of step in their selection, the degree of precision in their printing, and the margin of error allowed in a student's answer. (How many decimal points should an answer be taken to? Will the student's answer be accepted if it is a rounded form of the correct answer?) Some of this may seem a little unusual in a program which came into being as an aid to language teaching, but these features were requested by colleagues.

Scoring
Scoring was a catalyst for several enhancements to the program. It began as a simple statement to a student of the percentage score so far in a unit. Once scores were known, the option of stored records of a student performance was added to the program, with a separate program for initalising logging on selected units, and obtaining summaries of performance by unit, by student, or by class. At this point in the development of the program, the < PAGE command was extended to allow students the option of free movement within a unit. They could then omit questions by jumping past them, or repeat questions by going back. Clearly a record of just a score was inadequate, since a student could do only one

question, get it right, jump over the remainder, and emerge from a unit with an apparent score of 100%. Records were extended to include the number of questions attempted as well as the number correctly answered.

If student records were being logged, we had to include some means of student identification, without at the same time preventing visitors and casual users from having access to the units. The option of 'Give an I.D. or just press < RETURN >' was included. Then certain colleagues observed that students were entering the program as casual users, preparing the work thoroughly while incognito, and only then signing on with their I.D. to do the set work, and scoring very highly because it was all prepared. My reaction to these events was to welcome a situation in which a high level of achievement was being obtained through the use of the program. Some colleagues, however, thought that the students were somehow cheating, and asked me to include the option of preventing casual use of selected study units. This has been done, and the number of times each student uses a unit is now also recorded. Thus if the < SCAN option is OFF, and if casual use of a unit is not allowed, it can be used for formal testing in fairly tightly controlled conditions.

Throughout this period I also experimented with various ways of keeping students informed of their overall progress in a course - not how well they were doing in a particular unit, but which units they had completed, which, if any, needed to be done again, and so on. The < SCORE command took on another dimension whereby, if it is used in a contents unit (in which, by definition, no questions are asked except to invite a student to choose a study unit), it presents to a student his highest score so far on a named unit. As well as choosing a study unit from a list of titles, a student can now also see which ones have already been done, the highest score obtained so far on each of them, which units have not yet been attempted, and those which it would be a good idea to repeat. Scoring also allowed the inclusion of the < EXTRA command, details of which have been given above.

All of these developments were in terms of a single score built up during a study unit. But the < SCORE command can also be used to mark the beginning and end of a subset of questions, and assessment can now be in terms of a total score or a subset score. The subset can contain as many or as few questions as the user determines. It can even be one single question, and remedial work or extension work can be based on student performance on that single question.

Step by step, the < SCORE command and its cluster of parameters and satellites grew into a powerful tool for the assessment of learning and the diagnosis of problems.

Running other programs

It had to be admitted that, useful though it was, Proforma had its limits, and that users could well wish for other features to be available on occasion. For example, it would be a pity if their inability to show a sine curve on the screen would prevent them from using Proforma to teach trigonometry. But a sine curve is only one example among many, and the inclusion of all such features was out of the question. The solution was the inclusion of the command PROGRAM, which has the effect of chaining to the program named in the command, and later returning to the exact point at which the Proforma unit was left. Values can be passed to the outer program if needed. The documentation units include a sine curve, for example, for which it is possible to supply values for variables which determine its position on the screen, the vertical range of the curve which is drawn, and the width of each loop.

Use of Proforma at the University of Waikato

The eighteen units on French pronouns out of which the system grew are still in regular use. They have been revised from time to time to include new features as these became available. For example, the contents unit now lists a student's previous best score on each unit, making use of the revised < SCORE command. The topics dealt with in the set are:

1 Definitions	INTERROGATIVE PRONOUNS
	12 Variable
PERSONAL PRONOUNS	13 Invariable
2 Subject	
3 Direct object	DEMONSTRATIVE PRONOUNS
4 Indirect object	14 Variable
5 "y" and "en"	15 Invariable
6 Word order	
7 Reflexive	16 POSSESSIVE PRONOUNS
8 Disjunctive	

RELATIVE PRONOUNS	INDEFINITE PRONOUNS
9 "qui", "que"	17 Variable
10 "dont", "lequel"	18 Invariable
11 "ce qui", "ce que"	

By way of example, but it is not suggested that it is typical, since the units vary so much, Unit 3 on direct object pronouns has the following attributes. Length of file: 950 lines. Maximum number of pages, including two < EXTRA patches: 18. This would appear to average at about 50 lines per screen, which is clearly impossible on a 24 line screen. The explanation is that many of the lines in the data file are command lines and do not appear on the screen, and that in the patches of questions there is sometimes screen scrolling instead of clearing the screen with a < PAGE command. There are 28 questions, including those in the < EXTRA patches, seven < BOX commands, five < GRAPHICS commands, three < MOVE commands, and sixteen < HIGHLIGHT commands.

The use of at least fourteen of the eighteen units is formally required of students in certain classes. We have noticed that in such cases, where we specify a quantity to be done, the minimum requirement is rarely in question. Most students do far more than is set, with repeated use of units in nearly every case. Where no formal requirement is stated, far less use is made of a program. Conversation with students has revealed that by meeting the formal requirement, they come to realise that they are learning well and with enjoyment, and so they do more than they need to. They may try out the other programs to satisfy their curiosity, but do not use them enough to come to appreciate their value. We have even had students complaining because we did not formally require work on some other programs. They would do it, if it was set, and say that they know they would benefit from it, but it isn't, so they don't. It has also been noticed that in subsequent years students who got into the habit of using programs continue to do so, especially for revision purposes in the month or so before exams.

The pronouns units are a major component of the range of material available to our students. The potential of Proforma, however, extends much further, and the system is permanently available for the creation of teaching units in other areas of French studies. Professor F.W. Marshall has, for example, created study units on depuis, pendant, and related problems, and work is under way on the preparation of an on-line reference grammar with optional practice material on each section. The search for a published reference grammar to meet our various needs never having been completely successful. It is likely that this project will stretch to its fullest limits the "nested contents" feature of Proforma.

A tool of different kind, for information and guidance rather than teaching, has also been produced using Proforma - a guide to the French department, giving details of courses appropriate for students at different levels in different Schools, and information about the department and its activities. These units are especially useful during enrolment week.

Examples of other users on the Waikato campus are the Departments of Mathematics, Education, and Computer Science, and the School of Management Studies. In Mathematics, Proforma units in arithmetic, algebra, statistics, calculus, and general remedial maths are used by more than 200 students each year. Evaluative work done in the Mathematics Department is described below.

The Department of Education uses Proforma as a tool for training student teachers in the use of computers in general and of an author language in particular. The only pre-existing Proforma units they use are the documentation units. During their course on Computers in Education, the students are expected to produce a small set of sample teaching units, on a topic of their choice. We have had nearly a hundred students use Proforma in this way. The topics they have chosen range from standard curriculum topics (English spelling, punctuation and vocabulary, for example), through topics which, though less 'standard', are no less important (first aid, road safety), to a fascinating list of personal interests (rose growing, mixing drinks, and racehorse breeding are among my favourites). The assignments are assessed in terms of interest, clarity, and the range of Proforma features included.

In Computer Science, students in some courses are given assignments in which they are to produce a screened presentation of a given topic, thereby showing both their understanding of the topic and their ability to use a computer as a presentation medium. Each year the idea of using Proforma spreads like wildfire through the group of students, and nearly all of them use it as a vehicle for their assignment.

In the School of Management there are a hundred or so students making regular use of Proforma units over a wide range of topics. The major topics are Financial Accounting, the Mathematics of Finance, and Marketing, each of them with several subdivisions. It is interesting to note that they also offer several units on English, mainly in an attempt to meet the needs of Asian students in the School. The English of business letters, for example, has its own problems of style and vocabulary, and these units are not without relevance to the needs of some students whose first language is English.

The campus was recently open to the public for an Open Day. The many VAX terminals which are distributed around the campus were used for display purposes, and proved very popular. The Systems Manager had been asked only two days before if the computer could be used to advise visitors of events and points of interest. With such short notice, he was glad to be able to use Proforma. What with this, and various departments using Proforma units as an easy method of presenting samples of their activities, it was generally the case throughout the day that if one gave a $SYS command to obtain a listing of who was doing what and where on the system, about 70% of the sixty or so users were found to be using Proforma.

Evaluation of Proforma as a Teaching Aid

So much time has been spent on the development of the system that no formal evaluation of Proforma as an aid to learning and teaching has yet been possible in the French Department. I have been hoping to find a graduate student, with a background in French, Education and Computing, looking for a research topic suitable for a Master's degree or a doctorate. Such a student has recently been found, and in 1985 work began on an evaluation of computers in general and of Proforma in particular as an aid to teaching and learning French. This student is working in a High School in New Zealand, with students aged 13 to 15. The school has a set of BBC microcomputers, and the BBC version of Proforma is ready for field trials.

There has been continual informal assessment of the effectiveness of our programs. When a student shows an inability to handle correctly a particular pronominal structure, I have, on occasion, made enquiries as to whether the unit dealing with that point was found to be insufficiently clear, too brief, too hard, etc. "How did you know that I haven't done that unit yet?" is a common reaction. And when the student realises that the non-completion of the unit can be detected in this way, then that omission is usually soon remedied.

The Mathematics Department has done some formal evaluation of the effectiveness of their units. They have used pre- and post-tests in achievement, studied correlations between scores in the computer laboratory and examination performance, and attempted to measure attitudes to CAI work by the use of questionnaires and semantic differential analysis. This is not the place to report their findings, but a brief summary by Dr. J.C. Turner mentions that "strong positive attitudes are shown towards CAI", and they intend to continue the programme.

The Immediate Future

An on-line reference grammar has been mentioned above; it will take some time to complete. I am awaiting delivery (in New Zealand, by sea, from the UK!) of a Tandberg cassette player which will link to a microcomputer so that the important audio dimension can be added to some of our programs. Will it be possible to add new commands to Proforma, such as < LISTEN x,y, where x and y will be the starting and finishing points on the cassette counter, to produce a sound recording to support the screen image? Dictations, listening comprehension, sound discrimination exercises, and so on, should then be easy to construct and use.

Proforma is certainly going to be used by more departments on the campus. Staff training sessions are arranged for the near future, and undoubtedly more ideas for enhancements will be forthcoming. (Staff from Management Studies once brought me a list of twelve suggestions, ranging from the easy, "why didn't I think of that?" variety, to the almost impossible. Most of their requests have been met.)

And there is a list of other makes of microcomputer whose owners have asked me if and when Proforma will be adapted to run on their machine. A version for the IBM P.C. is under way. The process of the last three years or so is likely to continue in an attempt to increase the range of features available in the program, to maintain or improve its performance in terms of memory requirements and speed, and above all to keep it easy to use, so that it can be a really useful tool for teachers.

Appendix A: Examples of Proforma Input and Output

Some details relating to Pronouns Unit 3 on direct object pronouns are given in the text. The following samples of Proforma coding are drawn from the same unit. Command words are given in full for ease of reading. Explanatory comments inserted here are indicated by an exclamation mark.

SAMPLE 1: Input

```
< TITLE
Direct Object Pronouns

SUBJECT          VERB            DIRECT OBJECT

Pierre           prend           le train.
Je               mange           une glace.
Papa             arrive.
Paul             est parti.

<BOX 4, 10       ! Upper left corner of box; row 4,
                   column 10
10, 12, 14       ! Width of three vertical divisions
2, 2, 2, 2, 2    ! Depth of five horizontal divisions
```

SAMPLE 1: Output

DIRECT OBJECT PRONOUNS

SUBJECT	VERB	DIRECT OBJECT
Pierre	prend	le train.
Je	mange	une·glace.
Papa	arrive.	
Paul	est parti.	

SAMPLE 2: Input
Prenez-vous le train? Oui, je prends le train.

The second occurrence of   le
"le train" is unnecessary.
A pronoun would normally   la
be used instead.
                                  les

```
< BOX 11, 45             !Box around the column of three
                         !pronouns
5                        !Five columns wide
6                        !Six rows deep
< WAIT                   !The  impending  move  will  not
                         !occur  until  student  presses a
                         !key,  thus  giving time consider
                         !the example.
< MOVE 9,50,4            !Starting  from  row 9, column 50.
                         !There  will  be  four  stages to
                         !the move.
le train, DOWN, 3        !The moving text appears to pick
le train, LEFT, 4        !up the word "le" and change
le, LEFT, 3              !into it as it goes through the
le, UP, 4                !box.
< JUMP 12,49             !Empty string printed, to delete
                         !final  appearance  of  moving
                         !"train".
< JUMP 9,43              !Make  adjustments  to  final
                         !appearance of the modified
le prends                !sentence.
```

SAMPLE 2: Output before MOVE
Prenez-vous le train? Oui, je prends le train.

The second occurrence of   ┌─────┐
"le train" is unnecessary.   │ le │
A pronoun would normally   │ la │
be used instead.   │ les │
                              └─────┘

SAMPLE 2: Output after MOVE
Prenez-vous le train? Oui, je le prends.

The second occurrence of   ┌─────┐
"le train" is unnecessary.   │   │
A pronoun would normally   │ la │
be used instead.   │ les │
                              └─────┘

173

SAMPLE 3: Input

This direct object pronoun
can take the place of ANY
of the items in the box on
the left.

< GRAPHICS 10

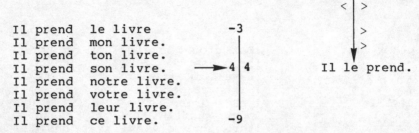

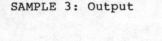

```
Il prend    le livre              -3                      >
Il prend    mon livre.                                    >
Il prend    ton livre.                                    >
Il prend    son livre.    ────▶ 4 │ 4        Il le prend.
Il prend    notre livre.
Il prend    votre livre.
Il prend    leur livre.
Il prend    ce livre.             -9
```

```
< BOX 3, 36     !We also managed to have "le" in "Il
28              !le prend" highlighted, which means
5               !that a graphics command and a
< BOX 9,20      !highlight command were operating in
13              !the same line. Many such
9               !combinations   are   possible,   but
                !details cannot be given here.
```

SAMPLE 3: Output

This direct object pronoun
can take the place of ANY
of the items in the box on
the left.

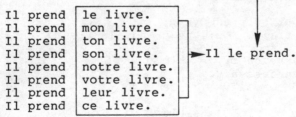

```
Il prend   │le livre.     │
Il prend   │mon livre.    │
Il prend   │ton livre.    │
Il prend   │son livre.    │──▶Il le prend.
Il prend   │notre livre.  │
Il prend   │votre livre.  │
Il prend   │leur livre.   │
Il prend   │ce livre.     │
```

Bibliography
The following references describe some of the French
programs at present in use by staff and students at
the University of Waikato.
COLLETT,   M.J.   (1980a),   Computers   in   Language
Teaching,   No.   2   (Seventh   Series),   Canterbury
Monographs   for   Teachers of French.   University of
Canterbury.
COLLETT, M.J. (1980b), "Examples of applications of

computers to Modern Language studies: 1. The step-
wise development of programs in reading, grammar and
vocabulary", System, 9, 1, 35-40.
COLLETT, M.J. (1981), "A sample run of the French
'TENSES' program on the University of Waikato PDP-
11/70 Computer". New Zealand Language Teacher, 7, 1,
10-12.
COLLETTE, M.J. (1982a), "A TENSES computer program
for students of French", The Modern Language Journal,
66, 2, 170-179.
COLLETT, M.J. (1982b), "Getting in the right mood: A
CAI program on the subjunctive in French", Computers
in the Humanities", 16, 137-143.

Articles on Proforma:
COLLETT, M.J. (1982c), "PROFORMA: A program to assist
non-specialists in the use of computers as a teaching
aid", British Journal of Educational Technology, 13,
3, 196-206.
This is an account of a very early version of the
program, and is now so out of date as to be totally
inaccurate and highly misleading.
COLLETT, M.J. (1983), "PROFORMA: An author language
for CAI", Proceedings of the Digital Equipment
Computer Users Society, 147-149, DECUS Australia
Symposium. DIGITAL Equipment Corporation, Maynard,
Massachusetts.
    Articles on author languages are so numerous
that no attempt will be made here to list them. An
excellent review, with an extensive bibliography,
can be found in:
BARKER, P.G. and SINGH, R. (1982), "Author languages
for computer-based learning", British Journal of
Educational Technology, 13, 3, 167-196.

Chapter Thirteen

MORPHOLOGY, MASKING, AND COMPUTER-ASSISTED LANGUAGE
INSTRUCTION

Robert Phillips, Department of Spanish and
Portuguese, The Miami University; Oxford, Ohio USA

I. Basic Types of Foreign Language CAI

There are several basic types of Computer-Assisted
Language Instruction (CALI). The most elementary is
"drill and practice", in which the user is presented
with a cue or stimulus, and responds with the
appropriate form, word, or phrase. In a vocabulary
drill, the stimulus might be a word or expression in
one language; the answer would be the equivalent word
or expression in the other language. For drills on
verb forms, the stimulus might be an infinitive and a
subject; the response would be that verb typed
properly in the tense chosen, showing the proper form
for the subject.

As programs develop in their complexity and
usefulness, the teacher finds it useful to add
"diagnostics" to the drill. If an error is detected,
diagnostic messages are presented to explain that
error to the student. For example, a simple
diagnostic message might tell the student of Spanish
that he has forgotten to use an accent mark.

The next logical progression is tutorial
programs, which attempt to take the student through a
lesson in much the way that a tutor would. Such
programs combine explanations with drills and
practice. They generally attempt to diagnose errors
for the student, and they generally make use of
branching techniques which move the student quickly
through material which presents no difficulty, but
give additional practice when the student encounters
difficulty with a certain concept. Such programs thus
try to emulate the way a personal tutor would act in
an individual session with a student; introducing a
topic and presenting practice items, giving
explanations when an error is made, and adjusting the
level of difficulty and the speed of the presentation
to the abilities of the student.

Drill and Practice

Basic drill and practice programs are fairly simple to code. They generally have an array of stimuli and another array of the correct answers. They also need to include directions for the exercise. ("You will be presented with a verb in the present indicative tense. Use the same subject and write the verb form in the imperfect tense.") In general, drill and practice programs should present items in random order, to prevent the student from learning the items by their position on the list.

There are several design considerations which the author must resolve: 1) how many wrong tries can the student have before the answer is displayed; 2) when the answer is displayed, should the student then enter it or merely look at it; 3) can the student ask for a hint; 4) can the student ask to see the correct answer; 5) when is an item removed from the pool of available items; 6) is a list kept of items the student missed, to be displayed at the end as a "prescription" of items that need further study; and 7) how is the student's score displayed and what type of record, if any, is to be kept? The resolution of these considerations depends both on the pedagogical objectives of the drill and on the minimum configuration of the equipment on which the program will run. In addition, the author must plan the screen display so that it is clear, attractive, and helpful to the goal of the drill.

An item should be removed from the active pool when the student gets it right on the first try; if items keep recurring, students become angered by the computer's apparent refusal to "believe" that they do know the form! Therefore, there must be some means of determining which items in the drill array are available and which are not. One common way of doing this is to have a "switch" array with as many elements as there are items in the drill; each element of this array is initialized to "on" (the value 1). When the student gets an item correct on the first try, the element corresponding to that item is switched "off" (set to zero). When the random number generator produces a number, it is checked against the array; if the switch in that position is off, the program asks for another random number. This may lead to quite a delay when few items remain active in the pool: the random number generator may have to try several hundred times before a valid number is produced. Furthermore, some means is needed to determine when all the switches are off; failure to detect that situation will produce an infinite loop.

More efficient is the use of a "queue" array and a variable which gives the current length of the queue. The array is different from most queues, however, in that any element in it has an equal chance of being chosen. When an element is chosen and subsequently removed from the queue, the element at the end of the queue is put in place of the removed element, and the effective length of the queue is decremented. To illustrate how this works, let us assume a drill with 30 items. The queue array (QU) will be 30 elements long; each element is initially assigned the number of its position: FOR I = I TO 30: QU(I) = I: NEXT I. The result of this operation is an array whose elements have the values 1, 2, 3 ... 29, 30. The queue length (QL) is initialized at 30 to record how many items are active in the queue. The program requests a random number between 1 and QL. (N = RND (1) * QL + 1) and then uses the value in the Nth position of the array as a subscript to point to the item in the stimulus and answer arrays.

To continue the example, assume that N comes up 13. At the start, the value 13 is in the 13th element of the queue, so the item presented to the student is the 13th one in the array of drill items. If the student gets that item right, it should be removed from the queue. To achieve this, the program takes the value at the end of the queue and places it in the 13th position. In our example, the value 30 would be placed in position 13, so that the array would now contain ... 11, 12, 30, 14, 15 ... Since one item has been removed from the queue, QL must be decremented to 29. If the next random number is 21 and the student gets it correct, then the number 29 would be put into the 21st position, and the length would be decremented to 28, and so on. If the student misses an item, neither the queue nor the length variable is changed. When the student has exhausted the queue, QL becomes 0, and the program can branch accordingly.

While random order is generally necessary in drill and practice, recent research suggests that student learning is optimized if items which have been missed are presented again fairly soon after they are missed. (See Stephen M. Alessi and Stanley R. Trollip, Computer-Based Instruction; Methods and Developments. Englewood Cliffs, New Jersey: Prentice-Hall Inc., 1985.) Some intervening time is needed, but it should be short. It is possible to randomize and to optimize at the same time: when a student misses an item, it is removed from the active queue (as above), and put into an error queue.

This means that an error queue is needed; a fairly short pointer array can serve for that queue. Also needed is a variable giving the length of the error queue. As items are missed, they are added to the "next" position in the queue, and the length variable is incremented. When an item is put into the error queue, a "clock" may be set by the random number generator to activate the error queue after 3 to 6 cycles through the drill. If items in the error queue are missed, they are put back on the end of the error queue; if they are written correctly by the student they are removed from the error queue and replaced in the active queue by adding them to end of the QU array and incrementing QL to reflect that. Thus, the student will have one more random opportunity to practice each "difficult" form.

Diagnostic Messages
Diagnostic messages can be developed in a program in two different ways. The first is that the author anticipates a specific error and tests for it. The second is that the error is detected in the program by masking; that is, the program first detects that an answer is wrong, then masks parts of the answer so that they are not processed. If the answer is correct with a part masked, the author can assume that the error was in the part that was masked, and can provide an appropriate diagnostic message. Part III of this chapter discusses masking techniques and the necessary algorithms.

Diagnostic messages can be fairly simple, from detecting a missing, incorrectly placed, unnecessary, or incorrect accent mark, to informing the student that the stem and/or ending of a verb form is incorrect. As programs become more complex, it is possible for the diagnostic part of the program to parse a sentence, and give messages about the various parts of the sentence, and about parts of words in the sentence.

Tutorial Programs
Tutorial programs require large amounts of file space, and a large number of items in the drill pool. Well written programs avoid presenting too much text to the student at one time: books do that very well, and the computer should not be used to duplicate what a book can do. A program generally should work with one concept at a time, and may have three parts to each concept: 1) explanation; 2) examples; and 3)

drill or practice. Because students learn at different rates of speed and need differing amounts of drill, it is generally good to have some type of branching mechanism in each part of a tutorial lesson. Two ways to do this are: 1) automatically; that is, the program detects that the student has achieved a desired level of proficiency, and automatically branches to the next part of the program; and 2) under student control; that is, the program presents the student with a number of items, then displays the student's performance, asking if the student wants to do some more items of the same type. It is obviously possible for an author to have a combination of the two types.

REASONS FOR USE OF FOREIGN LANGUAGE CAI

Although many studies have been done to determine what causes certain students to succeed and others to fail in learning a foreign language, there is no one answer which is readily apparent. Students have different motivation, different conceptions of the civilization which uses the language, different amounts of knowledge about their own language and about language systems, differing verbal abilities, and different study habits. All we know is that no one way is right for teaching all students a foreign language. CAI is one tool which can be used for students. I find it well indicated for the following things.

Vocabulary Acquisition
Some students have a difficult time acquiring new vocabulary in the foreign language: they cannot associate the words with the symbols; they have difficulty with the serial order of the letters and sounds within the words; and/or they have difficulty remembering the vocabulary. For all these difficulties, the use of CALI can be recommended. The computer requires the student to be active and to be accurate. While some students are able to learn vocabulary through passive study strategies, others require active use of the vocabulary to learn it. The computer program can require such students to work actively with the vocabulary. Those students who have a tendency to transpose letters and sounds seem to be helped by the fact that they have to enter the vocabulary into the computer one letter at a time, and the correct order is reinforced by this.

Verb Forms

In the Romance Languages, the verb form can generally be analyzed to contain three parts: 1) the stem (the action represented by the verb); 2) the tense-mode marker, which shows the tense and mood of the verb; and 3) the person-number marker, which indicates the subject of the verb. Spanish is different from the other European languages in that it does not require an explicit subject in a sentence; the verb form supplies this information. (For example, <u>hablábamos</u> contains information to mean 'we were speaking'.) This means that each verb in a Romance language may have some 50 different forms (combinations of modes, tenses, and subjects). Most Spanish verbs, for example, regularly have 45-48 unique forms, depending on the dialect. This contrasts (quite unfavorably, from the student point of view) with English, where the verb form generally does not show more than past or present tense. The other tenses are achieved by use of two verb forms: I will speak; I did speak, etc. All of this means that students who are learning foreign languages, especially of the Romance family, may experience difficulty in learning to manipulate the verb. There are so many different forms, so many different subjects, so many different tenses!

Although the process by which the verb forms are derived is fairly simple for students to understand, a considerable number of students have difficulty internalizing the process and learning to produce the correct verb form without thinking about it. Many students, indeed, never do internalize the process, and try to memorize all 45 forms of each of the verbs that they learn in the language. This is wildly inefficient (and unmanageable for most students), since the verbs can be reduced to a few different types, and can be generalized. That is, once a student has learned how to manipulate a "regular -<u>ar</u>" verb, he should be able to manipulate any other regular -<u>ar</u> verb in the language, since the forms are all completely predictable.

II **Morphology**

Morphology is the linguistic study of the forms of words in the language. The basic unit in morphology is the morpheme, which may be defined as any part of a word that carries some type of meaning in that word. In the form <u>books</u>, for example, it is easy to see two meaning units: 1) 'book,' a noun which is a symbol for a certain object; and 2) '-s', which means 'plural'. The basic difference between <u>book</u> and <u>-s</u> is that the former is a free morpheme, which means that it can stand alone, without any other morphemes attached to it. The plural '-s' is a bound morpheme: it does not have any meaning until it is attached to another morpheme. There are some morphemes which have purely grammatical function, such as the '-ly' which makes an English adjective ('rapid') into an adverb ('rapidly'); some others have both lexical meaning and grammatical function, such as '-less' which turns a noun ('fruit') into a adjective ('fruitless') with the meaning of 'not possessing that quality.'

   In learning any language, the students must learn the forms of the language and how to create them. When the learners understand the process by which morphemes are manipulated to create forms, then they are able to produce utterances which they have never heard before. That is, once students learn to make nouns plural by adding '-s', for example, they can then generalize to form the plural of any noun that adds '-s'. Learning the morphemes and how they combine is a vital part of language learning. Most teachers have as their ultimate goal the ability of their students to communicate in the foreign language. However, the student who cannot manipulate the forms correctly cannot hope to communicate; it is that type of student who may derive some help from "drill and practice" computer programs on morphology.

Spanish Verb Morphology
The Romance languages have verb morphology which is considerably more complex than that of the Germanic languages, and English-speaking students predictably have a difficult time learning to manipulate verb forms. The morphology of the Spanish verb is discussed here, but the same types of phenomena are also found in French and Italian.

   The verb in Spanish may be analyzed as having three morphemes: 1) the stem, which represents the action of the verb; 2) the tense-mode marker, which tells the tense and the mode of the action; and 3) the person-number marker, which indicates the subject of the verb. Thus, the form <u>hablábamos</u> ('we were speaking') contains three morphemes: 1) habl-, which is the stem and indicates that the action is 'speak'; 2) -ába-, which indicates that the tense is past indicative; and 3) -mos, which indicates that the subject is 'we'. If the subject were <u>ellos</u> ('they'), the form would be <u>hablaban</u>, since -n indicates a third-person plural subject. Similarly, if the tense were present indicative, the form would be <u>hablan</u>, since -a- (instead of -aba-) indicates present indicative.

Because English requires an explicit subject in a sentence, and because tense information is often carried in a separate word ('I will go', 'they did eat', etc.), the English-speaking student has trouble seeing that one Spanish word (<u>Iré</u>, for example) communicates exactly the same meaning as three English words ('I shall go'). Furthermore, there are different classes of Spanish verbs, and they use different forms to show the same meaning. For example, to form the imperfect indicative tense, verbs of the "-ar" class use the morpheme -aba- ('hablaban' - 'they were speaking') while verbs of the "-er" and "-ir" classes use -ía- ('comían' - 'they were eating').

Following is a chart which shows the morphemes that each of the three classes of verbs adds to the stem to form the present indicative tense in Spanish. This is a "three-slot" analysis; the verb form is composed of the stem, plus the tense-mode marker appropriate to the verb class, plus the person-number marker appropriate to the subject:

Subject Verb type:	-ar	T-M MARKER -er	-ir	P-N MARKER all types of verbs
yo	-o	-o	-o	
tú	-a-	-e-	-e	-s
él, ella, Vd.	-a	-e	-e	
nosotros	-a-	-e-	-i-	-mos
vosotros	-á-	-é-	(-í-)	-is
ellos, ellas, Vds.	-a-	-e-	-e-	-n

Many books (and teachers), however, find this system too complex for students to understand easily; they teach Spanish verb morphology using a "two-slot" analysis. That is, the student learns that the form consists of the stem and an ending; the ending consists of both the tense-mode marker and the person-number marker. The above chart changed to a two-slot analysis would be as follows:

Subject Verb type:	-ar	ENDING -er	-ir
yo	-o	-o	-o
tú	-as	-es	-es
él, ella, Vd.	-a	-e	-e
nosotros	-amos	-emos	-imos
vosotros	-áis	-éis	-ís
ellos, ellas, Vds.	-an	-en	-en

It doesn't matter whether the student learns the "two-slot" or the "three-slot" analysis. But the student must learn what endings combine with what stems, and what each combination of stem and ending means.

Using Pointer Arrays to Generate Verb Forms

The utility of "drill and practice" programs for providing students with opportunity to practice verb morphology is readily evident. However, each verb has, in Spanish, many different forms. If one wanted to provide drill in, say, nine different tenses, 54 forms would be necessary for each verb (9 tenses times 6 subjects). Thus, if one were to design a drill simply as an array 9 X 6 X N (N=number of different verbs available in the drill), the amount of memory needed would increase the same amount for each additional verb added to the drill. Ten verbs would require 540 elements in the array; 100 verbs would require 5400 elements, etc. This is a waste of memory: once the process is known how to form a regular -ar verb, all other regular -ar verbs are formed exactly the same way in all forms! Thus, instead of telling the program what all of the forms of the verb are, it is more efficient to tell the program how to generate the verb forms.

What is needed, then, is a collection of stems and endings, and a way to tell the program how to put them together. There are three variables which influence the choice of stem and ending morphemes: 1) the particular verb; 2) the tense; and 3) the subject of the verb. All three of these are important. A regular verb may use the same stem in all forms of all tenses, while an irregular verb may have several different stems for one tense, depending on the subject. (The verb tener, for example, has three different stems for the six forms of the present indicative: tengo; tenemos, tenéis; and tiene, tienes, tienen.)

As indicated above, groups of verbs follow the same pattern. One group will use the same stem for all forms of several tenses; another group will use two different stems, but in the same forms, etc. If two verbs work exactly the same way (except for their different stems), then it takes only one set of instructions to generate the forms of those verbs. There is also patterning in the endings as well as the stems.

My solution to the problem of writing a program to generate any verb form is to use pointer arrays.

All verbs which pattern exactly the same use the same pointers. For the stems, I use one multi-dimensional array of stems (it is necessary, because of several design decisions I made, to allow for as many as eight stems for a verb). That array (let's call it ST$) is dimensioned (N,8) where N stands for the number of verbs in the system. (The program from which the data in this paper are taken includes in it 55 verbs, so my array allows for 55 x 8 stems. The particular verbs and their stems are given in Listing 1.) Three pointer arrays are necessary to allow the program to identify the correct stem for each verb in each of the 54 possible forms. I call these pointer arrays S1, S2, and S3. S1 is a one-dimension array, with N elements in it; each element corresponds to a particular verb. The value of each element in S1 is a pointer (or subscript), which points to a row in S2.

S2 is a two-dimensional array: each row corresponds to a different pattern of verb and each column corresponds to a different tense. The first row, for example, is for those verbs which use the same one stem in all forms of the present indicative, imperfect indicative, preterit, present subjunctive, past subjunctive; use a different stem in all forms of the future and conditional; and have a past participle for use in the present perfect and past perfect tenses. (The foregoing is true of all completely regular verbs.) Another row is for those verbs which have a "stem-change" in the present indicative and present subjunctive, and so forth. The value in S1 in effect classifies the verb by type; it does so by pointing to a row in S2. The columns in S2 correspond to the different tenses. The number from S1 array points to a row in S2, and the tense points to a column; the value at the row/column indicated is another pointer which points to a row in S3.

S3 is another two-dimensional array: each row corresponds to a different pattern of subject-form use, and each column corresponds to a different subject. The first row, for example, would be for a verb and tense which uses the "infinite stem" for all persons in that tense; the second row might be for a verb and tense which uses an alternate stem for three forms in that tense, etc. The pointer from S2 points to a row in S3, and the subject chosen points to a column. The value at the row/column is a subscript, telling which of the eight possible stems of the verb is the one to be used.

The ending is generated in the same way, using a series of ending pointers which work the same as the

185

stem pointers. There is also an array of the endings themselves. Unlike the stems, which are in a two-dimensional array (since each verb is defined to have more than one stem), the endings are in a generalized, one-dimensional character array, EN$. The ending pointer arrays are E1, a one-dimensional array with one element corresponding to each verb in the series. The value in E1 is a number which points to a row in E2. The tense chosen points to a column in E2, and the value at that row/column is a pointer to E3. The number in E2 points to a row in E3, and the subject chosen points to a column in E3. The value at that row, column is the subscript to the ending array; it tells what ending is to be used. A simple concatenation operation then joins the stem and the ending to generate the form.

My system can generate forms for 9 tenses (present indicative, present subjunctive, imperfect indicative, preterit, past subjunctive, conditional, future, present perfect indicative, and past perfect indicative), using six subjects (first, second, and third persons, singular and plural). One design decision I had to make was how to handle the perfect tenses. The perfect tenses consist of two words: an auxiliary verb and a perfect participle (e.g. he hablada - 'I have spoken' and habían hablado - 'They had spoken'). One solution would be to have the program generate both the auxiliary forms (hemos, han, habías, etc.) and the perfect participle (hablado). A different approach would be to consider the entire perfect participle to be the "stem", and the entire auxiliary form to be a sort of "ending". Rather than concatenate the "ending" to the perfect participle, the auxiliary would be concatenated (with an intervening blank) in front of the perfect participle. I chose this second approach because it requires only two items ("stem" and "ending") for all verb forms. This approach is not actually correct from a strictly morphological point of view, and it does require a different concatenation procedure for the perfect tenses. In addition, the stem array must include the perfect participle for all verbs, rather than only the irregular ones.

To allow the greatest flexibility in what I can generate, I decided to use a stem array containing up to 8 elements per verb:

1   the infinitive ending (e.g. AR)
2   the infinitive stem (e.g. HABL)
3   the perfect participle, whether regular or irregular (e.g. HABLADO)

4   the future stem (infinitive or modified
     infinitive) (e.g. HABLAR)
5-8 irregular and alternate stems for tenses other
     than future, conditional, and the perfect
     tenses. These elements are null for verbs which
     do not require them. (Only one verb, of course,
     needs all eight!)

A concatenation of element 2 and element 1
generates the infinitive, which can be displayed for
the stimulus; element 1 can be used to identify the
verb by class in diagnostic messages.

My published drill using this method ("Hard Verb
Drill" in Practicando Español, 2nd edition; Iowa
City, Iowa: CONDUIT (Univ. of Iowa), 1984) contains
55 verbs, including every type of regular and
irregular verb in Spanish. My list is not inviolate;
any verb can be removed and any other verbs can be
added to or substituted into the list. The number can
be expanded to encompass as many verbs as the
programmer wishes to fit into memory. All that is
needed is the entry of the proper stems into ST$ and
the numbers for the S1 and E1 arrays. The other
arrays (EN$, S2, S3, E2, and E3) need no changing,
since they accommodate every verb type in Spanish.

For pedagogical purposes, I arrange the verbs in
the array so that the student can choose a "level of
difficulty". In my scheme, verbs 1-11 are completely
regular verbs; verbs 12-25 are stem changing verbs;
verbs 26-36 are spelling-changing verbs; and verbs
37-54 are 'irregular'. Verb 55 is averiguar, which is
a spelling-changing verb which requires a dieresis in
some forms; it is at the end of the list so that it
can be eliminated if there is no easy way to make a
dieresis.

Listing 1 gives the dimension, initializing,
and data statements necessary for the arrays. Once
the data are initialized in the arrays, any form of
these verbs can be generated easily, simply by using
numbers representing the verb desired, the subject,
and the tense. In my programs those numbers are
generated randomly (within the drill parameters
chosen by the student); I call them R1 (the verb), R2
(the tense) and R3 (the subject). It takes only one
statement to generate any form; however, since the
perfect tenses have the "ending" preceding the verb
while the other tenses have the ending attached to
the end of the stem, two different statements are
necessary.

The numbers used for the tenses are: 1=present
indicative; 2=imperfect indicative; 3=preterit;

4=present subjunctive; 5=past subjunctive; 6=future; 7=conditional; 8=present perfect; 9=past perfect. The subject representations are: 1=yo; 2=tú; 3=él/ella/Vd/.; 4=nosotros; 5=ellos/ellas/Vds.; 6=vosotros. (Vosotros is last, since U.S. students very often are not taught those forms, which are not used in Latin America. If a student does not want to drill them, it is easy to change the parameters to the random-number generator so that the number for vosotros is not generated.)

The actual statements needed to generate the forms are involved, since the variables are subscripts which serve as subscripts. The stem is S\$ = ST\$(R1,(S3(S2(S1(R1),R2),R3))) and the ending is E\$ = EN\$(E3(E2(E1(R1),R2),R3)). They are concatenated to produce the correct form as follows: IF R1 < 8 THEN FORM\$ = S\$ + E\$ ELSE FORM\$ = E\$ + " " + S\$

III **The Principles of Masking**
The technique of masking is an effective way of allowing the author to achieve the objectives of offering diagnostics and analyzing structure. Masking instructs the program to ignore parts of the student response: it covers certain parts with a "mask" and processes the answer, ignoring everything under the mask. As an example, in Spanish the use of the subject pronoun is optional and its position is variable. Because we cannot predict whether a given student will use a subject pronoun (nor in what position), we can construct a mask to cover the subject pronoun; this instructs the program to treat the student response as though no pronoun were used.

Masking techniques generally require two special characters to construct masks; I arbitrarily use "*" and "&". The asterisk (the "don't care" symbol) instructs the program to ignore any single non-blank character. The ampersand (the "wild-card") instructs the program to ignore everything (or even nothing) in that position. Examples of these are given below.

Using Masking
To use masking, a program must have access to an algorithm called a "match routine"; its purpose is to determine if there is a match between two strings. At its most simple, the match routine reports a "match" when the student response is exactly the same as the correct answer. It gets more complicated as masking characters are inserted. A match routine

works with two strings: the "target" string (the correct answer with or without masking) and the "response" string, the input from the user.

The mask can be used to isolate one word out of several. For example, if a student of Spanish is asked to give the Spanish equivalent of 'she speaks,' there are three correct answers: 1) habla; 2) ella habla; and 3) habla ella. Since pronoun use and position is optional, we tell the match routine to ignore everything but the verb by using the following masked target string: & HABLA &. This instructs the match routine to see if the form habla is present, and to ignore everything else. If the form habla is present, a "match" is reported; otherwise, there is "no-match."

If we get a no-match against the correct answer (thus indicating that the student response is wrong), we can successively mask parts to isolate the error. Then, if we get a match with one part masked, we know that the error is in that part, and we can provide the student with appropriate feedback. This technique can be used to mask individual morphemes in words, to mask words in a sentence, or both.

A short example will show how this is done for a word. As discussed above, Spanish verbs contain three morphemes: 1) the stem; 2) the tense-mode marker; and 3) the person-number marker. If, for example, the student is asked to write the 1st-person plural present subjunctive of hablar ('to speak'), the correct answer is hablemos. If the student makes a mistake and we want to find out precisely what mistake was made, masking can be used identify the error. Following are the steps that are taken and the masked target strings used:

1. HABLEMOS
   No masking; a "match" here indicates that the form is correct.
2. HABL*MOS
   This masks the tense-mode marker; a "match" indicates an error in it.
3. HABLE&
   The person-number marker is masked; a "match" here shows an error in it.
4. HABL&
   This masks all but the stem; a "match" indicates that both the person-number and the tense-mode markers are wrong; a "no-match" shows that the stem is incorrect.

In the construction of the mask and the

processing of input, leading and trailing blanks may be significant. If there is a possibility that the student may type both the pronoun and the verb form, (which means that the verb form would be preceded or followed by a blank), it is necessary for the mask to show a blank between the word and the masking characters: & HABLAN &. In such a case, it is necessary that the program concatenate preceding and trailing blanks to the student's answer, so that the match routine will find one whether or not the student used one. If we did not separate the mask from the word with a blank, the routine would report a "match" if it found it in the middle of a word. For example, if the student entered <u>chablan</u>, the mask &HABLA& would report a match while the mask & HABLA & would not.

Analyzing Sentences

To analyze sentences the ampersand is used to ignore optional elements of the sentence so that scanning is done only for the elements essential to the grammatical structure. An example of such scanning of sentences is the use of the subjunctive mode in Spanish. The English sentence, "He wants us to speak" is expressed in Spanish (translating literally) as 'He wants that we speak'. The second verb is generally in the infinitive form in English, but in the present subjunctive in Spanish.

There are a number of potential errors for the student to make in such a sentence: 1) a mistake in the form of the first verb; 2) the use of the infinitive for the second verb, rather than the conjunction and a finite verb form; 3) omission or misspelling of the conjunction; 4) use of the indicative rather than the subjunctive of the second verb; and 5) other mistakes in the form of the second verb, such as the incorrect stem or person-number marker. With two verbs in the sentence, there are nine possible correct combinations of 1st· verbs (+ subject) and 2nd verb (+ subject). To combine all of those to check for all possible wrong answers would be virtually impossible. For this reason, masking is essential. to check the sentence and to isolate and identify errors.

If the sentence given to the student were "He wants us to speak", the form of 'speak' would be hablemos. The entire sentence (without any subject pronouns) would be "Quiere que hablemos". Ampersands are used in the target string to mask the optional subject pronouns and any other extraneous words.

Following are the various "target" strings given to the match routine, and an explanation of what they show.

1.   & QUIERE & QUE & HABLEMOS &
If the routine returns a "match" at this point, the student has correctly used the essential grammatical structure. The match routine effectively masks any extraneous words and subject pronouns, checking only for the essentials, without wasting time on unpredictable and meaningless variations.
If the routine does not report a match for the correct answer, we want to find and identify the error. The most obvious potential error is for the student to translate literally from English by using the infinitive in Spanish; that's the first error to check:

2.   & HABLAR &
A match shows that the student has made this very basic mistake, and the program can present the appropriate diagnostic information and a reminder of Spanish structure.
If there was no match for that error, we need to go through each part of the sentence to find errors. I check the entire first verb rather than its parts, because the focus of an exercise like this is on the second verb:

3.   & QUIERE &
This masks everything but the first verb; a "no-match" here indicates that it is not correct.

4.   & QUE &
This checks the form of the conjunction; a "no-match" here indicates that the conjunction was either omitted or misspelled.

5.   & HABL*MOS &
This checks the tense-mode marker of the dependent verb; a "no-match" indicates that as the error.

6.   & HABLE&
This checks the person-number marker of the dependent verb.

7.   & HABL&
A "no-match" here indicates an error in the form of the stem of the second verb; a "match" shows that both ending morphemes are wrong.

As errors are isolated and identified in each step, appropriate diagnostic messages can be printed for the users, drawing their attention to the specific place the error(s) occurred.
One other possible error must be accounted for:

the correct words in the incorrect order. If the first use of the match string (checking the entire sentence) indicated that the sentence was not correct, but no further error was found by using masking, that indicates that all of the essential sentence elements were present and were correct, but that they were not in the correct order. The appropriate diagnostic message can then be displayed on the screen.

One word of caution must be given. When masking is used to separate out the non-essential parts of the sentence, the possibility exists that it masks an error in those parts. For example, in the example given above, it would be possible for the student to make a simple error in the subject pronoun by writing, for example, <u>Yo quiere que hablemos</u>. The form <u>yo</u> does not combine with <u>quiere</u>, but the masking would hide that error. To prevent such a thing from happening, I give my programs an "acceptable" answer string (without masking); if the student's answer varies from that, the program displays my answer and the student's so that the student can check the optional elements of the sentence. Several years experience has shown that the problem is very minor; virtually all student errors are uncovered by the masking process.

Examples of Other Uses for Masks

Once the concept of the mask is understood, it becomes very easy to see how to mask to identify virtually all types of errors. The following will show two examples of masking, one in Spanish and one in German, with a discussion of what each achieves and how it does it.

Checking Noun-Adjective Agreement in Spanish

In Spanish, adjectives must agree in grammatical gender (masculine or feminine) and in number (singular or plural) with the nouns that they modify. Since this phenomenon does not occur in English, it is a source of many student errors. The masking should check 1) gender; 2) number; and 3) adjective stem. For example, the student is asked to write 'white house' - <u>casas blancas</u>. The masking would be as follows:

1. & casas blancas & - the correct answer
2. & casas blanc*s & - masking the gender morpheme.
Match = the student has used incorrect gender

agreement.
3. & casas blanca& - masking the number morpheme.
Match = the student has not used the plural morpheme.
4. & casas blanc& - masks both agreement morphemes
in the adjective. Match = no agreement was done; the
correct word was used.
5. & casas & - masks the entire adjective. Match =
the student used the right noun, but probably used
the incorrect adjective.
6. & casa& - masks the plural morpheme on the noun.
Match = the student didn't make the noun plural.
7. & cas& - masks the end of the noun. No-match =
the student didn't use the right word for house.
8. & blanc& - masks the end of the adjective.
Match = the student did use the right adjective; if
step 7 shows the wrong noun, agreement here is
irrelevant.

Checking Object Pronoun Case in German

In German, object pronouns have different forms when
they are direct objects ("accusative case") and when
they are indirect objects ("dative case"); English
uses the same form for both. (Cf. 'He gave me the
ball' and 'He saw me yesterday'.) The indirect object
form corresponding to 'me' is mir; the corresponding
accusative form is mich. If the student were to write
the sentence meaning "They give me a book", the
German sentence should be Sie geben mir ein buch.
The masking procedure to check the indirect object in
the sentence would be as follows (note that this
example does not try to check all possible errors in
the sentence, such as the incorrect form of the
indefinite article):

1. Sie geben mir ein buch. - this is the correct
sentence. There are no options possible, so no
masking is needed.
2. Sie geben & ein buch. - this masks the object
pronoun. A "no-match" here indicates that there is an
error somewhere else in the sentence.
3. & mir & - this masks the rest of the sentence.
Although step 3 showed an error somewhere else in the
sentence, we need to see if the mir was correct.
4. Sie geben mi& ein buch. - this masks the crucial
part of the word. A match here shows that the error
is in the pronoun; it is necessary to go to step five
to find out whether the error was the wrong case or
simply a misspelling. A no-match shows that the
student is using the wrong stem morpheme, and step 5
should be skipped.

5. & mich & - this scans the sentence for the accusative mich. A match at this point shows that the student used the accusative form rather than the dative. A no-match indicates that the student misspelled the dative form mir.

IV. **Match Routines**
I present here two match routines which I have used. The first (Listing 2) is written in APPLESOFT, the dialect of BASIC used in the Apple II-family of computers. I originally wrote this routine in PL/1 (for use with an IBM 360 in interactive mode) and subsequently translated it to the micro-computer. When invoked (via a GOSUB), the routine expects the variable A$ (for "Author") to contain the target string, and the variable S$ (for "Student") to contain the response string. The result is reported via the variable R: 0 = "no-match"; 1 = "match". The routine may destroy the variables A$ and S$ during processing. It also internally uses the following variables; Z1, Z2, Z3, Z4, Z5, Z6, Z7, Z8, Z9, Z1$, Z2$, Z3$, Z4$, and Z5$.

This routine is not awesomely fast: on my Apple II, it takes about 1.4 seconds to compare the target string: & LE DECIMOS & QUE & SE ACUESTE & with the student responses: "Nosotros le decimos a Juan que se acueste temprano manana". (On the other hand, I have seen another match routine in BASIC that takes 14 seconds to make the same comparison on the same machine.) While 1.4 seconds is not too long, if the student makes errors, the student input will have to be compared to several target strings to isolate and identify the errors. It may take as long as six seconds in involved cases where the match routine has to be invoked four or five times. It is possible, of course, to obscure the time lapse by printing progress messages, such as "Sentence is incorrect; analyzing errors", "First verb is correct", etc.

Obviously, a match routine would run much faster in machine language. Dr.Joseph Simpson of the Miami University Academic Computer Services wrote such a match routine for me, and it is presented below in Listing 3. It is written for the Apple II Assembler, but can be used on any 6502-based computer by changing the routines which interface with the BASIC interpreter (that is, those routines which identify where in memory the strings are stored). In addition to the two masking characters (*, &) given above, Dr. Simpson added another: #, which is a word delimiter; it matches one or more blanks. Thus, #JUAN#HABLA# as the target string would "match" if those two discrete words were present.

Dr. Simpson wrote his algorithm so that it is accessed from APPLESOFT via the USR command. The USR vector is first initialized by a CALL to the starting address. (That is CALL 3960 for the listing given below.) From then on, the routine is accessed simply by USR (N), T$, R$ where N equals the starting byte (1st byte = 0) of the response string (R$) which is to be checked; I always use 0. T$ represents the target string (with or without masking), and R$ represents the response string. Any valid variable names are allowed for the three variables. The routine returns the position in the string where the first letter of the first match is found (first position = 1). A zero return shows no-match. To use the routine, I assign the target string to the variable A$ ("Author") and the student input to S$ ("Student"). It can be used in an APPLESOFT assignment statement such as R = USR (0), A$, S$ or in an if-statement such as IF USR (0), A$, S$ THEN GOTO 1040. This routine is very fast, and does not destroy any BASIC variables.

This routine can be located anywhere in memory. In my own programs (two packages of programs: <u>Practicando Español</u> and <u>Lecciones de Español</u>, both published by CONDUIT (Univ. of Iowa; Iowa City, Iowa); 1984), I use the Apple High-Resolution Character Generator (HRCG) to display Spanish accent marks, tildes, and inverted punctuation marks on the screen. The HRCG uses Hi-Res page 1, so my programs have to reside in memory above it. This leaves memory available below Hi-Res page 1. I put the HRCG itself immediately under Page 1, and have assembled this routine (as well as other short machine language routines that I have written) to reside below that.

Listing 1: Spanish Verb Generation
Statements numbered 4100-4170 dimension the arrays and initialize them.
Statements 5000-5999 are the DATA statements for the stems; 6000-6699 are the endings, 6100-7200 are the pointer arrays.
REM statements explain or introduce the arrays.
The stems and endings are printed here in lower-case so that the accent marks can be plainly shown. In actual practice, programmers need to convert all strings to one common case, so that use or not of capital letters will not cause a student response to be analyzed incorrectly.

```
4100 DIM ST$(55;8), S1(55), S2(23,9), S3(21,6)
4101 REM ST$ is the two-dimension array of the stems;
the others are stem pointer arrays.
4110 DIM EN$(79), E1(55), E2(17,9), E3(30,6)
4111 REM EN$ contains the endings; the others are
ending pointer arrays
4120   FOR  I=1  TO  54:  FOR  J=1  TO  8:  READ
ST$(I,J):NEXTJ: READ S1(I), E1(I):NEXTI
4121 REM Read in the stems, as well as the S1 and E1
pointers, for each verb
4130 FOR I=1 TO 79: READ EN$(I):NEXTI
4131 REM Read in the endings
4140 FOR I=1 TO 23: FOR J=1 TO 9: READ S2(I,J): NEXT
J: NEXT I
4141 REM Initialize S2 array
4150 FOR I=1 TO 21: FOR J=1 TO 6: READ S3(I,J): NEXT
J: NEXT I
4151 REM Initialize S3 array
4160 FOR I=1 TO 17: FOR J=1 TO 9: READ E2(I,J): NEXT
J: NEXT I
4161 REM Initialize E2 array
4170 FOR I=1 TO 30: FOR J=1 TO 6: READ E3(I,J): NEXT
J: NEXT I
```

Following are the DATA statements needed for the
initializing
```
5000 REM STEMS, S1,E1
5010 DATA ar,habl,hablado,hablar,,,,,1,1
5020 DATA ar,prepar,preparado,preparar,,,,,1,1
5030 DATA ar,particip,participado,participar,,,,,1,1
5040 DATA ar,estudi,estudiado,estudiar,,,,,1,1
5050 DATA ar,visit,visitado,visitar,,,,,1,1
5060 DATA ar,gust,gustado,gustar,,,,,1,1
5070 DATA er,com,comido,comer,,,,,1,2
5080 DATA er,comprend,comprendido,comprender,,,,,1,2
5090 DATA er,vend,vendido,vender,,,,,1,2
5100 DATA ir,viv,vivido,vivir,,,,,1,3
5110 DATA ir,escrib,escrito,escribir,,,,,1,3
5120 DATA ir,abr,abierto,abrir,,,,,1,3
5130 DATA er,deb,debido,deber,,,,,1,2
5140 DATA ar,pens,pensado,pensar,piens,,,, 3,1
5150 DATA ar,acost,acostado,acostar,acuest,,,,3,1
5160 DATA ar,cerr,cerrado,cerrar,cierr,,,,3,1
5170 DATA er,mov,movido,mover,muev,,,,3,2
5180 DATA er,volv,vuelto,volver,vuelv,,,,3,2
5190  DATA  er,entend,entendido,entender,entiend,,,,3
,2
5200 DATA ir,ped,pedido,pedir,pid,,,,4,3
5210 DATA ir,vest,vestido,vestir,vist,,,,4,3
5220 DATA ir,mor,muerto,morir,muer,mur,,,9,3
```

```
5230 DATA ir,prefer,preferido,preferir,prefier, pre-
fir,,,9,3
5240 DATA ir,divert,divertido,divertir,diviert, div-
irt,,,9,3
5250 DATA ir,dorm,dormido,dirmir,duerm,durm,,,9,3
5260 DATA er,le,leído,leer,ley,,,,2,5
5270 DATA ir,segu,seguido,seguir,sigu,sig,,,10,3
5280 DATA ar,empez,empezado,empezar,empiez,empiec,
empec,,16,1
5290 DATA ar,comenz,comenzado,comenzar,comienz, com-
ienc,comenc,,16,1
5300 DATA ar,jug,jugado,jugar,jueg,juegu,jugu,,17,1
5310 DATA ar,pag,pagado,pagar,pagu,,,,5,1
5320 DATA ar,cruz,cruzado,cruzar,cruc,,,,5,1
5330 DATA ar,busc,buscado,buscar,busqu,,,,5,1
5340 DATA ar,marc,marcado,marcar,marqu,,,,5,1
5350 DATA ír,re,reído,reir,rí,ri,,14,17
5360 DATA er,cre,creído,creer,crey,,,,2,5
5370 DATA ar,lleg,llegado,llegar,llegu,,,,5,1
5380 DATA er,quer,querido,querr,quier,quis,,,11,9
5390 DATA er,pod,podido,podr,pued,pud,,,11,9
5400 DATA er,tra,traído,traer,traig,traj,,,12,10
5410 DATA er,pon,puesto,pondr,pong,pus,,,12,9
5420 DATA ír,o,oído,oir,oig,oy,,,13,11
5430 DATA er,sab,sabido,sabr,sé,sup,sep,,15,12
5440 DATA er,ten,tenido,tendr,teng,tien,tuv,,18,9
5450 DATA ir,ven,venido,vendr,veng,vien,vin,,18,13
5460 DATA ir,dec,dicho,dir,dic,dig,dij,,19,14
5470 DATA er,hac,hecho,har,hag,hic,hiz,,20,9
5480 DATA er,s,sido,ser,e,fu,se,,21,15
5490 DATA eir,ido,fu,v,ib,vay,ib,22,,16
5500 DATA ar,d,dado,dar,,,,,1,4
5510 DATA ar,est,estado,estar,estuv,,,,6,6
5520 DATA ir,sal,salido,saldr,salg,,,,7,3
5530 DATA er,v,visto,ver,ve,,,,8,7
5540 DATA ar,and,andado,andar,anduv,,,,6,8
5550 DATA ar,averigu,averiguado,averiguar,averigü,,
,,5,1


6000 DATA REM ENDINGS
6010 DATA o,as,a,amos,an,es,e,emos,en,imos
6020 DATA oy,omos,aba,abas,abamos,aban,ia,ias,iamos,ian
6030 DATA é,ás,á,án,ímos,s,on,i,eron,aste
6040 DATA ó,aron,í,iste,ió,ieron,iera,ieras,iéramos
,ieran
6050 DATA era,eras,éramos,eran,ara,aras,áramos,aran
,he,has
6060 DATA ha,hemos,han,había,habías,habíamos,habían
,,io,és,én,íste
6070 DATA áis,éis,ís,abais,íais,asteis,isteis,ierais
```

```
6080 DATA erais,arais,ois,habéis,habíais,is,ais,eis
,isteis


6100 REM SPOINT2 (23,9)
6110 DATA 1,1,1,3,3,1,1,2,2
6120 DATA 1,1,4,3,3,1,5,2,2
6130 DATA 6,1,1,3,3,j6,1,2,2
6140 DATA 6,1,4,3,3,5,5,2,2
6150 DATA 1,1,7,3,3,5,1,2,2
6160 DATA 1,1,5,3,3,1.5,2,2
6170 DATA 7,1,1,3.3.5.1,2,2
6180 DATA 7,5,1,3,3,5,1,2,2
6190 DATA 6,1,8,3,3,9,12,2,2
6200 DATA 10,1,11,3,3,12,5,2,2
6210 DATA 6,1,12,3,3,j6,12,2,2
6220 DATA 7,1,12,3,3,5,12,2,2
6230 DATA 13,1,8,3,3,5,12,2,2
6240 DATA 6,1,14,3,3,9,12,2,2
6250 DATA 7,1,12,3,3,15,12,2,2
6260 DATA 6,1,16,3,3,17,1,2,2
6270 DATA 6,1,16,3,3,17,1,2,2
6280 DATA 13,1,15,3,3,5,15,2,2
6290 DATA 10,1,15,3,3,12,15,2,2
6300 DATA 7,1,18,3,3,5,12,2,2
6310 DATA 19,20,12,3,3,15,12,2,2
6320 DATA 5,21,3,1,1,15,3,2,2
6330 DATA 6,1,12,3,3,6,12,2,2


6400 REM SPOINT3 (21,6)
6410 DATA 2,2,2,2,2,2
6420 DATA 3,3,3,3,3,3
6430 DATA 4,4,4,4,4,4
6440 DATA 2,2,5,2,5,2
6450 DATA 5,5,5,5,5,5
6460 DATA 5,5,5,2,5,2
6470 DATA 5,2,2,2,2,2
6480 DATA 2,2,6,2,6,2
6490 DATA 5,5,5,6,5,6
6500 DATA 6,5,5,2,5,2
6510 DATA 2,2,5,2,5,2
6520 DATA 6,6,6,6,6,6
6530 DATA 5,6,6,2,6,2
6540 DATA 2,2,7,2,7,2
6550 DATA 7,7,7,7,7,7
6560 DATA 7,2,2,2,2,2
6570 DATA 6,6,6,7,6,7
6580 DATA 6,6,7,6,6,6
6590 DATA 2,1,5,2,2,2
6600 DATA 8,8,8,8,8,8
```

```
6610 DATA 6,6,6,8,6,6


6700 REM EPOINT2 (17,9)
6710 DATA 1,2,3,4,5,6,7,8,9
6720 DATA 10,5,11,4,5,12,13,8,9
6730 DATA 14,5,11,4,5,12,13,8,9
6740 DATA 15,2,16,4,5,17,13,8,9
6750 DATA 10,5,18,4,5,12,19,8,9
6760 DATA 20,2,21,4,5,22,13,8,9
6770 DATA 29,5,16,4,5,12,13,8,9
6780 DATA 1,2,21,4,5,6,13,8,9
6790 DATA 10,5,21,4,5,12,13,8,9
6800 DATA 10,5,23,4,5,12,19,8,9
6810 DATA 24,5,18,4,5,12,19,8,9
6820 DATA 25,5,21,4,5,12,13,8,9
6830 DATA 14,5,21,4,5,12,13,8,9
6840 DATA 14,5,23,4,5,12,19,8,9
6850 DATA 26,19,27,4,5,12,19,8,9
6860 DATA 15,30,27,4,5,12,19,8,9
6870 DATA 24,5,28,4,5,30,19,8,9


6900 REM EPOINT3 (30,6)
6910 DATA 1,2,3,4,5,63
6920 DATA 13,14,13,15,16,66
6930 DATA 21,30,31,4,32,68
6940 DATA 21,22,23,8,24,64
6950 DATA 17,18,17,19,20,67
6960 DATA 7,6,7,8,9,64
6970 DATA 45,46,45,47,48,72
6980 DATA 49,50,51,52,53,74
6990 DATA 54,55,54,56,57,75
7000 DATA 1,6,7,8,9,64
7010 DATA 33,34,35,10,36,69
7020 DATA 3,2,3,4,5,63
7030 DATA 37,38,37,30,40,70
7040 DATA 1,6,7,10,9,65
7050 DATA 11,2,3,4,5,77
7060 DATA 28,34,59,10,36,69
7070 DATA 21,6,21,8,9,78
7080 DATA 33,62,31,25,29,79
7090 DATA 41,42,41,43,44,71
7100 DATA 11,22,23,4,24,63
7110 DATA 7,34,1,10,36,69
7120 DATA 21,60,21,8,61,64
7130 DATA 7,34,1,10,29,69
7140 DATA 1,6,7,25,9,65
7150 DATA 58,6,7,8,9,64
7160 DATA 11,6,26,12,27,73
7170 DATA 28,34,7,10,29,69
```

```
7180   DATA 33,62,35,25,36,79
7190   DATA 1,6,7,8,9,78
7200   DATA 3,2,3,4,5,77
```

Listing 2: Match Routine in APPLESOFT BASIC

```
100   REM        MATCH ALGORITHM
102   R = 0: IF S$ = A$ THEN R = 1: RETURN
104   FOR Z1 = 1 TO LEN (A$): IF MID$ (A$,Z1,1) = "&"
      THEN GOTO 112
106   NEXT Z1:Z2 = 1:Z1 = 0:Z1$ = A$: = S$: GOSUB 156
108   Z5 = LEN (Z1$): IF MID$(?) (Z1$,1,Z5) = MID$
      (Z2$,1,Z5) AND LEN (Z2$) = Z5 THEN R = 1: RETURN
110   R = 0: RETURN
112   Z8 = 0: IF Z1 = 1 THEN A$ = MID$ (A$,2): GOTO 120
114   Z3$ = LEFT$ (A$,Z1 - 1):Z4$ = LEFT$ (S$,Z1 -
      1):Z1$ = Z3$:Z2$ = Z4$: GOSUB 156
116   IF Z1$ < > Z2$ THEN RETURN
118   A$ = MID$ (A$,Z1 + 1):S$ = MID$ (S$,Z1 +1)
120   FOR Z1 = 1 TO LEN (A$): IF MID$ (A$,Z1,1) = "&"
      THEN Z3$ = MID$ (A$,1,Z1 0-1):  GOTO 126
122   NEXT Z1:Z1 = 0: IF LEN (A$) = 0 THEN R = 1:
      RETURN
124   Z1 = 0:Z3$ = A$:A$=""
126   FOR Z4 = 1 TO LEN (Z3$) : IF MID$ (Z3$,Z4,1) =
      "*" THEN GOTO 138
128   NEXT Z4:Z4 = 0:Z6 = Z1 - 1: IF Z1 = 0 THEN Z6 =
      LEN (Z3$)
130   Z9 = LEN (Z3$): FOR Z7 = 1 TO LEN (S$) - Z9 + 1:
      IF MID$ (S$,Z7,Z9) = Z3$ THEN GOTO 134
132   NEXT Z7: RETURN
134   IF Z7 < Z8 THEN RETURN
136   Z8 = Z7: GOTO 152
138   Z5$ = LEFT$ (Z3$,Z4 - 1):Z6 = Z4 - 1:Z7 =1
140   Z9 = LEN (Z5$): FOR Z7 = Z7 TO LEN (S$) - Z9: IF
      MID$ (S$,Z7,Z9) = Z5$ THEN GOTO 144
142   NEXT Z7: RETURN
144   IF Z7 < Z8 THEN RETURN
146   Z8 = Z7: Z6 = Z1 - 1: Z4$ = MID$ (S$,Z7,Z6): Z2 =
      0:Z1$ = Z3$:
148   Z5 = LEN (Z1$): IF MID$ (Z1$,1,Z5) = MID$
      (Z2$,1,Z5) AND LEN (Z2$) < = Z5 + 1 THEN GOTO
      152
150   R = 0: RETURN
152   A$ = MID$ (A$,Z1 +1): GOTO 120
154   IF Z2 = 0 THEN GOTO 158
156   IF LEFT$ (Z2$,1) = " " THEN Z2$ = MID$ (Z2$,2):
      GOTO 156
158   FOR Z3 = 1 TO LEN (Z1$): IF MID$ (Z1$,Z3,1) =
      "*" THEN GOTO 162
160   NEXT Z3: RETURN
```

```
162  IF MID$ (Z2$,Z3,1) = " " THEN R = 0: POP :
     RETURN
164  Z1$ = MID$ (Z1$,1,Z3 - 1) + "/" + MID$ (Z1$,Z3 +
     1)
166  Z2$ = MID$ (Z2$,1,Z3 - 1) + "/" + MID$ (Z2$,Z3 +
     1): GOTO 158
```

Listing 3: 6502 Assembly-Language Match Routine

```
* ROUTINE    MS
* PURPOSE    STRING MATCH ROUTINE
* AUTHOR     JOSEPH C. SIMPSON; MIAMI UNIVERSITY,
*            OXFORD, OHIO
* USAGE      USR (INDEX), PPTR$, TARGET$
*            INDEX IS OFFSET INTO TARGET (NORMALLY
*            ZERO)
*            PATTERN$ IS A STRING VAR CONTAINING
*            STRINGS AND THE TOKENS *,#, &
*            TARGET$ IS A STRING VAR WHICH MAY CONTAIN
*            PATTERNS
*            USR RETURNS 0 IF PATTERN IS NOT IN
*            TARGET$ OR INDEX OF FIRST CHAR IN TARGET$
*            THAT MATCHES PATTERNS
* EQUATES AND ZERO PAGE
*
            MSB OFF
BLANKS      EQU '#'          ;ONE MORE BLANKS
NONBLANK    EQU '*'          ;EXACTLY ONE NON BLANK
WILDCARD    EQU '&'          ;ZERO OR MORE CHARS INCL.
                              BLANKS
PLEN        EQU $6           ;LENGTH OF PATTERN STRING
PPTR        EQU PLEN+1       ;PTR TO PATTERN STRING
VARPNT      EQU $83          ;APPLESOFT PTR TO VAR
DSCTMP      EQU $9D          ;TEMPORARY STRING DESCRIP-
                              TOR (APPLESOFT)
LENT        EQU DSCTMP       ;LENGTH   REMAINING   IN
                              TARGET
TSTART      EQU LENT+1       ;ADDR  OF  FIRST  CHAR  IN
                              TARGET  THAT  (MAY)  MATCH
                              PPTR$
INDEX       EQU $A0          ;POTENTIAL ANSWER
LENP        EQU $A1          ;CURRENT LENGTH OF P
FACLO       EQU $A1          ;APPLESOFT FAC BYTE
USRVEC      EQU $0A          ;APPLESOFT USR VECTOR
OUTMEM      EQU $D410        ;APPLESOFT OUT OF MEMORY
                              ERROR
CHKSTR      EQU $DD6C        ;APPLESOFT   CHECK   FOR
                              STRING
PTRGET      EQU $DFE3        ;GET A VAR
AYINT       EQU $E10C        ;INT(FAC) TO FACMO,FACLO
CHKCOM      EQU $DEBE        ;CHECK (TXTPTR) FOR ","
```

```
GIVAYF        EQU $E2F2     ;(A,Y) FLOAT-)FAC

* INITIALIZATION SEQUENCE
* SETS USR VECTOR IN APPLESOFT
* DO BASIC CALL TO ORG ADDRESS INITIALIZE
              ORG 3960      ;DECIMAL ADDRESS FOR BASIC
                            CALL
INIT          LDA $4C       ;JMP
              STA USRVEC
              LDA  MS
              STA USRVEC+1
              LDA (MS
              STA USRVEC+2
              RTS

* USR ENTRY FROM APPLESOFT BASIC
MS            JSR AYINT     ;CONVERT ARG TO ONE BYTE
                            POS INT IN X REC
              LDX FACLO     ;AND SAVE IT
              STX INDEX
              LDA #PLEN
              JSR GETSTR    ;GET PATTERN VAR
              LDA #LENT
              JSR GETSTR    ;GET TARGET VAR
              LDA INDEX
              CLC
              ADC TSTART
              STA TSTART
              LDA TSTART+1
              ADC #0
              STA TSTART+1
              LDA LENT
              SEC
              SEC INDEX
              STA LENT
              JSR MATCHIT   ;ACTUAL   STRING   MATCH
                            ROUTINE
              LDA #0
              LDY INDEX
              INY
              JSR GIVAYF
              RTS

* NOW MATCH THE STRINGS
MATCHIT       LDX #$40
              STX FFLAG     ;MARK FIRST ENTRY
SETDATA       LDA PLEN      ;INITIALIZE PATTERN
              STA LENP
              LDA PPTR
              STA PAT
              LDA PPTR+1
```

```
                STA PAT+1
                LDY #0          ;POINT TO FIRST CHAR OF
                                TARGET
                JSR PCHAR
COMPARE         CMP #NONBLANK
                BEQ AMP
                CMP #BLANKS
                BEQ PND
                CMP #WILDCARD
                BEQ WILD
                CMP (TSTART),Y
                BNE NOMATCH
ADVANCE         JSR PCHAR
                JSR TCHAR
                BNE COMPARE     ;ALWAYS
                AMP LDA#' '     ;HANDLE *
                CMP (TSTART),Y
                BNE ADVANCE
                BEQ NOMATCH     ;ALWAYS
                PND TAX         ;HANDLE
                LDA #' '
                CMP (TSTART),Y
                BEQ POUND
                BIT FFLAG       ;FIRST CHAR OF PATTERN?
                BPL NOMATCH     ;NO
                BMI POUND1      ;FIRST CHAR OF TARGET
POUND           TXA
                JSR TCHAR
                LDA #' '
                CMP (TSTART),Y
                BEQ POUND
POUND1          JSR PCHAR
                JMP COMPARE
NOMATCH         INC TSTART      ;BUMP POTENTIAL ANSWER
                BNE NM1
                INC TSTART+1
NM1             INC INDEX
                DEC LENT
                BEQ STRIKEOUT   ;OUT OF TARGET, QUIT
                JMP SETDATA

* SAVE CURRENT STATUS AND LOAD NEW ARGUMENTS
WILD            TSX             ;IS THERE ROOM ON THE
                                STACK?
                TXA
                SEC
                SEC 5
                BCS SETUP
                JMP OUTMEM      ;OUT OF MEMORY ERROR
SETUP           LDA LENP
                STA PLEN
```

203

```
                  LDA  PAT
                  STA  PPTR
                  LDA  PAT+1
                  STA  PPTR+1
                  TYA
                  CLC
                  ADC  TSTART
                  STA  TSTART
                  BCC  SETUP4
                  INC  TSTART+1
SETUP4            LDA  INDEX       ;SAVE INDEX
                  PHA
                  JSR  MATCHIT     ;NOW CALL MATCH ROUTINE
                                   AGAIN
                  LDX  INDEX       ;SAVE ANSWER TO ABOVE CALL
                  PLA             ;RESTORE OLD INDEX
                  STA  INDEX
                  INX             ;DID WE GET A MATCH?
                  BNE  MATCHED.    ;YES!

* EXIT ENTRIES
STRIKEOUT         LDA  #$FF
                  STA  INDEX
MATCHED           RTS

* NEXT CHARACTER ROUTINES
* WHEN STRING IS EXHAUSTED STACK IS LEVELLED AND
* JMP TO APPROPRIATE ACTION PERFORMED
PCHAR             LDA  LENP
                  BEQ  P2          ;OUT OF PATTERN
                  ASL  FFLAC       ;MOVE FIRST ENTRY FLAC OUT
                  PAT  EQU *+1     ;IMBEDDED DATA TRICK HERE
                  LDA  PAT
                  INC  PAT         ;BUMP PATTERN POINTER
                  BNE  P1
                  INC  PAT+1
P1                DEC  LENP
                  RTS
P2                PLA              ;OUT OF PPTR, DISCARD
                                   RETURN ADDR
                  PLA
                  JMP  MATCHED
TCHAR             INY              ;GET NEXT TARGET CHAR
                  CPY  LENT
                  BEQ  TEND
                  RTS
TEND              TAX
                  PLA              ;OUT OF TARGET
                  PLA
ENDTEST           LDA  LENP
                  BNE  STRIKEOUT
```

```
              TXA
              CMP #'#
              BEQ MATCHED
              CMP #'&'
              BEQ MATCHED
              BNE STRIKEOUT  ;ALWAYS
* SET STRING VAR AND STORE DESCRIPTOR AT STPOOL,X
GETSTR        PHA
              JSR CHKCOM
              JSR PTRGET
              PLA
              TAX
              LDY #0
GS1           LDA (VARPNT),Y
              STA 0,X
              INX
              INY
              CPY #3
              BNE GS1
              RTS
* LOCAL VARIABLES
FFLAC         DS1            ;FIRST ENTRY FLAG
```

Chapter Fourteen

A SYSTEM FOR MORPHOLOGICAL ANALYSIS AND SYNTHESIS OF GERMAN TEXTS

Harald Trost, Georg Dorffner, Vienna University

Introduction

In this chapter we describe a system for automated morphological analysis and synthesis of German. Since German is a language rich in inflectional and derivational endings this is a non-trivial task. Integrated into the system are a spelling corrector (Dorffner 1985) and a semi-automated system for the introduction of new vocabulary (Trost, Buchberger 1985). The same data structures are used for both analysis and synthesis guaranteeing the consistency of the data. The system forms part of VIE-LANG (Trost et al. 1983), a German language dialogue system developed at the University of Vienna, but the approach is general, so the system could be used in another context as well.

German Morphology

To help the reader with no knowledge of German we will start with a short overview of German morphology.

In contrast to English the German language has very few restrictions on constituent order, having instead a rich inflectional system. Apart from that there is a large set of derivational endings some of which are very productive. Another characteristic feature is the possibility of creating complex compound words.

Our system takes care of inflexion and (to some extent) of derivation. Word composition is not considered, therefore compound words are treated like single words.

Inflexion

Generally there are three types of flexion:

- conjugation of verbs,
- noun declension,
- and adjectival declension.

Articles and some pronouns have a declension similar to adjectives. All other word types do not inflect. Inflexion is realized in the following way:

- endings,
- prefixes,
- so-called 'Umlautung' (substituting the main vowel of the stem by another vowel according to certain rules),
- and suppletion (stem changing).

By far the most frequent means of inflection are endings, as in other European languages. The only prefixes to be considered are 'ge-' for building the past participle and 'zu' for the infinitive (though the latter is usually written as a separate word). 'Umlautung' is fairly frequent for plurals of nouns, verb tense and mode, and adjective comparison. The most regular type of 'umlautung' is the substitution of the vowels 'a', 'o' and 'u' by the corresponding 'Umlaute', 'ä', 'ö' and 'ü' respectively (also written as 'ae', 'oe' and 'ue'). There are other substitutions, too, like changing 'e' to 'i', but they do not follow such a regular pattern. Suppletion is restricted to articles, some pronouns, auxiliary verbs, and a very few others.

Another feature of German is the fact that some compound verbs split into inflected stem and particle under certain conditions. The reason for this is that the verb complex always forms the last part of the sentence, whereas the finite verb in main clauses is put into the second position. In case the verb complex consists of only one verb (e.g. in present tense, active voice) only the inflected stem of the compound verb takes the second position while the particle takes the last one (e.g. 'einkaufen' (= to buy) leads to 'kaufe' ... 'ein'). These verbs also have the prefixes 'ge-' and 'zu' between particle and verb stem ('einzukaufen', 'eingekauft') in the respective forms.

Derivation

As mentioned above the German language has a large set of productive derivational endings. Since new words can be formed with some of these endings in an ad-hoc manner (especially nominalizations) the system must be able to process these endings automatically.

Most important is the way in which the semantics of a word are changed by derivational endings. It is a prerequisite for a useful treatment, that the meaning of the new word can automatically be derived from the old one. This condition holds true only for some of the endings.

An example for such an ending is '-er', transforming verbs into nouns. The meaning is 'the actor of the action described by the verb' (e.g. 'arbeiten' (=to work) - (Arbeit<u>er</u> (= worker)).

Several endings can be applied to a word consecutively e.g. Arbiet<u>er</u> - Arbeiter<u>in</u> (= female worker) - arbeiterinnen<u>los</u> (= without female workers). This last adjectiv<u>e</u> is constructed from the plural of the noun, so there is the inflectional ending '-en' in between.

The Lexicon

Our system uses a lexicon-based approach, i.e. the algorithm relies on a dictionary comprising all words to be processed.

There are two different ways to organize a lexicon:
- A lexicon containing explicitly all the possible forms of every word. The advantages are fast access and (with the exception of data errors) no wrong associations. Disadvantages are the large amount of memory space consumed and the impossibility of analyzing ad-hoc derivations.
- A lexicon containing only one canonical form per word (plus some irregular forms). All other forms are reduced to that form (analysis) or derived from that form (synthesis) algorithmically. This approach results in slower access but uses up less memory space per word.

Since the actual savings depend on the size of the dictionary as well as on the number of forms possible for each entry the second approach compares even more favourably for German that for English. Therefore we decided to use that approach. Each entry consists of the canonical form plus some numerically coded morphological and syntactical information.

To make it easier to build up a new dictionary we implemented a system for semi-automatic acquisition of new words.

The Algorithm
In this section we will describe the algorithms in some detail. We will start with the part concerned with the analysis of flexional endings, since this is the more complicated task. The next part shows how the same data structures are used for synthesis as well. In the last part the analysis of derivational endings is explained.

Inflexion
Although German has a rich morphology there is only a small set of flexional endings. This is because suffixes are often used in more than one way (e.g. the suffix '-en' can express the plural for nouns - Frau<u>en</u> - but also a flectional form of verbs - geh<u>en</u> - and adjectives - schoen<u>en</u>). What is more, many of them are similar in form (e.g. '-n' and '-ten' are inflectional endings, too, which contain 'en' or are part of it). Therefore the best way to guide the analysis is to construct a tree out of the set of German flexional endings. The root of the tree is the 'no ending'-node, so all words other than the inflecting ones are found in the first search step. All endings containing another ending as their last part are successors to that ending. This tree is shown in figure 14.1.

Figure 14.1:

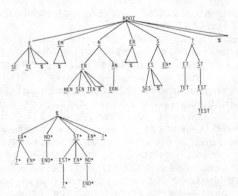

Note: The underlined letters mark the string that has to be split off in addition to what already has been taken away from the word form. The meaning of the asterisk is explained in the section on 'multiple inflection'.

Analysis is performed by searching for a path through that tree. This is done by consecutively splitting off characters from the end of the word and matching those character groups against the tree nodes. Every time this match proves successful a procedure is evoked that checks whether the rest of the word is equal to an entry in the dictionary and - in case one is found - if the ending is compatible with that entry. If this procedure succeeds the interpretation of the found combination of stem and ending is returned. Otherwise the algorithm tries to continue searching the tree. If that is not possible the analysis fails.

As shown in the first part suffixes are not the only possibility for inflection in German. Changing of roots, the so-called 'umlaut' and the prefixes have to be considered as well. Furthermore those compound verbs must be considered from which particles can be split off (e.g. 'aufgeben' - 'gebe ... auf') and where the prefixes 'ge-' and 'zu' become infixes (aufgegeben).

Many changes in word stem are similar to 'umlaut', e.g. the verb root 'fang' (=catch) is transformed into 'fing' when put into past tense. This particular example could be handled as a change from 'a' to 'i' (like the 'umlaut' transformation converts an 'a' to an 'ä', but in general this kind of transformation does not follow precise rules that would allow the phenomenon to be captured in a simple algorithm. The verb 'fahr' (to go by car), for example, becomes 'fuhr' in the past tense, i.e. a transition from 'a' to 'u'.

Therefore only the 'umlaut' transformation is handled by the search algorithm, all other root changes are treated like suppletion, the change into a completely different word form.

As mentioned above the analysis algorithm must not only search the dictionary but also check if the right form is used ('umlaut', suppletion, prefix). For every word the dictionary must contain the root form (canonical form) plus entries for all transformed forms (suppletion, 'Umlautung'), e.g. 'fang' and 'fing' are both found in the lexicon. All entries that belong to one lexeme are connected by pointers so that every form that is found can easily be reduced to its root form.

If a word is not found directly in the dictionary the word is checked for the occurence of an 'umlaut' or prefix (they exclude each other). If one is found, the word form without 'umlaut' (or without prefix) is searched for in the lexicon. As

only some of the possible endings of a word can co-
occur with 'umlaut' or prefix it has to be marked
that such a feature was found.

Suffix and Interpretation Lists. In spite of the
occurence of form changing most of the inflectional
information is expressed by endings. Every root form
can take a specific set of endings, depending on its
category and its special type (e.g. verbs can be
'stark' (strong), 'schwach' (weak) or 'gemischt'
(mixed). According to school grammar there should be
only about 10 'inflectional classes' (3 for verbs, 6
for nouns, 1 for adjectives) that cover all the
possible cases of inflection by suffixes. But when
one takes into consideration those cases where
endings change due to phonological reasons (e.g.
'-st' becomes '-est' when attached after a 't': 'geh'
- 'gehst' (= you go), but 'reit' - 'reitest' (= you
ride)), and cases where one has to distinguish, which
form is used (e.g. 'geh' can take '-st' for 2nd
person, but 'geb' cannot, because it changes to
'gibst') then there are about 50 different sets of
suffixes constituting the same number of
inflectional classes (Kunze, Rudiger 1968).
     For this reason at the heart of the algorithm
there is a data structure that looks like the
following:
     For every inflectional class a pair of lists is
constructed: Each pair consists of one list
containing all the suffixes (end-list) and another
one containing coded interpretations to convey the
information every suffix in this list stands for when
attached to a root (thus called interpretation-
list). Every pair of lists is identified by a number
that is stored with every word form in the dictionary
belonging to that class. In some cases it happens
that there is an end-list, where the endings express
different syntactical information when attached to
different roots. For example, the list consisting of
ST and NIL - NIL stands for zero ending - is the set
of possible endings of'kann' (= can for singular
present tense) and also for 'hoch' (= high). But in
the former case ST expresses the 2nd person ('du
kannst' = you can), in the latter case the
superlative ('höchst' = highest). To make it clear
which interpretation is meant there have to be two
distinct lists consisting of ST and NIL, each with
its own corresponding interpretation-list.
     This data structure allows for the use of the
inflectional information for both morphological

analysis and synthesis. For analysis the suffix that was split off is searched for in the end-list bearing the number that is stored with the root. If it is found that means it is correct and the information is returned from the corresponding element of the interpretation-list.

The 'umlaut' and prefix have not yet been considered. Thus, before the final interpretations (there can be more than one) are returned those where the required 'umlaut' or prefix does not fit to what was really found in the word have to be filtered out (see next paragraph).

For synthesis it has to be done the other way round: The interpretation expected is looked for in the interpretation-list and the corresponding suffix is returned (for more details see the paragraph about synthesis).

Morphological and Syntactical Information. There are two kinds of information that the dictionary and the data structures within the morphological procedures have to provide: the properties of each lexeme that tell how it is used in the grammar of the language, and the properties of a word form that is expressed by inflection. The former has to be stored in the data base of the lexicon, the latter has to be part of the analysis procedure.

The information stored with each lexicon entry is divided between morphological and syntactical information, the latter being a feature of the lexeme itself (and not expressed by inflection), for example the gender of a noun. The morphological information consists of several numbers that tell how the lexeme can be changed. These are the following:

KL: The number of the class of suffixes
UM: A code, that informs about 'umlaut'
PF: A flag, if the prefix 'ge-' is possible
FM: Information about new forms (suppletion)
SP: The number of letters that can be split off
    (for verbs with separable particles)

KL, UM and PF are given for each lexicon entry (i.e. also for each word form like 'fang', 'fing', etc.), the other two numbers, FM and SP, only for the primary entries (the root forms).

UM and FM are numbers of an element in a list of possible cases (e.g. 'umlaut' for 2nd 3rd person singular and for subjunctive past tense).

UM and PF serve for filtering out those

interpretations delivered by the end-list that
cannot co-occur with 'umlaut' or prefix. E.g. the
possible interpretations for '-t' as a suffix of
'lauf' (= to run) are:
(a)   3rd person sing. present tense,
(b)   2nd person plural present tense.

But for a) to be the right interpretation, there
has to be an 'umlaut' (läuft), while b) occurs
without (lauft). This filtering can be done by
comparing UM and PF with the markers that - in the
way described above - tell if an 'umlaut' or a prefix
was found in the word and detached from it.

The syntactical information (which is
independent of inflection) can be retrieved only at
the primary entries and consists of the following
possible features:

-     Word category (verb, noun, pronoun, etc.)
-     Gender of nouns (masculine, feminine, neuter)
-     Transitivity of verbs
-     Subcategory (e.g. auxiliary verb, demonstrative
pronoun, etc.)

This information is coded into one number (12)
where the first digit represents the word category
and the other ones are dependent on it (e.g. gender
only for nouns).

The syntactical information that is given by the
ending is coded into a number as well and stored in
the above mentioned interpretation-lists. It has to
be retrieved and decoded by the analysis algorithm.
The following figure shows the encoding for verbs:

Figure 14.2

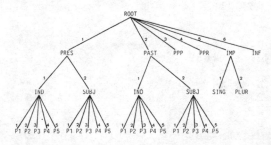

Note: P1 to P5 stand for the grammatical person: P1,
P2 and P3 mean 1st, 2nd and 3rd person sing., P5
means 2nd person plural, while P4 stands for 1st and
3rd person plural, for these two forms are always the
same.

As an example, code 212 would stand for past tense, indicative, 2nd person. The only exceptions to that scheme are some pronouns and other word types, where inflection is done only by suppletion and without suffixes. For these kinds of words, which are not very many, the interpretation code is stored directly in the dictionary with the specific form and retrieved from there (e.g. the article 'der' (masculine singular nominative) inflects into 'des' (masc./neuter singular genitive), 'dem', and so on. Therefore the lexicon entry for 'des' will contain the code for (masc./neuter singular genitive)).

A Detailed Example. The function of the morphological analysis will be demonstrated using the same word 'geben' (=to give): there are three entries in the dictionary (from now on every entry or variable from the procedure is written in upper case):

GEB the root for present tense and past participle
GIB the root for 2nd and 3rd person (present tense)
GAB the root for past tense

and their dictionary entries have the following form:

```
GEB: No: LXM#889
     KL: 22
     UM: 0
     PF: 1
     FM: 8
     12: 500
     FORR: (LXM#718 LXM#754)

GIB: No: LXM#718
     KL: 26
     UM: 0
     PF: 0
     STAMM: LXM#889

GAB: No: LXM#754
     KL: 23
     UM: 3
     PF: 0
     STAMM: LXM#889
```

The numbers are the identification of the entries in the lexicon. The items FORR and STAMM represent the pointers between the entries. This means that, for example, GAB can be reduced to the primary entry GEB (where the syntactical information

12 is found).

KL stands for 'Klasse' (class) and tells the number of the suffix list and interpretation list. For this example the following lists are used:

```
END22 (for GEB):     (E EN END EST ET T)
INT22:               E: (111 121 123)
                     EN: (3 7 114 124)
                     END: (4)
                     EST: (122)
                     ET: (125)
                     T: (115 52)

END26 (for GIB):     (NIL ST T)
INT26:               NIL: (51)
                     ST: (112)
                     T: (113)

END23 (for GAB):     (NIL ST T EN E EST ET)
INT23:               NIL: (211 213)
                     ST: (212)
                     T: (215)
                     EN: (214 224)
                     E: (221 223)
                     EST: (222)
                     ET: (225)
```

The numbers in the interpretation list are the codes obtained by applying the scheme given in figure 14.2. E.g.:

```
'gebt' :
root: GEB    suffix: T
looking up lists 22:  INT = (115 52)
```

That means, 'gebt' is either 2nd person plural present tense, or the imperative plural.

Items UM and PF tell about possible 'umlaut' or prefix 'ge'. When one of them is 0, the corresponding feature is impossible. E.g. the root GEB cannot have an 'umlaut', GAB cannot take the prefix 'ge'. If PF is 1, this prefix can be attached (for forming the past participle). This is true for GEB, because the past participle is 'gegeben' (given). UM is a number in a list of possible cases for 'umlaut', UM=3 for GAB means that it takes an 'umlaut' (A becomes AE) for subjunctive past tense. The filtering process to get the correct interpretations can be explained in four examples:

```
'gegeben':
```

```
root: GEB suffix: EN   prefix GE found
interpretation list: INT = (3 7 114 124)
filter: if GE was found pick out number 3 if it
is an element of the list and it will be the
correct interpretation.
result: past participle
```

```
'geben':
root: GEB  suffix: EN  no prefix found
interpretation list: INT = (3 7 114 124)
filter: if no prefix was found then exclude
number 3 from the list and the rest will be the
correct interpretation.
result: infinitive or  1st/3rd person plural
present tense
```

```
'gaben':
root: GAB suffix: EN  no 'umlaut' found
interpretation list: INT = (214 224)
filter: if no 'umlaut' was found then the set
difference on the list and (221 222 223 224 225)
will be the right interpretation.
note: the list (221 222 223 224 225) can be
extracted from UM=3 and is the list of all
subjunctive past tense endings.
result: 1st/3rd person plural past tense
```

```
'gäben':
root: GAB  suffix: EN  'umlaut' AE was found
interpretation list:  INT = (214 224)
filter: if an 'umlaut' was found then the
intersection of the list and (221 222 223 224
225) will be the right interpretation.
result: 1st/3rd person plural past subjunctive
```

I2 as the inflection–independent syntactical information labels all three roots to be of type verb (No.5), and that no particles can be split off (0). The auxiliary verb for the past tense is 'haben' (0). This information is printed together with the interpretation of the inflection.

FM is necessary only for the morphological synthesis. FM=8 means that a new root has to be taken for 2nd/3rd person singular present tense (GIB) and for the past tense (GAB).

Multiple Inflection. Usually inflection takes place only once for each word at the outermost level. (i.e. first composition and derivation can be applied and finally the whole word is inflected). This rule would exclude the possibility of more than one inflectional suffix.

But there are some exceptions:
- Comparison when handled like inflection produces a word that itself can be inflected. E.g.: Klein-er (=smaller) - klein-er-es.
- Participles (present and past) are usually also considered within the paradigm of inflection, but are words that behave like adjectives. E.g.: gegeben (=given) -gegeben-es (like in: 'a given book').

For easy handling of multiple inflection there are some nodes in the search tree (marked with an '*' in Fig. 14.1) where the procedure has to consider more than one ending. Every time it gets to an '*' node it builds up a stack of the suffixes that already have been analyzed. E.g. when the EN* node is reached after the ER-node the stack consists of EN and ER (written (EN ER), where the left element is the outermost one). After a stem has been found the checking procedure must be applied several times, each time popping a suffix from the stack. The highest depth of multiple inflection of that kind is 3 (participle + comparison + adjectival inflection).

The following example shows how the stack of endings is built:

```
input:    GEFRAGTERES
prefix GE can be detached (FRAGTERES)
ROOT-NODE: FRAGTERES not found
S-NODE:    FRAGTERE is not found
ES-NODE:   FRAGTER is not found
ER*NODE:   FRAGT is not found for this is a '*'-
           node
           the stack must be built: (ER ES)
T*NODE:    FRAG is found
           stack is augmented: (T ER ES)

           checking if T fits to FRAG: ok
           (while also considering prefix)
           checking if ER fits to GEFRAGT: ok
           checking if ES fits to GEFRAGTER: ok

result:    past participle of FRAG
           + comparative
           + adj. inflection ES
```

Note: It is important to distinguish between 'no ending' (word has the end-list NIL) and 'zero ending' (word has an end-list containing NIL). For example an adjective has NIL among its inflectional endings and therefore can get a 'zero ending', while an adverb, that cannot be inflected, gets 'no ending'. Thus a participle with 'zero ending' (like 'gefragt') is not found in the T-NODE, but in the T*NODE, because there a stack consisting of (T NIL) is built and the adjectival inflection by 'zero ending' can be recognized. This distinction must be included in the algorithm to avoid finding a participle with 'zero ending' twice (both in T-NODE and T*NODE). See also the next section.

Ambiguous Word Forms. Up to now we have described in detail how a word form that has one single interpretation can be analyzed. But sometimes word forms are ambiguous, so that there is more than one solution. For instance, the word 'Gefahren' can be the plural of the noun 'Gefahr' (= danger) or the past participle of the verb 'fahren' (= to go by vehicle). Therefore a control structure is needed to handle the search for multiple solutions.

There are two possibilities to cover ambiguities: Either to go through the whole search tree, collecting all solutions that are found and returning them afterwards, or to search until the first solution is retrieved and to continue the algorithm when this solution is rejected by the system superordinated to morphological analysis.

Since ambiguous words are not very numerous and therefore the mean time of analysis can be kept lower when the first solution is returned immediately we have implemented the second way: the procedure returns the first interpretation it can find leaving the spot marked where it would have to continue when another solution is wanted (Schuster 1984).

In addition to this the analysis was separated into three passes: first the whole tree is gone through while trying to find the unmodified stem, second it is searched for after an 'umlaut' was removed and third after a prefix was detached (only if this is possible). The advantage of this algorithm is that in most cases the first solution is found very fast, because only a small fraction of words contain an 'umlaut'. The prefix occurs even more seldom.

This can best be shown by following the analysis of our sample word GEFAHREN:

```
input: GEFAHREN
first pass: 'normal' (GEFAHREN)
ROOT-NODE:  GEFAHREN is not found directly
```

```
N-NODE: GEFAHRE is not found
EN-NODE: GEFAHR is found
checking if EN is correct: ok

first solution returned: Plural of GEFAHR

procedure continued (another solution wanted):

no child of EN-NODE can be taken
(neither NEN, SEN or TEN can be split off)

backtracking to ROOT
EN*NODE: GEFAHR is found
because this is an '*'-node, a stack of
endings is built: (EN NIL)
checking if EN is correct: ok
checking if NIL is correct: no
(because GEFAHREN cannot take more
endings)

second pass: 'umlaut' removed

it is not possible to remove an 'umlaut'

third pass: prefix detached: (FAHREN)
ROOT-NODE: FAHREN is not found directly
N-NODE: FAHRE is not found
EN-NODE: FAHR is found
checking if EN is correct: ok
prefix GE has been detached
solution would be past participle
but this can obtain more endings and
cannot be found in a node without an '*'

backtracking to ROOT
EN*NODE: FAHR is found
building a stack of endings: (EN NIL)
checking if EN correct: ok
checking if NIL correct: ok
new solution returned: Past participle of FAHR
```

Morphological synthesis. As opposed to analysis synthesis means producing the correctly inflected form when the root and some syntactical information are given. For an isolated word this usually can be done faster, because the procedure has to look for the root in the dictionary only once or twice (primary entry and suppletion form). As already mentioned the data structures of the morphological component were built in a way that they can be used

219

for both analysis and synthesis, keeping the system consistent. So we can still refer to the lists and items described above.

The algorithm works in the following way:

The given root is looked up in the dictionary and thus the suffix and interpretation lists are known. Now the syntactical information has to be coded by following the tree depicted in figure 14.2. At this point the item FM is important, because the correct root form has to be found (which implies a different suffix list). And, too, it has to be decided if this root should obtain an 'umlaut' or prefix. This can be done by checking the items FM, UM and PF at the corresponding nodes in the coding tree. E.g:

wanted: GEB inflected into past subjunctive 3rd person sing.

FM=8, that means new root forms for 2nd/3rd person singular present tense, and for past tense

in the coding tree the 'past'-arc is taken and in node PAST the item FM is checked if it possibly is 8 (besides other code numbers)

this is true, therefore GAB as the new root is taken

next the 'subjunctive'-arc is taken and in node SUBJ the item UM is checked to see if it is 3 (that means 'umlaut' for past subjunctive)

this, too, is true and a flag is set that marks the requirement for an 'umlaut'

When all the syntactical information is coded, the code number is now searched for in the interpretation list. If it is found the corresponding suffix is returned. The last step of the procedure is attaching the suffix at the chosen root and, depending on the flags, including an 'umlaut' or a prefix.

example continued:
Coded information: 223
found in list with: E
'umlaut'-flag is set
result: GAEBE

To handle multiple inflection this procedure has to be applied recursively several times.

Derivation

Derivation by suffixes was included in the morphological analysis in those cases where it adheres to the upcoming restrictions:

- it has to be productive, i.e. the suffix must not be restricted to only a few word roots.
- the syntactical (and semantical) transformation done by the derivation suffix has to be somewhat clear.
- the suffix must not change the root (except 'umlaut')

Under these preconditions a set of derivational endings was chosen and an analysis procedure was built. Contrary to the case of inflection, it has to be considered now that derivation can happen fully recursively. This means a derived word can obtain again a derivation suffix, and so on. This recursion is not restricted by syntax but only by pragmatics and understandability.

Derivation endings usually change the word category and are themselves dependent on which category they can be attached at. E.g.:

-bar can be attached at verb roots and produces an adjective (les-bar = readable)
-los can be attached at noun roots and produces an adjective
-heit
-keit can be attached at adjective roots and produce a noun (Krank-heit = illness)
recursion: Dank-bar-keit = thankfulness

Some derivation suffixes require an 'umlaut' in the word root, as was the case for the inflection. For example, 'Haus' (= house) - 'Häuschen' (= little house). Another morphological property of derivation that sometimes occurs is an additional letter between root and ending (or between two endings). For instance, 'Arbeit' (= work) + los = 'arbeitslos' (= without work). This can easily be handled by introducing some pseudo-suffixes (like '-slos') that have the same properties as the corresponding suffix (like '-los').

For analyzing a derived word a new item (as a property of the lexicon entry) was invented, called

DV, that tells which suffixes can be attached to the root. This must be done because the endings, though productive, are restricted to certain classes of words (e.g. the ending '-bar' requires a transitive verb).

The derivation suffixes are separated into three groups, dependent on the category they require: the de-verbal (e.g. (-bar'), the de-adjectival (e.g. '-heit') and the de-nominal endings (e.g. '-los' that occurs with nouns)). The suffixes of each group are given in a fixed order so that one digit of DV can refer to one suffix. The values of those digits give the following information:

0   ... the corresponding suffix cannot be attached
1   ... the suffix can be attached
2   ... the suffix can be attached but requires an 'umlaut'

E.g. HAUS (= house) has DV=210210 that refers to the de-nominal endings:
CHEN HAFT IN LEIN LOS SLOS
that means:
HAUS can take HAFT and LOS without 'umlaut'; can take CHEN and LEIN with 'umlaut'; cannot take IN or SLOS
so HAUSLOS AND HAEUSCHEN are correct; HAUSIN is not

If one of the digits of DV is non-zero, this does not mean that the word with the corresponding ending is a word often used in practice, but only that it is syntactically right.

As has been explained before, derivation can be applied recursively several times, each time transforming the word category into another. And in addition, which suffixes can be attached to a derived word, depends on that category. So it can be said that attaching a derivation suffix transforms not only the word category, but also the item DV. For example, a word derived by '-bar' will get a new DV that tells which de-adjectival endings the new word can obtain (in this case only '-heit').

The Analysis Procedure. Based on these considerations the analyzing can be done as follows:

Beginning from the end of a word the procedure tries to find a derivation suffix. If it succeeds the rest of the word must be a lexicon entry or a derived word itself. The former is found in the dictionary, the latter must be analyzed by starting the procedure again. When a root is found, the word category and the item DV are known and one can check if the innermost suffix has been correctly attached. Then the two transformations (category and DV) are done and, following the backtracking of the recursive calls of the procedure, the next suffix is checked, etc. E.g:

```
Checking MEINUNGSLOS
SLOS is found
Checking MEINUNG
UNG is found
Checking MEIN
MEIN found in the dictionary
UNG fits - MEINUNG correct
SLOS fits
result: MEIN-UNG-SLOS
Checking MEINUNGBAR (wrong)
BAR is found
Checking MEINUNG
UNG is found
Checking MEIN
MEIN found in the dictionary
UNG fits - MEINUNG correct
BAR does not fit (not de-nominal)
result: Word wrong
```

Conclusion

We have presented a system for the automated morphological analysis and synthesis of German words. The basis is formed by a classification scheme for inflexion (resulting in about 50 classes) and derivation. The main data structure is a lexicon of canonical forms. Words are derived and generated from these forms by procedures relying on explicitly stored morphological and syntactical data. This makes the approach apt for easy modification and extension.

References

Dorffner G. (1985) 'Schreibfehlerverbesserung als Komponente eines Sprachverstehenden Systems' Masters Thesis, University of Technology Vienna.

Kunze J., Rudiger B. (1968) 'Algorithmische Synthese der Flexionsformen des Deutschen' *Zeitschrift für Phonetik, Sprachwissenschaft und Kommunikationsfor-schung* 21, 245-303.

Schuster H. (1984) 'Morphologische Analyse für das

Sprachverstehende System VIE-LANG' Masters Thesis, University of Technology Vienna.
Trost H., Buchberger E., Steinacker I., Trappl R. (1983) 'VIE-LANG: A German Language Dialogue System' Cybernetics and Systems 14, 343-357
Trost H., Buchberger E. (1985) 'Knowledge Acquisition in the System VIE-LANG' in H. Trost (ed.), Austrian AI-Workshop 85, Springer, Berlin.

Appendix 1: Some Useful Publications

Ahmad, K., Corbett, G.G., Rogers, M., Sussex, R.,
Computers, Language Learning and Language Teaching
(Cambridge University Press, Cambridge, 1985). An
excellent work, by some of the pioneers of CALL for
Russian.
Davies, G., Talking BASIC (Cassell, London, 1985).
Another pioneer of CALL. Aimed at the 'non-numerate'.
Davies, G., Higgins, J., Computers, Language and
Language Learning (CILT Information Guide No. 22,
London, 1982). John Higgins with Tim Johns (below)
was behind the idea of Storyboard. Being rewritten
with a comprehensive bibliography for release in late
1985.
Higgins, J., Johns, T., Computers in Language
Learning (Collins, London & Glasgow, 1984). An
excellent book, with a number of imaginative
approaches to computers as language-teaching aids.
The programs included are designed for the ZX
Spectrum (TS2000), but may be easily rewritten.
Kenning, M.J., Kenning, M.-M., An Introduction to
Computer Assisted Language Learning (Oxford
University Press, Oxford, 1983). Rather traditional
in its approach to CALL. Includes a full introduction
to BASIC for intending CALL system designers.
Last, R., Language Teaching and the Microcomputer
(Basil Blackwell, Oxford, 1984). A good, no-nonsense
survey by a pioneer in the field.
CALLBOARD, edited by G. Davies. A very useful
newsletter, issued irregularly. Subscriptions (£1
for six issues) from: Roger Savage, CALLBOARD
treasurer, 19 High Street, Eccleshall, Stafford ST21
6BW.

Appendix 2

SOME SOURCES OF CALL SOFTWARE

Acornsoft, Technopark, 645 Newmarket Road, Cambridge CB5 8PD

Arnold Wheaton Software, Parkside Lane, Leeds LS11 5TD

AVC, PO Box 415, Harborne, Birmingham B17 0HD

BBC Publications, 35 Marylebone High Street, London W1M 4AA

Beebugsoft, PO Box 109, High Wycombe, Bucks. HP10 8NP

CALL, Lanchester Poly, Coventry CV1 5FB

Cambridge Micro Software, Cambridge University Press, The Edinburgh Building, Shaftesbury Road, Cambridge CB2 2RU

Chalksoft, PO Box 49, Spalding PE11 1NZ

Educated Owl, 62 Airedale Avenue, Tickhill, Doncaster, S. Yorks

ESM, 32 Bridge Street, Cambridge CB2 1UJ

Hargreaves, Updown, Pewley Way, Guildford, Surrey

Heinemann, Windmill Press, Kingswood, Tadworth KT20 6TG

Hodder and Stoughton, Mill Road, Dunton Green, Sevenoaks, Kent

Kosmos Software Ltd., 1 Pilgrims Close, Harlington, Dunstable, Beds LU5 6LX

Longman, Burnt Hill, Harlow CM20 2JE

Macmillan, Little Essex Street, London WC2R 3LF

Medstat, City House, Maid Marian Way, Nottingham NG1 6BH

Micro-aid, 25 Fore Street, Praze, Camborne, Cornwall

MUSE, PO Box 43, Hull HU1 2HD

Primary Programs, Claypits, Debden Road, Saffron Walden, Essex

Private Tutor, 29 Hollow Way, Lane, Amersham HP6 6DJ

Silversoft, Unit 7D Kings Yard, Carpenters Road, London E15 2HD

Sulis, c/o Wiley Software, Baffins Lane, Chichester PO19 1UD

Wida Software, 2 Nicholas Gardens, London W5 5HY

INDEX

accents, French 70
animation 18, 25
audio output 13, 28, 114, 141, 143, 148, 171
author languages 17, 155

bi-lingualism, educational policy issues 54

CALL usage 1
character codes, standards for 10
cloze technique 124, 126, 140

deaf students, use of computer in teaching 26
dialogue generation 23, 27
dictionary design 73, 208
'drill and practice' techniques 177

educational materials, production of 39
evaluation of CAI software 66

games, computer
    adventure 18, 26, 69
    general 62
grammar
    on-line reference 171
    teaching 22
graphics
    criteria for use in CALL 47
    files, cataloging of 41
    for digitalised images 43
    general 13, 24-5, 141

integration with text 34
group work, effectiveness compared to individual 23, 29, 85

images, see graphics
incompatibility of CALL systems 5
input methods 11

keyboards, for non-Latin character sets 111, 127

learning, theories of 78

mainframe, future of 7
migrant workers, problems of language learning 59
mixed ability groups 79
morphemes 182, 206

networks 4, 6, 14

orthography
    non-European 29
    role in language instruction 38

pictures, see graphics
plasma display screens 105
Plato system 105, 140

research results in second-language teaching 27, 58

sex differences in CAI 63
speech synthesis, see audio